PENGUIN BOOKS

THE HUNDRED YEARS WAR

Desmond Seward was born in Paris and educated at Cambridge University. He is the author of *Richard III: England's Black Legend*, *The Monks of War*, and *The Wars of the Roses*.

DESMOND SEWARD

The Hundred Years War

THE ENGLISH IN FRANCE
1337–1453

PENGUIN BOOKS

For my godsons

Mark Kendall
Tobias Riley-Smith
Paul Seward

PENGUIN BOOKS
Published by the Penguin Group
Penguin Putnam Inc., 375 Hudson Street,
New York, New York 10014, U.S.A.
Penguin Books Ltd, 27 Wrights Lane,
London W8 5TZ, England
Penguin Books Australia Ltd, Ringwood,
Victoria, Australia
Penguin Books Canada Ltd, 10 Alcorn Avenue,
Toronto, Ontario, Canada M4V 3B2
Penguin Books (N.Z.) Ltd, 182–190 Wairau Road,
Auckland 10, New Zealand

Penguin Books Ltd, Registered Offices:
Harmondsworth, Middlesex, England

First published in Great Britain by Constable and Company Limited
First published in the United States of America by Atheneum Publishers 1978
Published in Penguin Books 1999

10 9 8 7 6 5 4 3 2 1

Copyright © Desmond Seward, 1978
Maps and battle diagrams drawn by Patrick Leeson.
All rights reserved

(CIP data available)
ISBN 0 14.02 8361 7

Printed in the United States of America
Set in Janson

Contents

Illustrations

Acknowledgements

My first debt is to two Benedictine monks, Dom Marcel Pierrot and Dom Jean Bequet of Ligugé, who took me over the battlefield of Poitiers sixteen years ago. I am sincerely grateful to them for starting my interest in the Hundred Years War, and to their monastery for its memorable hospitality.

I am especially indebted to Mr Reresby Sitwell for much encouragement, for many useful ideas, and for reading the typescript and the proofs; to Mrs Prudence Fay for her invaluable editorial criticisms; to Sir Iain Moncreiffe of that Ilk for the suggestion that Charles VI's madness may have been caused by porphyria; and to Commander W. F. Patterson, RN (Retd), Chairman of the Society of Archer-Antiquaries, for the diagrams of the long-bow and crossbow and for advice on the technical points of medieval bowmanship.

Among those who gave me information about the part played by their families in the Hundred Years War were Lord Mowbray, Segrave and Stourton, Lord Dunboyne and the Hon Nicholas Assheton. Lord Mowbray supplied me with material about the life of his ancestor the first Lord Stourton, who had an unusually profitable career during the later stages of the War, Lord Dunboyne provided me with details about the Butlers and other Irishmen in France, while Mr Assheton drew my attention to Sir John Assheton who served with Henry V in Normandy.

I must also thank Mr Michael Thomas, Mr Christopher Manning, Mr Hubert Witheford and Mr David Beynon, and Miss Mollie Luther who helped find the illustrations.

Finally I would like to express my gratitude to Mr Richard Bancroft of the British Library, to Mr Esmond Warner, the Honorary Librarian of Brooks's, and to Miss E. V. Baird and Miss E. A. Hollingdale of Brighton Library.

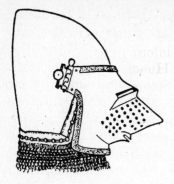

Foreword

Do you not know that I live by war and that peace would be my undoing?

Sir John Hawkwood

This is a short, narrative account of the Hundred Years War for the general reader. Other studies have either been translated from the French, and dismiss Agincourt in a few lines, or are too scholarly. However, while this book is not for the specialist, it nevertheless makes full use of the recent research which has radically altered the traditional picture of the War.

The phrase 'The Hundred Years War' only gained currency during the late nineteenth century. In fact it gathers together a series of wars which lasted longer than a hundred years. They are generally assumed to have begun in 1337 when Philip VI of France 'confiscated' the English-held Duchy of Guyenne from Edward III, who then claimed the French throne, and to have ended in 1453 when the English finally lost Bordeaux. For most of the period England enjoyed a remarkable military superiority thanks to the fire-power of the long-bow.

Some of the battles are part of the English legend, like the glorious victories of Crécy, Poitiers and Agincourt, but there are also the little known (to Englishmen) defeats at the end when French cannon routed their once invincible archers. The protagonists are among the most colourful in English and French history : Edward III, the Black Prince, and the even more formidable Henry V ; the splendid but inept John II who died a prisoner in London, the sickly, limping intellectual Charles V, who very nearly overcame the English, and the enigmatic Charles VII (Joan of Arc's Dauphin) who at last drove them out. The supporting English cast included such men as Sir John Chandos, John of Gaunt, the Duke of Bedford and Old Talbot, as well as Sir John Fastolf—the original of Shakespeare's Falstaff. On the French side were figures like the Constable du Guesclin, the Bastard of Orleans and the witch-saint from Domrémy.

While the chronicler Froissart paints a pageant of glittering court life, 'a Bourgeois of Paris' tells of times when wolves entered Paris to eat the corpses. The world of the *Très Riches Heures du Duc de Berry* was as bloody as it was beautiful. For the French, unlike the English, the War was more than a mere saga of battles ; it was a dreadful experience, which like modern warfare, involved the entire community.

For over a century one Western country systematically plundered another. A distinguished modern historian has written that the contemporary English attitude to the War was as a 'speculative, but at best hugely profitable, trade that was shared by all who joined the mercenary armies of Edward III and Henry V . . .' He adds that by 1450 'among those who had done best out of the war were the great landed families', while as for 'needy adventurers of obscure birth and no inherited property ; scores of them made notable fortunes'. Indeed generations of Englishmen of every class went to France to seek their fortunes, in rather the same way that their descendants would one day go to India or Africa. Of course there were other incentives besides greed, as anyone who has read Froissart or *King Henry V* will realize—knight-errantry, feudal loyalty or a primitive patriotism. If the emphasis on material motives in this book may sometimes seem excessive, it is partly because their role has been underestimated in popular accounts of the Hundred Years War ; and partly because recent research has given us much more information about the extent and nature of 'spoils won in France' and how they were spent in England.

Whatever the motives, a sustained—and, on the whole, extraordinarily successful—offensive was waged for over a century by a poor and scantily populated little country against a richer, more populous and ostensibly far more powerful enemy. It is arguable that the Hundred Years War was medieval England's greatest achievement.

Valois or Plantagenet?
1328–1340

Dare he command a fealty in me?
Tell him the Crown that he usurps is mine,
And where he sets his foot he ought to kneel.
'Tis not a petty Dukedom that I claim,
But all the whole dominions of the realm;
Which if with grudging he refuse to yield
I'll take away those borrowed plumes of his
And send him naked to the wilderness.

The Raigne of King Edward III

Sir, does it not seem to you that the silken
thread encompassing France is broken?

Sir Geoffrey Scrope

On the first day of February 1328 King Charles IV of
France, third son of King Philip the Handsome and last of
the Capetian dynasty, lay dying. He had no children but his
wife was pregnant. On his deathbed Charles said, 'If the
Queen bears a son he will be King, but if she bears a
daughter then the crown belongs to Philip of Valois.'

Philip, Count of Valois, Anjou and Maine, was thirty-
five, a tall, handsome nobleman who was famous for magnificence and for prowess in the tournament and on the
battlefield. He was a great-grandson of St Louis and King
Charles's first cousin; his father, Charles of Valois, had not
only been a Prince of the Blood Royal but also, because of
his second wife, titular Emperor of Constantinople; while
Philip's mother had been a daughter of the Capetian house

which ruled Naples. He had inherited vast wealth and estates. Cold and calculating, he was very different from the flashy and incapable knight-errant of popular tradition.

On All Fool's Day 1328 the widowed Queen gave birth to a posthumous daughter. Philip at once summoned a well-chosen assembly to Paris, who swiftly acknowledged him as their King—Philip VI. They did not know how much misery and destruction they had thereby brought upon France.

Across the Channel an even more dramatic scene took place two years later. Parliament had met at Nottingham in October 1330 and Isabel, the Queen Mother, and her lover Roger Mortimer, Earl of March, who was the real ruler of England, had taken up residence in the castle. On a dark night the eighteen-year-old King Edward III and a band of young lords entered the fortress through a secret passage and, after cutting down the guards, burst into the pregnant Queen Isabel's bedchamber to seize Mortimer—Edward personally broke down the door with a battle-axe, though he tried to avoid being seen by his mother. Despite Isabel's plea, 'Fair son, fair son, have pity on gentle Mortimer,' Roger was hanged, drawn and quartered on the Common Gallows at Tyburn. The young King had at last won control of his kingdom.

Edward had every reason to hate both Mortimer and his mother. The 'She Wolf of France' seems always to have despised her husband, Edward II—the loser at Bannockburn, a peculiarly inept ruler and a reputed homosexual. In 1326 she and Mortimer had forced Edward to abdicate, replacing him with his son as a puppet monarch; a year later the deposed King was horribly murdered, being buggered with a red-hot poker. Mortimer, perhaps the nastiest man ever to rule England, had governed by fear; not only had he killed Edward II but he had tricked his brother, the Earl of Kent, into a conspiracy and then legally murdered him. To cap everything he had got the Queen Mother with child. However, Edward was merciful to Isabel, allowing her to withdraw to a luxurious retirement at Castle Rising in Norfolk where he visited her once a year.

Isabel was the link between the Kings of England and France, for she was Philip VI's first cousin. She was also the late King Charles's sister and many thought that she or her son should have inherited the throne of France, and not the Valois. At this date there was no problem of nationality : Anglo-Norman French was still a living tongue, spoken and written by the English ruling class until the last quarter of the fourteenth century. It was the first language of Edward III and his sons, probably of his grandsons, and even perhaps of his great-grandsons ; Edward himself had to be taught English as part of his childhood education. Moreover, as Duke of Guyenne and Count of Ponthieu, Edward was one of the Twelve Peers of France and a French magnate.

During the assembly which Philip had summoned to Paris on the death of Charles IV, two English envoys had demanded the crown for Queen Isabel. There was only one instance in France of a female claim being set aside and that was very recent—when John I had died in 1316, after ten days of life and kingship, his sister had been excluded from the succession by an assembly. They were unable to produce any convincing legal argument in support of their decision, but the girl's guardian conveniently renounced her claims on her behalf. The English spokesman, Bishop Adam Orleton of Worcester, argued a plausible case ; that the precedent of 1316 was no true precedent as no woman had ever been *legally* excluded from wearing the crown of France, even if there was no instance of a female sovereign in French history ; and that it was undeniable that every feudal fief in the land, not excepting the mightest duchy, could be inherited by a woman. (The Salic Law of the ancient Franks, which forbade inheritance by a woman or through the female line, was not disinterred from the mists of time until much later.) But the assembly 'put clean out' Queen Isabel of England. According to Froissart they 'maintained that the realm of France was of so great noblesse that it ought not by succession to fall into a woman's hand'. They had had the opportunity to see Isabel and her appalling lover—with

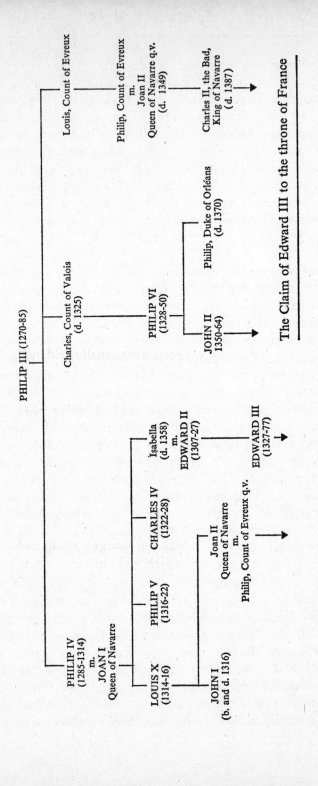

PHILIP III (1270-85)

PHILIP IV (1285-1314) m. JOAN I Queen of Navarre

Charles, Count of Valois (d. 1325)

Louis, Count of Evreux

LOUIS X (1314-16)

PHILIP V (1316-22)

CHARLES IV (1322-28)

Isabella (d. 1358) m. EDWARD II (1307-27)

PHILIP VI (1328-50)

Philip, Count of Evreux m. Joan II Queen of Navarre q.v. (d. 1349)

JOHN I (b. and d. 1316)

Joan II Queen of Navarre m. Philip, Count of Evreux q.v.

EDWARD III (1327-77)

JOHN II 1350-64

Philip, Duke of Orléans (d. 1370)

Charles II, the Bad, King of Navarre (d. 1387)

The Claim of Edward III to the throne of France

whom Orleton was known to be hand-in-glove—when they had visited the French court in 1326, and had no wish to be ruled by them.

When the young King of England won control of his kingdom, it was only as a leader of dissatisfied barons. He was far too weak to challenge Philip VI. Indeed, at this date Edward III merely hoped to retain his Duchy of Aquitaine (or Guyenne) which since 1259 the Kings of England had held as feudatories of the Kings of France. This last fragment of Henry II's Angevin empire consisted of a long, narrow strip of coastal territory, stretching from just south of La Rochelle to Bayonne and the Pyrenees—the western parts of Guenne proper, the Saintonge and Gascony—defended by a string of frontier *bastides*, carefully sited and strongly fortified town colonies.

However, Guyenne was in no sense a colony. Though the highest administrative posts were usually held by Englishmen—those of the Seneschal of Guyenne, the Constable and Mayor of Bordeaux, and the Seneschal of the Saintonge; and those of a number of under-seneschals and of the captains of most fortresses—in all these amounted to perhaps 200. The majority of officials were locally recruited. No Englishman was ever Archbishop of Bordeaux, and though there were plenty of English merchants there were few English landowners. All the important *seigneurs* were Guyennois, some of whom also had estates in England.

The duchy was an important source of income for Edward. There were royal toll-bridges along the entire Garonne which extracted a rich yield in taxes, for wine was to Guyenne what wool was to England; sometimes (as in 1306–1307) the revenue from Guyenne was larger than that from England. Bordeaux, the ducal capital with a population of 30,000, owed its prosperity to the English connection; wine flowed into England in such quantities as to make it cheap for all save the poorest—the fourteenth-century English drank several times more claret per head than they do today. Not only Bordeaux but Bayonne (which built the ships) and many other towns benefited from the wine trade, as did

countless *seigneurs* who owned vineyards, for claret was then
a blended wine which made use of such far-off vintages as
those of Gaillac or Cahors. Indeed there was not a sufficient
market at home for all their produce. On the other hand
Guyenne depended on England for grain—in 1334 it took
50,000 quarters—and bought English wool, leather, resin
and salt. The duchy's language was not really French but
Gascon, a form of Provençal. In fact it was a separate
country of its own, whose inhabitants had few ties with the
French Crown or the northern French. Many Guyennois
found jobs in England, serving in the King's armies during
the Scottish campaigns or as merchants, especially in
London; the Guyennois Henri le Waleys was Mayor of
both Bordeaux and London. It was possible to appeal to
England against a decision by a Guyennois court. The
Plantagenets regarded Guyenne as a far more integral part
of their domains than Wales or Ireland, and Froissart often
refers to Guyennois as 'the English'.

Nevertheless in 1329 Edward had to go to Amiens and
pay homage to 'our right dear cousin', swearing in the
cathedral to become 'the King of France's man for the
Duchy of Guyenne'. He also did homage for his County
of Ponthieu at the mouth of the Somme; its capital was
Abbeville and another of its towns was Crécy, of which more
will be heard. After Mortimer's fall, Edward had to agree in
a document drawn up in March 1331 'to bear faith and
loyalty' to the Valois. If he had refused, he might well have
lost both Guyenne and Ponthieu. Since 1259 there had been
incessant wrangling over the duchy's boundaries and over
the respective powers of the Duke–King and his overlord—
whether the Plantagenets held Guyenne in full sovereignty
or as tenants who must obey the King of France. From time
to time fighting broke out. In 1325 the English Governor
of Guyenne, the Earl of Kent, had been forced to surrender
to Charles IV at the *bastide* of La Réole during the 'War of
Saint-Sardos', which had been largely brought about by
Edward II's refusal to pay homage. King Charles had then
contented himself with retaining the Agenais (the border

area between the rivers Garonne and Dordogne), but Edward III must have recognized that the conquest of Guyenne was a logical step in the unification of France. In the latter part of 1331, disguised as a wool merchant, he again crossed the Channel to meet Philip secretly at Pont-Saint-Maxence and try to negotiate a lasting peace.

At that time the French monarchy appeared to be far stronger than the English. Matthew Paris, the famous thirteenth-century chronicler, wrote that: 'The King of France is the King of all earthly Kings,' and the French King was undoubtedly the first ruler in western Europe. He far outshone the Holy Roman Emperor and more or less controlled the Papacy which since 1309 had been established at Avignon—the French King being both the Pope's protector and quasi-gaoler. And for over a century there had been no unruly nobles in France as there were in England, but a steady bringing to heel of the counts and barons. If Flanders and Brittany—and of course Guyenne—remained semi-autonomous, Philip VI none the less inherited direct control of more than three-quarters of his mighty realm.

Since the tenth century new agricultural techniques had enabled the peasants of north-western Europe to exploit their rich soil, bringing more and more forest land under the plough. Until the early fourteenth century the area under cultivation expanded every year, with an accompanying rise in the birthrate. Nowhere was this more evident than in France which in the 1330s had a population of perhaps 21 million—five times that of England. French merchants and artisans multiplied, creating the most beautiful cities and cathedrals this side of the Alps; Gothic Paris became the capital of northern Europe, with perhaps 150,000 inhabitants. Froissart, who travelled a good deal, comments: 'One may well marvel at the noble realm of France, therein are so many towns and castles, both in the distant marches and in the heart of the realm.'

By contrast, medieval England was an underpopulated land, rather like modern Norway, with more forest and moor than arable; a poor little country whose wealth was its wool.

London held some 30,000 souls. The King, unlike Philip in France, ruled with difficulty. Edward III was not the absolute monarch his grandfather had been—that had gone under Edward II. Edward III always had to take into careful account the wishes of his 'Lords in Parliament', about a hundred barons, bishops and abbots. Froissart observed : 'Any man who is King of that country must conform to the will of the people and bow to many of their wishes. If he fails to do this, and misfortune comes to the country, he will be thrown over.'

The French knighthood—'good chivalry, strong of limb and stout of heart, in great abundance'—was Philip's most daunting asset. The man-at-arms and his giant warhorse (a particularly expensive item costing as much as £200 and trained to bite, kick and trample) constituted a unit of heavy armour which was the medieval equivalent of the tank : a massed formation of such units concentrated on a narrow front had a shattering impact. Their cult of chivalry, which has been likened to the bushido of the Japanese samurai— one should forget the fantasies of the *Morte d'Arthur*—made for excellent morale and a most formidable fighting spirit. For nearly three centuries heavy cavalrymen of this type had won almost every important victory in Christendom ; they had even wrested Palestine from the infidel for a brief moment and had all but reconquered Spain from the Moors. During the last hundred years France had possessed an enormous knighthood for whom war—whether in the tournament, in the King's host or as a mercenary—was a way of life. On at least one occasion it had broken an English army beyond recovery. In 1328 Philip VI and his men-at-arms had annihilated an army of Flemish pikemen at Cassel. In consequence Philip now enjoyed a reputation as a military leader comparable to that of Guderian and Patton at their zenith, besides commanding the largest, best equipped, most enthusiastic and most successful heavy armour in western Europe. During the early years of his reign he must have seemed invincible.

In contrast England had a dismal military record. The

Earl of Kent's poor showing in Gascony has already been mentioned. Still more serious were England's repeated thrashings at the hands of the Scots. After Bannockburn in 1314 until a truce was negotiated in 1323, they frequently raided as far south as Yorkshire, inflicting widespread devastation. In 1327 young Edward was reduced to tears by a humiliatingly unfortunate campaign against them; the very peace he had to negotiate was called the 'Shameful Peace of Northampton'. If only a poor and barbarous little country, Scotland nevertheless appeared to be a most effective ally against England at this time.

But, for all their undoubted fighting qualities, the Scots have been beaten more often than not by the English and in July 1333 at Halidon Hill, near Berwick, King Edward crushed them. Not only did he taste victory for the first time, but he saw what could be done by a combination of archers and dismounted cavalry defending a strong position—even though the Scots were only spearmen and light horse and not to be compared with the magnificent heavy cavalry of France. The King also systematically burnt and laid waste all Lowland Scotland—later his troops would employ the same vicious tactics in France. Jean le Bel, a chronicler who actually took part in the campaign, records the joy of the English at avenging Bannockburn and says that when Edward returned to his own country he received a triumphant reception, being 'universally loved and honoured by high and low, as much for his noble words and deeds as for his greatness of heart and for the fair assemblies of ladies and maidens that he held, so much so that one and all said that he was King Arthur come again'.

However, Edward still had no wish to fight Philip. He was too busy trying to conquer Scotland, campaigning there in person until 1336. For several years he tried sincerely to negotiate a lasting settlement in Guyenne, whose frontiers remained vague and where his main aim seems to have been to regain the border territory of the Agenais. Philip was no less peaceably disposed. In 1332 both Kings decided to go on crusade together, a plan which met with the Pope's

enthusiastic encouragement, and a fleet was slowly
assembled at Marseilles. Yet it was inevitable that war
would eventually break out between France and England.
The growing centralization and institutionalization of both
countries was making the old feudal relationship unwork-
able between France and Guyenne. As the outstanding
modern authority on the Hundred Years War, Dr Kenneth
Fowler, has written : 'Slowly but inexorably, and perhaps
with only an imperfect knowledge of the consequences of
what they were doing, the kings of France in the thirteenth
and early fourteenth centuries were reducing the dukes'
lordship to landlordship, erecting their suzerainty into
sovereignty . . . . It was an impossible situation for the King
of England.'

In May 1334 the ten-year-old David II of Scotland took
refuge in France at the invitation of Philip VI, who
announced that any future negotiations between himself
and the English must take into consideration the interests
of the King of Scots. Edward, infuriated at being encircled,
henceforward regarded the French King as his enemy. For
a time Pope Benedict XII managed to keep an increasingly
angry Philip quiet; in November 1335 Papal envoys
succeeded in arranging a truce between England and
Scotland. But in March 1336 the Pope reluctantly announced that as there was no genuine peace between King
Edward and King Philip the Crusade would have to be
postponed. A few weeks later the erstwhile Crusader fleet
sailed out of Marseilles, bound for new moorings in the
Norman ports. Though the fleet itself remained inactive,
French privateers began to terrorize the Channel and the
Bay of Biscay—oared galleys made quick work of becalmed
English merchantmen. In July the Archbishop of Rouen
announced in a sermon that Philip was going to send 6,000
men to Scotland. In September a great council at Nottingham, supported by an assembly of merchants, condemned
the perfidy of the King of France and voted special taxes of
a 'tenth' and a 'fifteenth' to enable Edward to fight the
French. In March 1337 a Parliament at Westminster would

renew these taxes for three years. But it was not yet open war.

What finally made Edward go to war? Some modern commentators credit him with an excessively sophisticated policy, that of a holding operation ; they assume that by attacking France he hoped for no more than to deflect the attention of the French from Guyenne. But this 'maintenance of the *status quo*' interpretation is a little too subtle. Personal motives still seem more plausible. Probably Edward really did feel cheated of his rightful inheritance and had every intention of reconquering France if it was possible ; at the least he was determined to hold Guyenne against the Valois.

Edward III was one of England's most formidable kings, somewhere between Edward I and Henry VIII. Nobody will ever know what drove him—a father complex or simple megalomania—but for over thirty years he showed a demonic energy. After dispossessing Mortimer, he swiftly established his authority over the barons, and by his mid-twenties he had reached the height of his powers. In person he was an immensely tall, strikingly handsome young man with a pointed yellow beard and long drooping moustaches, his features 'like the face of a god' according to a contemporary. He had abundant dignity and charm, speaking English as well as he spoke French, in a caressing voice. (He also spoke and wrote Latin and seems to have understood German and Flemish.) His esoteric cult of chivalry, so much admired in his day, has obscured the man beneath, yet a personality nevertheless emerges—extravagantly elegant, warm in friendship, mercilessly cruel and hardhearted in enmity. He was at the same time self-indulgent, a relentless womanizer, who eventually ruined his health. One can only guess at what must have been a Napoleonic confidence in himself and an oddly self-conscious determination to be a hero-king. With all this he was also realistic—his motto was 'It is as it is'.

Edward's glittering court, a constant round of banquets and jousting, provided him with an excellent general staff. His friends, professional soldiers by virtue of their birth and class, knew how his mind worked and had been tested by him on the Scottish campaigns. Although the old feudal structure was dissolving, society was still a military hierarchy and great lords were *ex-officio* generals. It is significant that in 1338, preparing for a campaign, the King created six new earls. But not all Edward's commanders were earls. There were men like Sir John Chandos, a poor knight from Derbyshire; and Sir Thomas Dagworth, 'a bold professional soldier', did not come from anything like a noble background, belonging to a family of small Norfolk squires. The Belgian—as we would now term him—Sir Walter Manny (born Gauthier de Masny), who had come from Hainault with Edward's Queen Philippa and remained as her carver, was another commander of comparatively humble origins.

One of the more striking foreign ornaments of Edward's court was the ill-famed Robert of Artois, a French Prince of the Blood who was King Philip's brother-in-law and 'his chief and special companion'. According to Jean le Bel, he had done a great deal to obtain the crown for Philip. But in 1330 Robert tried to gain possession of Artois, which had been inherited by his aunt, through forged documents and his fraud was discovered. Two years later the aunt died, supposedly poisoned. Robert was found guilty of her murder, condemned to death and 'chased out of the realm of France' as Froissart puts it; there were allegations, probably justified, of witchcraft. He came to England in 1336, to be warmly welcomed by Edward who made him Earl of Richmond and presented him with three castles and a pension despite Philip's threat that he was the enemy of anyone who sheltered Robert. The exile is said to have fanned Edward's growing enmity towards Philip into white heat; 'He was ever about King Edward and always he counselled him to defy the French King who kept his heritage from him wrongfully.' It was Robert who, in 1338, stage-managed the Oath of the Heron during a banquet at Windsor, when the entire English court swore to do deeds of valour to help their King regain the crown which three of

his uncles had worn. Robert was also a most useful contact
with disaffected noblemen in northern France. Years later,
Froissart heard how King Edward had had the greatest
confidence in 'Sir Robert'.

Edward's Queen was of considerable value as a contact
in the Low Countries. Philippa of Hainault had fallen in
love with the King when she was only twelve and he fourteen, and they had been married in 1328 ; two years later
she bore him the first of their many sons, the future Black
Prince. A tall Belgian beauty with a retroussé nose, dark-
brown eyes and hair and a winning nature, she remained
devoted to her husband despite his many infidelities.
Shrewd and sensible, her only faults were a certain extravagance and a taste for over-dressing. As the daughter of
William the Good, Count of Hainault, of Holland and of
Zeeland, she provided Edward with some extremely useful
relations.

The English saw Flanders much as the French saw
Scotland—an ally in the event of war. Edward sent letters
to the Imperial nobles of the adjoining Low Countries at the
end of 1336, complaining of the French King's injustice
and of his 'great plot' against him and his intention of
stealing Guyenne. But many of these lords remained faithful
friends of Philip VI, so in the spring of 1337 Edward sent
carefully chosen envoys to Hainault—sixty knights led by
the Earls of Salisbury and Huntingdon and the Bishop of
Lincoln. They soon found that ready money could buy allies
against France, including the Counts of Guelders, Juliers
and Limbourg ; they actually paid the Duke of Brabant
£60,000, a sum equal to the combined revenues of England
and Guyenne for an entire year. They also offered to install
the Staple (the official depot where England's raw wool was
stored and marketed) at Antwerp.

Edward was a skilful exponent of the trade embargo. The
Flemish were the cloth-makers of Europe and depended on
English wool. The Count of Flanders, the unpopular Louis
de Nevers, stayed obstinately loyal to Philip and arrested
English merchants in his territory. So in August 1336

Edward forbade the export of raw wool—of which England enjoyed a near-monopoly—to Flanders; neighbouring centres of cloth-manufacture like Brabant were only allowed English wool on condition that it did not go to Flanders. Soon starving Flemish weavers were begging all over the countryside and in all the towns of northern France. City patricians and cloth-workers were united by the threat of utter ruin. In January 1338 the men of Ghent elected Jacob van Artevelde, a rich merchant and brewer of mead, to be their *Hooftman* (Captain), and he quickly took control of Bruges and Ypres as well; according to Froissart, Jacob had soldiers in every town and fortress of Flanders who were in his pay and acted as both spies and hatchet men—'he put to death anyone who opposed him'. In 1339 Count Louis and his family were forced to flee from Flanders which was then ruled by the three towns as a kind of republic; in December of the same year Edward agreed to allow exports of wool to Flanders and to transfer the Staple to Bruges, in return for a military alliance with Jacob van Artevelde and his pikemen—'good men and expert in arms' as even Froissart admits.

Wool was 'the sovereign merchandise and jewel of this realm of England', and the best part of the kingdom's wealth. Since the country was already overtaxed as a result of his Scottish campaigns, Edward decided to plunder the wool trade. At Nottingham in 1336 he obtained a loan on every sack produced, which he hoped would bring him in £70,000 per annum. The King also negotiated a somewhat dubious bargain with a group of wealthy English merchants, who were to buy, export and sell sacks of wool for him in return for a monopoly in exporting wool; to obtain the sacks, he arbitrarily requisitioned the stock at Dordrecht, the unwilling owners being compensated by bonds which exempted them from the *maletote* or export duty. (A woolsack, which was of the sort on which the Lord Chancellor still sits, was then worth about £10.) The scheme was expected to bring in at least £200,000, but in the event it proved a costly failure.

In borrowing, Edward III resorted to even more dubious expedients. He raised vast loans from Lombard bankers—the Bardi, the Frescobaldi and the Peruzzi—from merchants in the Netherlands, from English wool merchants, pledging either English wool or the duties on Guyennois wine as security. Almost everyone who lent him money went bankrupt. The only thing that mattered to Edward III was to obtain sufficient funds to wage war. It is astonishing that he ever hoped to find it. In fairness, it has to be admitted that he did at least consult his subjects before taxing them. The troubles of Edward I, and his own father's ruin, had shown him the need for such consultation. Time and again he explained his needs to both Council and Parliament, often to some effect; in 1343 one of his ministers was able to remind Parliament that the War had been 'undertaken by the joint assent of bishops, lords and commons'. Edward even went so far as to explain himself at local level; in the autumn of 1337 a royal proclamation was read in every English county court, telling how 'the King of the French, hardened in his malice, would assent to no peace or treaty'. But all these explanations did little to make anyone readier to pay more taxes.

Another of Edward's difficulties was mobilization. The old system of feudal military service had practically disappeared and Edward had to use the 'indenture' method, hiring leaders who, by the terms of a carefully drawn up contract, raised a given number of troops of a specified type to serve for a fixed period and for a fixed scale of pay. However, to begin with, his infantry—whether Welsh knifemen or English archers—were conscripted by the traditional 'commissions of array'. The commissioner, usually a local gentleman with military experience, chose what in theory were the most likely-looking men among the population between sixteen and sixty, who were called together by the constables and bailiffs of the district. In practice these included a very dubious element—it has been estimated that as many as 12 per cent of Edward III's troops were outlaws, most of whom were condemned murderers serving in hope of a 'charter of pardon'. Even these conscripts had to be clothed, equipped and paid by the King.

In theory Philip VI should have had no financial worries. But though France was rich, it was none the less extremely difficult for her rulers to tap her wealth. Unlike England there was no single tax system and no single consultative assembly. The centralization of the previous century, which had taken over the powers of the dukes and counts, had left largely intact the local fiscal systems and assemblies. In 1337 Philip actually found himself unable to pay his officials, partly because some local assemblies refused to pay as much as he had asked, partly because some of them refused to pay at all. Philip then instructed his officials to strike bargains, to restore old privileges and grant new ones, to promise future exemption, and to be 'pleasing, gentle and meek' when negotiating. He allowed provincial assemblies to become recognized 'Estates' of nobles, clergy and commons, permitting the growth of the idea that the Estates' consent was necessary for any extraordinary taxation. Eventually he managed to impose and collect an adequate revenue from hearth taxes, from *maletotes* and other subsidies and—later in his reign—from the *gabelle* or duty on salt. On a number of occasions he also devalued the currency, calling in his silver *gros tournois* and reissuing them in debased metal. He extracted more money from the clergy by keeping benefices vacant and appropriating the income. After all these measures Philip still had to borrow a million gold florins from the Pope.

The French King needed every *sou* to pay his soldiers. The feudal system, of a lord holding land from the crown in return for military service, had been breaking down in France since the twelfth century; for generations many nobles had refused to go to the wars. Those who did come expected to be paid, while as in England troops were increasingly hired by *lettres de retenue*—indentures. But somehow Philip found the money to raise a mighty army. In 1340, for example, he had nearly 20,000 heavy cavalry on the borders of Guyenne and over 40,000 on those of

Flanders. Indeed, possibly the real drama of the early stages of the Hundred Years War is the herculean effort of both protagonists to harness the resources of their bewilderingly ramshackle and unwieldy states for a confrontation.

Slowly France and England lumbered into war. On 24 May 1337 King Philip declared that Guyenne had been forfeited by Edward 'because of the many excesses, rebellious and disobedient acts committed by the King of England against Us and Our Royal Majesty', citing in particular Edward's harbouring of the sorcerer Robert of Artois. This declaration is generally considered to be the beginning of the Hundred Years War. In October Edward responded with a formal letter of defiance to 'Philip of Valois who calls himself King of France', laying claim to the French throne.

Philip VI immediately began a formidable onslaught on Guyenne, which lasted for three years. In 1339 his troops took Blaye on the north bank of the Gironde estuary, threatening Bordeaux's access to the sea, and in 1340 took Bourg at the mouth of the Dordogne. On the Garonne, La Réole was again captured by the French who then besieged Saint-Macaire nearer the ducal capital. Besides disrupting the main lines of transport and communication, they laid waste the rich vineyard country of Entre-Deux-Mers and Saint-Emilion and made a determined attempt to take Bordeaux itself. Guyenne only survived because after 1340 Philip was busy elsewhere.

Meanwhile, Edward encircled France with a string of alliances. In August 1337, with a massive bribe, he landed no less a catch than the Holy (though excommunicated) Roman Emperor Ludwig IV, who was Philippa's brother-in-law. After establishing himself and his Queen at a splendid headquarters in Antwerp, Edward went with much pomp to meet Ludwig at Coblenz, where the Emperor promised to help him against Philip 'for seven years', making Edward Vicar-General (or Deputy) of the Empire with jurisdiction over all Imperial fiefs outside Germany. In theory Edward could now summon as his vassals all the lords of the Low Countries and even the Counts of

Burgundy and Savoy ; in practice the post gave him hardly more than a dubious prestige. Nevertheless Edward and Philippa returned to Antwerp to hold court in the winter of 1338–1339 and 'kept their house right honourably all that winter, and caused money, gold and silver, to be made at Antwerp, great plenty'.

If the English King was enjoying diplomatic triumphs, his country was enduring raids by enemy privateers. In March 1338 Nicolas Béhuchet and his sailors burnt all Portsmouth save for the parish church and a hospital. A few months later Hue Quiéret took five rich ships off Walcheren, including the great cog *Christopher*—'richly laden with money and wool'—which had been built for Edward himself. In October 1338 Southampton went up in flames, then Guernsey was occupied. The following year the French raided from Cornwall to Kent, attacking Dover and Folkestone, putting the entire Isle of Wight to fire and sword, and even appearing in the Thames Estuary. French warships became an increasingly serious menace to the vessels which took wool to Flanders, and to the great wine fleet which every summer sailed between Southampton and Bordeaux. Furthermore, any English expedition to France had to reckon with being intercepted en route.

In fact England was facing a full-scale invasion. Informed Englishmen had feared one by Philip's Crusader fleet as early as 1333, and the raids of 1338–1340 caused grim rumours to circulate among the coastal folk—tales of kidnapped Kentish fishermen being mutilated and then paraded through the streets of Calais were not without foundation. A home-guard was organized for every southern county, the *garde de la mer*. On 23 March 1339, Philip VI issued an *ordonnance* for the conquest of England. Suggestions for the destruction of English merchant shipping (including even fishing boats) put forward by Béhuchet and costed as nearly as possible, were set aside—the 'Grand Army of the Sea' took precedence. Within little more than a year a fleet of over 200 vessels were assembling off Sluys on the Zeeland sea-coast, at the mouth of the river Zwyn. (In those days

Sluys was an important seaport, though today the Zwyn has long been closed by silt.)

The English avenged the raids with gusto, sacking Le Treport in the spring of 1339. In the autumn of the same year they sailed into the harbour at Boulogne, burning thirty French ships at anchor, hanging their captains and leaving the lower town in flames. But the French invasion fleet continued to grow. Mille de Noyers, Marshal of France, planned to take 60,000 troops over the Channel.

Edward tried desperately to find enough money to fight Philip on land. His first expedition, in 1337—15,000 men under William de Bohun, Earl of Northampton, sent to harry the lands of the Count of Flanders—proved ruinously expensive. In 1339 he pawned the crown made for his coronation as King of France; he had already pawned the Great Crown of England. In September of that year he at last managed to invade France from the Low Countries in person, his troops consisting of a small English army which joined him at Antwerp, together with some noticeably unreliable German and Dutch mercenaries and the Duke of Brabant. He advanced slowly into Picardy, deliberately destroying the entire countryside of the Thiérache and besieging Cambrai. Philip moved up to meet him from Saint-Quentin with an army of 35,000 cavalry and foot.

King Edward, only too anxious to be attacked, drew up his army before Flamengerie in three lines; the English in front, the German princes and their men behind, and in third place the Duke of Brabant with his Brabançons and Flemings. (The English formation was dismounted men-at-arms in the centre and archers on the wings—obviously Edward hoped to employ the tactics he would use at Crécy six years later). Philip titillated the English lords' appetite for chivalrous glory by issuing a challenge to trial by battle between the respective paladins of each army—a challenge which he then unsportingly withdrew. Still more damaging, he refused to fight at all, though his army outnumbered Edward's by more than two to one. After a campaign of hardly more than a month, the English King was forced to retreat.

What makes the 1339 campaign of particular interest is the misery inflicted on French non-combatants. It was the custom of medieval warfare to wreak as much damage as possible on both towns and country in order to weaken the enemy government. The English had acquired nasty habits in their Scottish wars and during the campaign Edward wrote to the young Prince of Wales how his men had burnt and plundered 'so that the country is quite laid waste of corn, of cattle and of any other goods'. Every little hamlet went up in flames, each house being looted and then put to the torch. Neither abbeys and churches nor hospitals were spared. Hundreds of civilians—men, women and children, priests, bourgeois and peasants—were killed while thousands fled starving to the fortified towns. The English King saw the effectiveness of 'total war' in such a rich and thickly populated land; henceforth the *chevauchée*, a raid which systematically devastated enemy territory, was used as much as possible in the hope of making the French sick of war. (Exactly the same principle inspired General Sherman's March through Georgia four centuries later.) The English were obviously satisfied with what they had achieved on this occasion. One of Edward's advisers, the great judge Sir Geoffrey Scrope, took a French cardinal 'up a great and high tower, showing him the whole countryside towards Paris for a distance of fifteen miles burning in every place'. 'Sir,' asked Scrope, 'does it not seem to you that the silken thread encompassing France is broken?' At this, the cardinal fell down 'as if dead, stretched out on the roof of the tower from fear and grief'.

Some more detached observers were equally horrified. Pope Benedict XII sent 6,000 gold florins to Paris for the relief of the refugees. The Archdeacon of Eu, who distributed the Papal bounty, left a report which speaks of 7,879 victims, mostly destitute, whom he relieved (though he does not give any estimate of the number of dead); nearly all were simple peasants or artisans. He tells of destruction by fire in 174 parishes, many of which had been entirely demolished together with their parish churches.

Edward now found himself even more alarmingly short of money than usual. After buying with his last remaining cash the alliance with Jacob van Artevelde, the King returned to England to try and find new funds, though he had to leave his children and pregnant wife at Ghent as surety for his debts. (His third son to survive, born at Ghent in his absence, was consequently named 'John of Gaunt'.) The great historian of the Hundred Years War, Professor Edouard Perroy, writes how at this time, 'anyone except Edward III would have been discouraged'.

Before leaving for England, Edward held an imposing assembly at Ghent on 6 February 1340. Here he publicly assumed the arms of France, quartering the golden lilies on their blue ground with his own gold lions on red, and styled himself King of France. (He is said to have done so on the advice of Jacob van Artevelde, who pointed out that by doing this he would become not merely the ally of the gallant Flemish pikemen but their King.) In addition Edward issued a cunningly worded proclamation addressed not only to the French lords but also to the common people of France; he promised to 'revive the good laws and customs which were in force in the time of St Louis our ancestor', to reduce taxation and to stop debasing the coinage, and to be 'guided by the counsel and advice of the peers, prelates, magnates and faithful vassals of the kingdom'. He was posing as a champion of local independence against Valois centralization, offering an alternative monarchy.

Edward then sent yet another insulting letter to Philip, challenging him to trial by battle as 'we do purpose to recover the right we have to the inheritance which you so violently withhold from us'. The combat was to be either between the two kings—chivalrous but hardly fair as Philip was forty-seven and Edward only twenty-eight—or else between a hundred of Philip's best knights and a hundred of Edward's.

The challenge was never withdrawn, and henceforward

Valois and Plantagenet were locked in an unrelenting struggle. Edward III had shown extraordinary determination and opportunism, even if he had failed to bring the French King to battle. In contrast Philip VI, now approaching old age by medieval standards, had remained entirely on the defensive. Despite his much advertised taste for the tournament, Philip successfully used a strategy of tempting Edward to invade and then refusing battle until the enemy's money ran out.

2

Crécy 1340–1350

Therefore Valois say, wilt thou yet resign,
Before the sickle's thrust into the corn?

The Raigne of King Edward III

From battle and murder, and from sudden
death, Good Lord, deliver us.

The Litany

The next stage of the Hundred Years War is the story of
Edward III's relentless perseverance despite setbacks both
at home and abroad, and of how he was eventually rewarded.
Blocked in Flanders, this dogged and rather terrifying man
attacked in Brittany, in Guyenne, in Normandy and even in
the Ile de Paris. First, however, he won a great victory at
sea.

When the King arrived back in England from Ghent in
the spring of 1340, he summoned Parliament and told it that
unless new taxes were raised he would have to return to the
Low Countries and be imprisoned for debt. Parliament made
plain that it was very unhappy about Edward's extravagance,
but reluctantly granted him a 'ninth' for two years—the
ninth sheaf, fleece and lamb from every farm, and the ninth

part of every townsman's goods. In return the King had to promise to abolish certain taxes and make a number of reforms in government. However he could now return to Ghent to redeem his wife and children and recommence operations against Philip. He collected reinforcements, assembling a fleet on the Suffolk coast for their transport. En route he intended to deal with the French armada at Sluys.

Contrary to what the chronicler Geoffrey le Baker seems to have heard, the King had been planning this move for some time. The enemy invasion fleet was now dauntingly large; it included not only French but also Castilian and Genoese vessels, Castile being an ally of France while the Genoese were mercenaries under the veteran sea-captain Barbanera (or '*Barbenoire*' as the French called him). Edward had requisitioned all the ships he could find, literally pressganging men to sail and to fight on them. Even so, his sailing masters, Robert Morley and the Fleming Jehan Crabbe, warned him that the odds were too high. The King accused them of trying to frighten him, 'but I shall cross the sea and those who are afraid may stay at home'. On 22 June 1340 he finally set sail from the little port of Orwell in Suffolk, he himself on board his great cog *Thomas*. En route he was joined by Lord Morley, Admiral of the Northern Fleet, with fifty vessels—together their combined force amounted to 147 ships.

Probably these vessels were nearly all cogs. The English government had commissioned a number of converted cogs, the 'King's Ships', which for all their shortcomings were intended for war. The cog was basically a merchant ship, designed for carrying cargoes which ranged from wool to wine and from livestock to passengers. Shallow-draughted and small-sized—usually 30 to 40 tons, though sometimes as big as 200—it could use creeks and inlets inaccessible to bigger ships. Clinker-built, broad-beamed and with a rounded bow and poop, it was a boat for all weathers and for the North Sea. But while the cog made an excellent troop transport, it was hardly a warship—even though special fighting tops could be built on the fore and stern castles.

Tactics were brutally simple—to move to windward of the enemy ship and then try to sink her by ramming or by running her aground.

With its single square sail and rudimentary rudder, a cog was slow to manœuvre. The King's Ships were particularly at risk when confronted by a purpose-built battle-craft, like the Mediterranean galley which was armed with a proper ram and a stone-throwing catapult, and whose oars gave it superior speed and manœuvrability. For the last forty years the French had maintained a royal dockyard, constructed by Genoese experts, which specialized in producing these galleys—the Clos des Galées at Rouen—and a battle on the open sea might have placed Edward at a considerable tactical disadvantage.

The English fleet anchored off the Zeeland coast, opposite Blankenberghe, on 23 June. Scouts were landed and sent out to reconnoitre. They returned to report how they had seen at Sluys 'so great a number of ships that their masts seemed to be like a great wood'. Edward stayed at sea and spent all day discussing what to do.

The French Admirals, Hue Quiéret and Nicolas Béhuchet, were 'right good and expert men of war' but no seamen—Béhuchet was a former tax collector—and there was a marked lack of liaison with their Castilian and Genoese colleagues. Barbanera begged the Admirals to put to sea, no doubt so that he could use his three galleys against the English cogs, but they insisted on staying in the estuary where they could fight a land battle, which was just what Edward wanted. The French massed their fleet in three squadrons, one behind the other, the ships lashed together with chains and barricaded by planks and by small boats weighted with stones. The first squadron had captured English cogs at one end of the line, each vessel mounting four cannon and defended by crossbowmen and crewed by Flemings and Picards. The second squadron was manned by men from Boulogne and Dieppe, the third by Normans. But the 20,000 men on board were largely pressganged and few of them had ever seen a battle. There were no more than

150 knights and 400 professional crossbowmen all told in the whole of this Grand Army of the Sea—the rest were frightened fisherfolk, bargees and longshoremen.

That night King Edward divided his own fleet into three squadrons, marshalling his ships in threes—two filled with archers flanking one of men-at-arms. He kept in reserve a fourth squadron, of ships defended entirely by archers. Then at 5 in the morning he tacked away from his anchorage into the wind and waited for the tide to turn. When his sailing-masters finally put their helms over and steered towards Sluys, they had the wind and the sun behind them and the tide running with them. Barbanera at once realized the danger. 'My Lord', he told Béhuchet, 'the King of England and his fleet are coming down on us. Stand out to sea with your ships, for if you remain here, shut in between these great dykes, the English, who have the wind, the tide and the sun with them, will hem you in and you will be unable to manœuvre.' But this last desperate warning went unheeded, whereupon the Genoese galleys slipped anchor and escaped just in time.

At about 9 o'clock the English fleet sailed straight into the French ships who, still at their moorings, were 'arrayed like a line of castles'. According to an enthralled English chronicler, 'an iron cloud of quarrels from crossbows and arrows from long-bows fell on the enemy, dealing death to thousands'. Then the English ships crashed into the French and grappled together. The men-at-arms boarded with swords, axes and half-pikes, while the bowmen continued to shoot flight after flight and seamen threw heavy stones, iron bolts and quicklime from the mast-tops; there were even divers who tried to sink the enemy ships by boring holes in their hulls below water. The battle surged backwards and forwards from one vessel to another.

An early casualty was a fine English cog which was carrying 'a great number of countesses, ladies, knights' wives and other damosels, that were going to see the Queen at Ghent'. Although strongly guarded by archers and men-at-arms, their ship was sunk—it is said—by cannon. The screams of the drowning ladies must have maddened the English.

Froissart, who had met men who were there, writes: 'This battle was right fierce and terrible [*moult felenesse et moult orible*]; for the battles on the sea are more dangerous and fiercer than the battles by land; for on the sea there is no reculing nor fleeing; there is no remedy but to fight and to abide fortune, and every man to shew his prowess.' The King was in the thick of the mêlée and was wounded in the leg—his white leather boots were covered in blood. There was an especially murderous struggle to regain the great cog *Christopher* which was defended by Genoese crossbowmen, but at last it was 'won by the Englishmen, and all that were within it were taken or slain'. The English found considerable difficulty in capturing the Castilian ships because their sides were so tall. The battle 'endured from the morning till it was noon, and the Englishmen endured much pain'.

Eventually archers gave the advantage to Edward's men —they could shoot two or even three arrows for every one crossbow quarrel—and the first French squadron was overwhelmed. Many of the enemy jumped overboard, their wounded being thrown after them. The sea was so full of corpses that those who did not drown could not tell whether they were swimming in water or blood, though the knights must have gone straight to the bottom in their heavy armour. Hue Quiéret, after being badly wounded, surrendered—to be beheaded immediately. Béhuchet was also captured, to be strung up by English knights within a matter of minutes.

The sight of their Admiral's corpse swinging from the yardarm of the *Thomas* (the King's flagship) caused panic among the French second squadron, many of whose crews leapt overboard without resisting. The onset of dusk went unnoticed, so bright was the light of the burning ships. When darkness fell the King remained before Sluys, 'and all that night abode in his ship . . . with great noise of trumpets and other instruments'.

During the night thirty enemy vessels slipped anchor and fled, while the *Saint-Jacques* of Dieppe continued to fight on in the dark—when she was finally taken by the Earl of Huntingdon, 400 corpses were found on board. Those French ships who stayed were attacked from the rear by Flemish fishermen in barges. When morning came Edward sent Jehan Crabbe and a well-armed flotilla in pursuit, but he had no reason to be dismayed that a few enemy vessels escaped. The entire French fleet, with the exception of those who had fled during the night, had been captured or sent to the bottom, while thousands of its men had died—'there was not one that escaped but all were slain', Froissart boasts with pardonable exaggeration.

Edward made a pilgrimage of thanksgiving to the shrine of Our Lady of Ardembourg. Later he commemorated the battle of Sluys on a new gold coin, the noble of six shillings and eight pence; he is shown on board a ship floating on the waves, crowned and bearing a sword and a shield which quarters the royal arms of France and England. These coins so impressed contemporaries that some people said they had been made by alchemists in the Tower of London. They gave rise to a jingle:

Foure things our Noble showeth unto me,
King, ship, and sword, and power of the sea.

But Sluys had not won Edward command of the Channel, let alone of the seas—only two years later the French sacked Plymouth for a second time. None the less, he had rid England of a very real threat of invasion. With hindsight one can see that Sluys marked the passing of the initiative to the English—indeed, to the men of 1340 God had shown he was on their side.

However, King Edward still seemed no nearer to achieving the conquest of France. Towards the end of July, accompanied by seven earls and an army which included 9,000 archers, several thousand Flemish pikemen, and a multitude of mercenaries, he laid siege to Tournai.

But though he may have had as many as 30,000 troops, he had no siege engines—mangonels or battering-rams—and could do little apart from camping before the walls. And, as in 1339, his army included Dutch and German lords who had been hired under the indenture system ; these quarrelled incessantly with each other, insisted on being paid on time, and left when they felt like it.

Meanwhile Philip who was 'very angry at the defeat of his navy'—only his court jester had dared tell him the news —marched to relieve Tournai with an army even bigger than Edward's and mustering nearly 20,000 men-at-arms. The French King adopted his usual tactics, refusing to offer battle and keeping his troops in the surrounding hills from where they raided Edward's outposts and ambushed his supply lines. The English King grumbled to the young Prince of Wales, in a letter : 'He dug trenches all round him and cut down big trees so that we might not get at him.' Edward's army was already unpaid and mutinous, and soon supplies and fodder began to run out. Shorter of money than ever and totally unable to pay his angry mercenaries, the English King was forced to negotiate a truce, at Espléchin on 25 September. For once even Edward seems to have been discouraged ; in October he had told the Pope's envoys that he was ready to surrender his claims to the French crown if Philip would give him the Duchy of Aquitaine (as it had been in Henry III's day) in full sovereignty. For he could expect no money from England ; many of his subjects had refused to pay the promised ninth and in some places tax collectors had been met with armed resistance. Two months later, Edward fled secretly from the Low Countries to escape his clamorous creditors.

The King returned to England in a fury. As he saw it, years of work had been ruined by the failure of his govern-ment to find him enough money. The chief villain in his eyes was the Chancellor, John Stratford, Archbishop of Canter-bury, whom he believed to have mishandled the taxes. Edward actually informed the Pope that Stratford had deliberately kept him short of money in the hope that he would be defeated and killed; incredibly, the King insinuated that the Archbishop had adulterous designs on the Queen and had tried to set her against him. Stratford saved himself by bolting to Canterbury where he took sanctuary, but many of his officials were arrested. However, after casting himself as a second Thomas à Becket, the wily prelate then managed to shift the dispute from the administrative to the constitutional field—he accused Edward of infringing Magna Carta, insisted on the right of ministers to be tried by Parliament, and manoeuvred him into summoning one in April 1341. The Archbishop found massive support in the Parliament, and the King was wise enough to give way in return for supplies; soon he was reconciled with Stratford. Edward knew very well that he had to keep his subjects' support, above all that of the magnates, not only to continue with his French ambitions but to keep his throne.

Despite the subsidies granted in 1341, King Edward could not repay his loans. These included £180,000 which he had borrowed from the Florentines. In 1343 the Peruzzi, who were owed £77,000 (quite apart from interest) went bankrupt; the Bardi followed them three years later. For a short time the small group of native English financiers— among them an enterprising Hull merchant, William de la Pole, whose family will be heard of later—who controlled the wool trade tried to make a profit by lending money to the King, but in 1349 they in their turn crashed. However, by then Edward was at least able to rely on the *maletote* or export duty on wool. The Parliament, which included many wool producers, had at last grown reconciled to this hateful tax becoming an annual subsidy, partly because they had wrested from the King the right of controlling taxes. Indeed the growth of parliamentary power was one of the most important side effects of the Hundred Years War for the English.

In the spring of 1341 Duke John III of Brittany died. The ducal succession was disputed by Jeanne, Countess of Blois, the daughter of the late Duke's younger brother who had predeceased him; and by John, Count of Montfort, the

Duke's half-brother. Jeanne was the niece of Philip VI, who—with a certain irony, in view of his inheritance through an exclusively male line—recognized her as Duchess of Brittany. John of Montfort thereupon sailed to England, where he acknowledged Edward to be the rightful King of France; in return he was accepted as Duke of Brittany and was also created Earl of Richmond (Robert of Artois having recently been killed). There were sound economic and strategic reasons why Edward should intervene in this struggle. On their way to Bordeaux, or to Portugal and Castile, the little English ships dared not cross the stormy Bay of Biscay but hugged the coast; it was essential that they should be able to put in at Breton ports and sail without fear of Breton privateers. A friendly Duke had to reign at Rennes if the Gascon sea-route was to be guaranteed, just as later British communications with India depended on a biddable Cairo and a biddable Aden.

A vicious little war ensued in Brittany, the lesser nobles and the peasants of the Celtic west rallying to John of Montfort, the great lords and French-speaking bourgeois of the east supporting Jeanne of Blois. In November 1341 Count John was besieged in Nantes by the French, who catapulted the heads of thirty of his knights over the walls which so terrified the defenders that they surrendered, John being taken prisoner to Paris. However, his gallant Countess kept his cause alive. She was saved by the arrival of Edward III in person in the autumn of 1342, bringing 12,000 men with him. He launched a savage *chevauchée*, and laid siege to the duchy's three great cities—Rennes, Nantes and Vannes. King Philip's son and heir, John, Duke of Normandy, marched to relieve them with a host which outnumbered the English army by at least two to one. Edward thereupon copied Philip's precedent by digging in at a strong position. Autumn turned into a wet midwinter and soon both camps were waterlogged. In these dismal conditions Papal envoys were able to negotiate a truce in January 1343. The King returned to England, but he left troops behind him in well-chosen fortresses, under the redoubtable Sir Thomas

Dagworth, to keep the Montfort cause alive. When John of Montfort died in 1345, his young son took refuge at the English court where he was brought up; eventually he regained his duchy. In consequence Edward could always count on finding support in Brittany.

In 1334 Pope Clement VI succeeded in arranging a peace conference between the English and the French. It took place in the autumn at Avignon. The English tried to discuss Edward's claim to the throne of France, but the French refused even to consider the matter. Then the English asked for compensation in the shape of an enlarged Guyenne, free of any obligations to the French King and in full sovereignty. Indeed Edward may well have been ready to settle for this. But Philip was not prepared to give away a single foot of French soil—his final offer was a slight enlargement of Guyenne's frontiers on condition that the duchy was held not by Edward but by one of Edward's sons as a vassal of France. Philip VI believed that he was negotiating from a position of strength.

Edward now adopted a new strategy, attacking in France on three fronts with comparatively small armies. His interim objective may have been to strengthen his position in Guyenne while reinforcing the alliance with Flanders. In the spring of 1345 his Plantagenet cousin, Henry of Grosmont, Earl of Derby and future Duke of Lancaster, assisted by Sir Hugh Hastings, struck in upper Gascony. He caught the French off guard, capturing Bergerac and many other towns and castles; the latter included La Réole, which the English had lost in 1325 and which only fell after a determined siege of nine weeks. This stronghold, high above the river Gironde and forty miles from Bordeaux, enabled the English to regain the long-disputed Agenais. They also penetrated as far north as Angoulême, which they took by storm. Simultaneously Sir Thomas Dagworth took the offensive in Brittany, overrunning French garrisons.

The following spring there was a massive French counterattack in the south-west, Duke John of Normandy besieging the Earl of Derby at Aiguillon (where the rivers Lot and

Garonne meet). The Duke may not have had 100,000 troops as Froissart tells us, but he could well have had 20,000—a considerable proportion of the French military might. Edward now prepared his third front. Reading the chronicles with all their tales of chivalry and knightly deeds, one tends not to realize the surprisingly modern thoroughness and professionalism of his strategy.

The French anticipated an English invasion from Flanders. But Jacob van Artevelde had been overthrown and a pro-French count returned. Against all expectations Edward chose to launch his third front, and main attack, in Normandy. It may have been an accidental choice. Froissart heard that Edward actually set sail for Guyenne, but was blown back to the marches of Cornwall, where, while waiting, he was advised to try Normandy instead by an important Norman lord, Godefroi d'Harcourt, who had fallen foul of Philip VI and fled to England. He told Edward that the people of Normandy were not used to war, and that 'there shall ye find great towns that be not walled, whereby your men shall have such winning, that they shall be the better thereby twenty years after'.

When King Edward sailed from Porchester on 5 July 1346 he had with him 'a thousand ships, pinnaces and supply vessels', carrying about 15,000 men. (This was a considerable logistic achievement; even the great host which his father had led—on land—to defeat at Bannockburn thirty years before had numbered no more than 18,000.) As one of the most successful expeditionary forces in English history its composition—knights, lancers, bowmen (mounted and on foot) and knifemen—is worth examining in detail. It is significant that there was a far larger proportion of volunteers than hitherto, attracted by the prospect of plunder; noblemen had no difficulty in recruiting big companies under 'indentures of war'.

In 1346 an English man-at-arms was still armoured mainly in 'chainmail' of interlinked metal rings. A shirt of this mail, over a padded tunic, covered him from neck to knees and was laced on to a conical helmet which was open faced but which occasionally had a visor. (The great barrel helm was seldom worn in battle nowadays.) He had steel breastplates and plates on his arms, together with elbow pieces and articulated foot-guards over mail stockings. Over all he wore a short linen surcoat. English knights were noticeably old-fashioned compared to the French, for across the Channel Philip VI's paladins had their shoulders and limbs also covered by plate, and helmets (*bascinets*) with hinged, snout-like visors which had breathing holes. Their surcoat had been replaced by the shorter leather *jupon*. The horses also wore armour, with plate for their heads and mail or leather for their flanks. The basic weapon of both English and French was a long straight sword, hung in front at first but later moved to the left side and balanced by a short dagger on the right (called a *misericord* or 'mercy' on account of being used to dispatch the mortally wounded). On horseback, a ten-foot lance was carried and a small, flat-iron-shaped shield, and sometimes a short, steel-hafted battle-axe. On foot the principal weapon was usually the halberd—a combined half-pike and axe.

Only the men-at-arms—a term which covered knight-bannerets (paid 4s a day), knights bachelor (2s a day) and esquires (1s a day)—could afford this enormously expensive equipment which (in theory at least) also required two armed valets and three mounts per man-at-arms—a warhorse, a packhorse for the armour and a palfrey to ride when not on the battlefield. Some men-at-arms who could only afford a single horse wore instead the lighter, cheaper brigandine which was a leather jacket sewn with thin, overlapping metal plates. The light lancers or *hobelars* (also 1s a day), who rode with the men-at-arms, made do with a metal hat, steel gauntlets and a 'jack'—a short quilted coat stiffened with iron studs and rather like a modern flak-jacket.

The jack was the armour of the more fortunate archers, whether mounted or on foot. Their weapon, the famous English long-bow, was to revolutionize military tactics. It was in fact of Welsh rather than English origin, having first come to attention in the twelfth century during campaigns in Gwent, where its ability to send an arrow through the thickness of a church door had much impressed the English. Since Edward I's reign every village in England had contributed to a national pool of archers, every yokel being commanded by law to practise at the butts on Sundays. By 1346 the long-bow had become standardized, each archer carrying as many as two dozen arrows; further supplies were carried in carts. The long-bowmen could shoot ten or even twelve a minute, literally darkening the sky, and had a fighting range of over 150 yards with a plate-armour-piercing range of about sixty. There was a huge arsenal of bows and arrows in the Tower of London ; perhaps it was ironical that many of the bow-staves had been imported from Guyenne. The archer also carried either a sword, a billhook, an axe or a maul—a leaden mallet with a five-foot-long wooden handle.

Mounted archers on ponies first appeared in Edward III's Scottish campaigns. They carried a lance and were paid 6d a day—the wage of a master craftsman. The King valued these archers so highly that he had a bodyguard of 200 mounted bowmen from Cheshire in green and white uniforms. Together, horse-archers and men-at-arms combined fire power and armour with the utmost mobility. Yet although increasingly employed, mounted archers were probably always outnumbered by foot archers. Nor must it be forgotten that they had to dismount when in action as they could not shoot from the saddle. It cannot be too much emphasized that all long-bowmen were essentially defensive troops who could only play a decisive part in a battle if they were attacked by an enemy advancing towards them over the right terrain.

The long-bow and its murderous potential were so far unknown outside the British Isles. The favourite missile weapon of the French was the crossbow, a complicated instrument with a bow reinforced by horn and sinew ; to draw it the crossbowman had to place his foot in the stirrup at the front end of the bow, fasten the string on to a hook on his belt, which meant crouching down by bending his knees

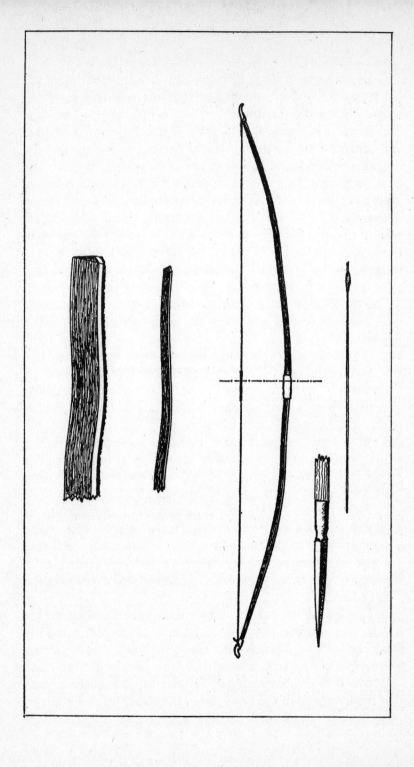

and back, and then stand up, pulling the string until it could be engaged in the trigger mechanism. The crossbow had sights and fired small, heavy arrows known as quarrels. Its advantages were its longer range and greater accuracy and velocity, its disadvantages being its weight (up to 20 lbs) and slow rate of fire—only four quarrels a minute, at best.

In addition King Edward seems to have had guns in 1346. This has been disputed, but the previous year he definitely ordered the manufacture of 100 *ribaulds*. The *ribauld* was a bundle of many small-bore tubes—a bit like the *mitrailleuse* of the 1870s—mounted on a cart. Such weapons were seldom lethal, except to those firing them,

Long-bow

Though various woods were used in their construction, yew was the best. Bows were made from the main trunk or from thick boughs. Under the scaly bark is a layer of white sapwood that withstands tension very well. Beneath this is the red heartwood that is resistant to compression and gives drive to the bow. It is the combination of these two characteristics that results in the excellence of yew for making bows. The maker, or bowyer, had to follow the run of the grain in the wood so as to leave a layer of the sapwood, about $\frac{1}{8}''$ in thickness, on the outside of the heartwood. For this reason there are, almost invariably, irregularities in the curve of the yew long-bow.

The left-hand drawing shows a section of yew split from the main trunk. The next sketch shows a part of the rough stave with the thin layer of sapwood left on the outer surface. The two limbs were tapered to give a smooth curve when the bow was drawn. Horn tips with notches—or nocks, as they were called—for the bowstring were fitted to the better bows, but alternatively grooves were cut into the wood. The length of bows varied from about 5′ 8″ to about 6′ 4″.

The arrows were about 30″ in length and though many forms of head have been found, the so-called bodkin was generally accepted as the most deadly in warfare. It was basically a four-sided, case-hardened steel spike, as shown in the illustration. The string was of hemp with a spliced loop at one end and secured with a timber hitch at the other. The centre was served with thread to protect the strands from the abrasion of the arrow nock and from the fingers of the drawing hand, on which a leather shooting-glove was often worn.

With a typical war bow, having a draw-weight of 80–100 lb, the instantaneous thrust on the string at the moment it checks the forward movement of the two limbs when it is shot is in the order of 400 lb, so it needed to have a breaking strain of about 600 lb to allow an adequate safety margin.

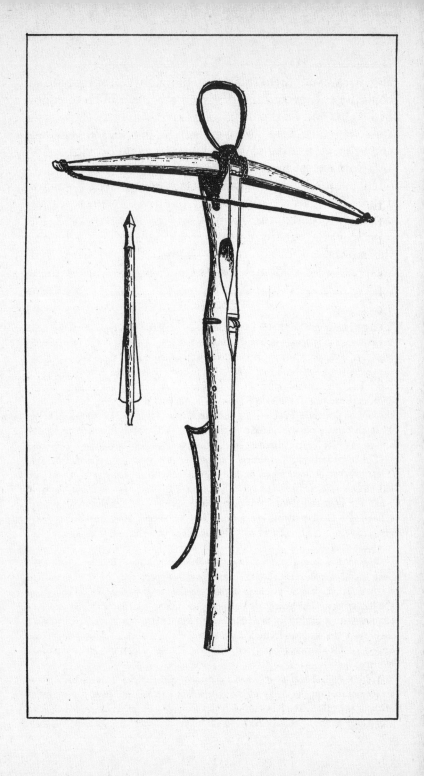

but they produced plenty of noise, flame and acrid black smoke.

Edward's army also included large numbers of light infantry, who were paid 2d a day. These scouts and skirmishers were Welsh, Cornish and even Irish 'kern', armed with dirks and javelins—'certain rascals that went on foot with great knives'. Their speciality was creeping beneath the men-at-arms' horses and stabbing them in the belly, though they seem to have spent most of their time cutting the throats of the enemy wounded.

Modern research has revealed a far greater degree of sophistication in medieval logistics than one might expect from reading Froissart's 'honourable and noble adventures of feats of arms'. Even if most armies lived off the country, supply depots were needed while their troops were assembling. Victuals included salted and smoked meat, dried fish, cheese, flour, oats and beans, together with vast quantities of ale. These were gathered from all over England, usually by the sheriffs, and sent to the embarkation point in wagons along the rough, muddy roads, in barges down the rivers, or by sea—in the latter case on board commandeered ships. In addition there were fuel and munitions—among the latter being siege engines (springalds, arbalests, trebuchets and mangonels), weapons (especially bow-staves and arrows and bow-strings), gunpowder and shot. Huge numbers of horses

Crossbow

A military crossbow, one of the types used in the latter half of the fourteenth century and during the fifteenth century. The length overall is about 30", the span of the bow about 26", the weight about 4¾ lb.

The stock or tiller is of wood, surfaced along the top with antler. The actual bow, or lath, is of composite construction, employing wood, horn and sinew. The fore end is fitted with an iron stirrup in which the foot is placed to facilitate spanning the bow—or drawing the string—with the belt and claw back to the revolving nut mechanism.

The bolt shown was the most widely used form for military purposes. It is about 15" long, the shaft is of wood and the flights, or vanes, are of leather, horn or wood. The rear end is tapered to fit between the lugs of the nut, while the fore end of the shaft is supported by a grooved rest, made from antler.

were needed for such an expedition. The ships to transport them, and also the men and their supplies, were requisitioned by royal sergeants-at-arms, who 'arrested' them together with their crews, their original cargoes being compulsorily unloaded. The requisitioning took time and troops often had to wait at the ports for long periods before they could cross the sea.

On 13 July 1346 the English armada landed at La Hogue, on the north of the Cherbourg peninsula. As at D-Day in 1944, they were completely unexpected by the Normans, many of whose towns—as Godefroi d'Harcourt had told Edward—proved to be unwalled. The following day the King launched a *chevauchée* through the Cotentin, deliberately devastating the rich countryside, his men burning mills and barns, orchards, haystacks and cornricks, smashing wine vats, tearing down and setting fire to the thatched cabins of the villagers, whose throats they cut together with those of their livestock. One may presume that the usual atrocities were perpetrated on the peasants— the men were tortured to reveal hidden valuables, the women suffering multiple rape and sexual mutilation, those who were pregnant being disembowelled. Terror was an indispensable accompaniment to every *chevauchée* and Edward obviously intended to wreak the maximum '*dampnum*'— the medieval term for that total war which struck at an enemy King through his subjects. All ranks of the English army tasted the sweets of plunder. When Barfleur surrendered it did not escape from being sacked and burnt, 'and much gold and silver was found there, and rich jewels : there was found so much riches, that the boys and villains of the host set nothing by good furred coats'. They then burnt Cherbourg and Montebourg and other towns, 'and won so much riches that it was marvel to reckon on it'. A party of 500 men-at-arms rode off with Godefroi d'Harcourt for a distance of 'six or seven leagues' to lay waste and to plunder, and were astonished by the plenty which they found—'the granges full of corn, the houses full of all riches, rich burgesses, carts and chariots, horse, swine, muttons and other beasts . . . but the soldiers made no count to the King nor to none of his officers of the gold and silver that they did get'. The burgesses were probably sent back to England to be ransomed, a fate which seems to have been the lot of the entire town of Barfleur.

On 26 July Edward's army reached Caen, larger than any town in England apart from London, and soon stormed their way through the bridge gate. When the garrison surrendered, the English started to plunder, rape and kill, 'for the soldiers were without mercy'. The desperate inhabitants then began to throw stones, wooden beams and iron bars from the rooftops down into the narrow streets, killing more than 500 Englishmen. Edward ordered the entire population to be put to the sword and the town burnt, 'and there were done in the town many evil deeds, murders and robberies'— although Godefroi d'Harcourt persuaded the King to rescind his order. The sack lasted three days and 3,000 townsmen died. One chronicler says that the English took 'only jewelled clothing or very valuable ornaments'. The plunder was sent back to the fleet by barges. Edward seems to have done better than anyone : Froissart relates how from Caen the King 'sent into England his navy of ships charged with clothes, jewels, vessels of gold and silver, and other riches, and of prisoners more than 60 knights and 300 burgesses'—the latter for ransom.

One of the prisoners was the Abbess of Caen, who must surely have complained that her captivity was against all the usages of Christian war. The King had issued the customary order to spare churches and consecrated buildings, but even so, nuns were raped and many religious houses suffered. The priory of Gerin was burnt to the ground and later the strongly defended monastery town of Troarn fell by storm.

Among the spoils of Caen was Philip VI's *ordonnance* of 1339 for the invasion of England. Edward, who possessed an almost modern flair for propaganda, at once had copies made to be read in every parish church in England; in London, after a splendid pontifical procession, it was read at St Paul's by the Archbishop of Canterbury 'that he might thereby rouse the people'.

The English King then continued his march in the direction of Paris, still slaying and burning. He was able to pay his soldiers generously in addition to their loot, Jean le Bel tells us. The approach of the English was announced by flames in the distance and by mobs of terrified refugees. Philip massed as many troops as possible and sent reinforcements to Rouen—it seems likely he feared that if Edward captured the Norman capital he would control the lower Seine and be able to obtain fresh troops of his own from Flanders. Edward's main objective had been achieved—to distract the French from Guyenne and Brittany, and lessen the pressure on Lancaster and Dagworth.

The English army finally stopped at Poissy, advance parties burning Saint-Cloud and Saint-Germain within sight of the walls of Paris. The English King had no intention of attacking the French capital—he had no proper siege train, and in any case his troops were hopelessly outnumbered by the vast army which Philip was assembling at Saint-Denis just outside Paris. The French had demolished all the bridges along that part of the Seine, hoping to trap the English. However, Edward managed to repair the bridge at Poissy over which he retreated northwards, destroying everything he could; at Mareuil he burnt the town, the fortress and even the priory. He next found his way barred by the river Somme, along which the bridges had also been broken down. Fortunately a local peasant showed him a sandy-bottomed ford just below Abbeville—'the Passage of Blanche-taque'. The opposite bank was defended by several thousand enemy troops including Genoese crossbowmen, but after some volleys from their own archers the English forced their way across 'in a sore battle' : Philip was snapping at their heels and even captured some of their baggage, but luckily the river rose and prevented the French from crossing too.

Once over the Somme Edward thanked God. Although outnumbered he was no longer frightened of a battle—the

way was now clear for him to retreat to Flanders if things
went wrong. In any case a halt was essential, as his men were
exhausted by their forced march ; it is known that their food
and wine, and even their shoes, were used up. Accordingly
he camped on the downs near the little town of Crécy-en-
Ponthieu.

The English King had found a perfect position, on rising
ground. In front of him was the 'Valley of the Clerks', both
his front and his right were protected by the little river Maie,
while his flank was guarded by the great wood of Crécy which
was ten miles long and four miles deep. The most obvious
direction from which he might be attacked, the front, led up
a downland slope which gave his archers an admirably clear
field of fire. His army, now somewhat reduced, consisted of
about 2,000 men-at-arms and perhaps 500 light lancers
together with something like 7,000 English and Welsh bowmen and 1,500 knifemen—approximately 11,000 men,
though estimates vary. The enemy was obviously near, so
Edward drew up his troops in order of battle. On the right,
on the slope above the Maie, he placed 4,000 men under the
sixteen-year-old Black Prince (supported by such veterans
as Sir Reynold Cobham, Sir John Chandos and Godefroi
d'Harcourt). The centre of this division consisted of 800
men-at-arms on foot in a long line, probably six deep ; 2,000
archers were placed on the flanks—deliberately, so they
could shoot at the French from the side when the latter
attacked the centre—while behind these archers stood the
knifemen. On his left Edward sited a second division, under
the Earls of Northampton and Arundel, with 500 dismounted men-at-arms and 1,200 archers in the same formation as the division on the right. The archers of both
divisions dug a large number of small holes, a foot deep
and a foot square, in front of their positions in order to make
the enemy horses stumble. Edward himself commanded the
third division—700 men-at-arms on foot, 2,000 archers and
the remaining knifemen—which he stationed somewhere
behind to serve as a reserve.

Edward, having drawn up his army, says Jean le Bel,

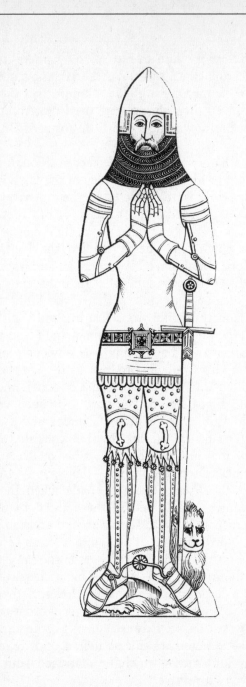

'went among his men, exhorting each of them with a laugh to do his duty, and flattered and encouraged them to such an extent that cowards became brave men'. He also warned them not to plunder the enemy wounded until he gave permission. 'This done,' adds the chronicler, 'he allowed everyone to break ranks so that they could eat and drink until the trumpets sounded.' (Large supplies of wine had been found at the nearby town of Le Crotoy by the quartermasters, while herds of cattle had been driven into the camp.) 'Then', says Froissart, 'every man lay down on the earth and by him his helmet and bow to be the more fresher when their enemies should come.' Meanwhile Edward established his command post at a windmill on the high ground on which his own division was stationed, from where he could see the entire battlefield. At noon news reached him that the French were coming up, whereupon he ordered the trumpets to sound and everyone rejoined his ranks.

It was Saturday 26 August 1346. King Philip, who had spent the night at Abbeville, had some reason to feel confident as his troops outnumbered Edward's by nearly three to one—at least 30,000 including 20,000 men-at-arms. Unfortunately for Philip, when he rode out of Abbeville at sunrise after hearing Mass, his army was still arriving and it continued to do so throughout the day. With his usual caution the French King sent four men to investigate the enemy position. One, a knight called Le Moine de Bazeilles, reporting that the English were waiting in a carefully arranged order of battle, told Philip: 'My own counsel, saving your displeasure, is that you and all your company rest here and lodge for this night for . . . it will be very late and your people be weary and out of array, and ye shall find your enemies fresh and ready to receive you.' The knight continued that next morning the King would be able to form

Thomas Cheyne, shield-bearer to King Edward III. He is wearing armour of a type that came in a few years after Crécy and stayed in fashion for the rest of the century, with a tight fitting cloth *jupon* over a steel breastplate on top of a chainmail shirt. Brass of 1368 in the parish church of Drayton Beauchamp, Buckinghamshire.

up his troops and look for the right place to attack the English, 'for, Sir, surely they will abide you'. Philip thought this excellent advice and gave orders for his troops to halt and make camp.

But there was always a problem in controlling excessively large medieval armies, and by now 'the flower of France' was completely out of control. While those in front tried to halt, the men-at-arms behind kept on coming and the front had to move on again. 'So they rode proudly forward without any order or good array until they came in sight of the English who stood waiting for them in fine order, but then it seemed shameful to retreat.' At the same time all the roads between Abbeville and Crécy were jammed with peasants and townsmen waving swords and spears, yelling 'Down with them! let us slay them all!' Eventually Philip, who was up in front, realized that he had lost any hope of restraining his troops. In desperation he ordered an attack— 'Make the Genoese go on before, and begin the battle, in the name of God and Saint Denis.' By then it was evening. The sun was beginning to set.

Trumpets, drums and kettledrums sounded, and a line of Genoese crossbowmen advanced to within 200 or even 150 yards of the English. As they did so they were drenched to the skin by a short but violent thunderstorm. At the same moment that they began to discharge their quarrels the English archers stepped forward and shot with such rapidity that 'it seemed as if it snowed'. The Genoese had marched long miles carrying their heavy instruments, and it is probable that they had discarded the pavises or large shields which crossbowmen normally used to protect themselves while reloading. Highly vulnerable, they at once began to drop beneath the arrow-storm, which they had never before experienced. Tired, demoralized—even the setting sun, which had reappeared, was in their eyes—the survivors started running. This stage of the engagement may have lasted no more than a minute.

The Count of Alençon was so shocked by what he considered to be cowardice on the part of the crossbowmen that

A panel of the Wilton Diptych, *c.* 1390. Richard II kneels before three saints. It is possible that Edward the Confessor (centre) is an idealized portrait of Edward III, and that Edmund of East Anglia (right) is a similar portrait of Edward II. John the Baptist may be the Black Prince.

'The noble King Edward III' (1312–1377) whose face was said to be 'like the face of a god'.

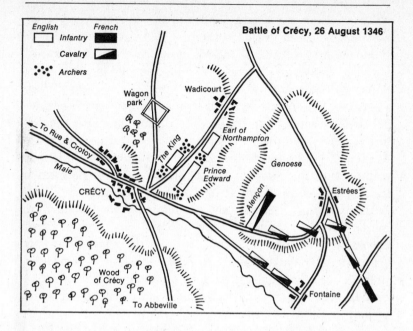

English French
□ Infantry ■ Cavalry
◦•◦• Archers

Battle of Crécy, 26 August 1346

Wadicourt

Wagon park

To Rue & Crotoy

Maie

The King

Earl of Northampton

Genoese

Prince Edward

CRÉCY

Alençon

Estrées

Wood of Crécy

Fontaine

To Abbeville

he shouted, 'Ride down this rabble who block our advance!' His fellow men-at-arms immediately responded to his appeal with a hopelessly disorganized charge. The shrieks of the miserable crossbowmen trampled under horses' hooves made the French in the rear think that the English were being killed, so they too pressed forward. The result was a struggling mob at the very foot of the slope where the English archers were positioned and from where they shot with murderous precision, not wasting a single arrow; each one found its mark, piercing the riders' heads and limbs through their mail and above all driving their mounts mad. Some horses bolted in a frenzy, others reared hideously or turned their hindquarters to the enemy. 'A great outcry rose to the stars.' Jean le Bel, who had spoken to men who were there, tells of horses being piled on top of one another 'like a litter of piglets'.

Almost certainly Edward's guns added to the confusion. At least one chronicler says that the King's cannon—only three are mentioned—terrified the horses. If of little use as weapons, their noise and smoke must have appalled those who had never experienced them.

Surprisingly, some French knights reached the forward English divisions, where the men-at-arms hacked them down with axes and swords. Either in this charge or during a later one the sixteen-year-old Prince of Wales was knocked off his feet, whereupon Richard de Beaumont, the standard-bearer, in a magnificent gesture covered the boy with the banner of Wales and fought off his assailants till the Prince could stand up. Froissart has a romantic tale of how when the Prince's companions sent to Edward for help, the King refused, saying, 'Let the boy win his spurs for I want him, please God to have all the glory.' However another chronicler (Geoffrey le Baker) says that the King did in fact send twenty picked knights to relieve his son. They found the boy and his mentors leaning on their swords and halberds, recovering their breath and waiting silently in front of long mounds of corpses for the enemy to return.

An enemy who reached the English lines was the blind King John of Bohemia. He ordered his attendant knights to lead him forward 'so that I may strike one stroke with my sword'. Somehow the little party, tied to each other by their reins, managed to ride through the archers and then charge the English men-at-arms. There the Bohemians fell with their King, save for two who cut their way back to the French lines to tell his story. The bodies were found next day, still tied together. The Prince of Wales was so moved that he adopted the old King's crest and motto—the three feathers with the legend *Ich dien*—I serve.

The French charged fifteen times, 'from sunset to the third quarter of the night', each charge beginning as well as ending in hopeless disorder beneath the arrow-storm. Froissart says that no one who was not present could imagine, let alone describe, the confusion, especially the disorganization and indiscipline of the French. The slaughter was heightened by the Welsh and Cornish knifemen who 'slew and murdered many as they lay on the ground, both earls, barons, knights and squires'. The last French attacks were launched in pitch darkness. By then there were few French knights left—apart from those who were dead, many had been quietly slipping away since the onset of dusk. King Philip, who had been hit in the neck by an arrow and had had at least one horse killed under him, found that he could only muster sixty men-at-arms when he tried to mount a final desperate charge through the gloom. The Count of Hainault took hold of the King's bridle and persuaded him to leave the field—'Sir, depart hence, for it is time. Lose not yourself wilfully ; if ye have loss at this time, ye shall recover it again at another time.' They rode to the royal château of La Broye six miles away. When he arrived there, with only five companions, Philip shouted to the castellan, 'Open your gate quickly, for this is the fortune of France.' The King only stopped to drink and then rode on through the night to find a safer refuge at Amiens.

The English who, because of the dark, did not realize the fearful casualties which they had inflicted, slept at their positions, so relieved at having escaped annihilation that they prayed to God in thanksgiving. They had lost less than a hundred men themselves. Next morning they awoke in such thick fog 'that a man might not see the breadth of an acre of land from him'. Edward forbade any pursuit. He sent out a scouting force, 500 men-at-arms and 2,000 archers under the Earl of Northampton, who soon found themselves facing some local militia and then a force of Norman knights who had arrived too late. Northampton's men quickly routed these last opponents, killing many. The King now saw the extent of his victory and ordered heralds to count the slain. They identified the bodies of more than 1,500 lords and knights, among them the Duke of Lorraine and the Counts of Alençon, Auxerre, Blamont, Blois, Flanders, Forez, Grandpré, Harcourt, Saint-Pol, Salm and Sancerre. Froissart exaggerates the number of 'common people' on the French side who died, but it was certainly well over 10,000.

Edward had won one of the great victories of Western history. Until Crécy the English were very little thought of as soldiers, while the French were considered the best in

Europe. Tactically and technologically the battle amounted
to a military revolution, a triumph of fire-power over armour.
The King of England became the most celebrated commander in Christendom.

However, Edward was in no position to exploit his
victory. Although Philip's army had been destroyed, he
dared not march on Paris with his tired troops. On 30
August he set off for the coast to capture a port. He chose
Calais, which he reached on 4 September. It was only a few
miles from the Flemish border and was the nearest port to
England. Soon English ships arrived with reinforcements
and took home the wounded as well as prisoners and
plunder. The King had expected to take the town without
much trouble but found that it was stronger than he had
thought—surrounded by sand dunes and marshes on which
it was impossible to erect siege engines. Deep dykes made
mining out of the question. Moreover it had a strong
garrison commanded by a gallant Burgundian knight, Jean
de Vienne, who was determined to hold out until winter
came and the English would be forced to withdraw. But
Edward was equally determined, and built wooden huts to
house his troops during the winter. Jean le Bel says that he
'set the houses like streets and covered them with reed and
broom, so that it was like a little town'; it even had market
days which did a thriving trade. Many Englishmen died
from disease, but the rest kept on grimly with the siege
throughout the winter, devastating the country for thirty
miles around. In the spring Edward brought over more
reinforcements, in case Philip should try to relieve the town.
Parliament was co-operative, supplying the necessary funds,
and by mid-summer 1347 the English had over 30,000
men outside Calais. All this represents a remarkable administrative achievement—not only the new troops but also vast
quantities of food to feed them had to be ferried across the
Channel.

King Edward's real weapon was a ruthless blockade by his
ships, calculating that 'hunger, which enters closed doors,
could and should conquer the pride of the besieged'

according to the Oxfordshire chronicler Geoffrey le Baker. Palisades running out into the sea prevented small boats from bringing supplies along the shore to the beleaguered garrison. A large English fleet was always waiting outside the harbour, and they built a wooden tower with catapults to destroy any vessel which might possibly slip through. The citizens expelled 500 of their poor to save food, but by the spring supplies were running out ; they decided that they would have no option other than to surrender if Philip did not relieve them by August.

One reason why Edward was able to find so many troops was the recent elimination of any danger from Scotland :

For once the eagle England being in prey
To her unguarded nest the weasel Scot
Comes sneaking, and so sucks her princely eggs.

In October 1346 David II had invaded Northumberland and Co. Durham, to meet with the fate of all Scottish invaders at Neville's Cross near Durham. The Scots were annihilated, their King being taken prisoner to the Tower of London where he spent nine years. His nation's most sacred relic, the Black Rood of Scotland, was triumphantly hung up in Durham Cathedral.

In July 1347 Philip at last marched to relieve Calais. His army was neither so large as that of the previous year nor so eager for battle. Looking down on Edward's camp from the cliffs at Sangatte only a mile away, he set up his own camp and then sent a challenge to the English King to come out and fight, but Edward refused to leave his snugly fortified siege lines. Philip knew that to attack would be to invite another Crécy and tried unsuccessfully to negotiate a truce. On 2 August he ordered his men to strike camp and set fire to their tents. The retreating French army could hear the lamentations of the doomed people of Calais as they rode away—its garrison threw the royal standard down into the ditch.

By now even the richest of those inside Calais were dying

from lack of food and the day after Philip's withdrawal Jean de Vienne appeared on the battlements to shout that his garrison was ready to negotiate. He was told how the English King was so furious at the town's resistance that its people would have to submit to being killed or ransomed as he chose. Eventually Edward was persuaded to limit his punishment to the six chief burgesses, who had to appear before him clad only in their shirts and with halters round their necks. 'The King looked felly on them, for greatly he hated the people of Calais.' Then he commanded their heads to be struck off. They were only saved by the intercession of the pregnant Queen Philippa who knelt before her husband in tears and pleaded, 'Ah, gentle sir, since I passed the sea in great peril, I have desired nothing of you; therefore now I humbly require you in honour of the Son of the Virgin Mary and for the love of me that ye will take mercy of these six burgesses.' Nonetheless Edward turned all the inhabitants out of the town in the clothes they had on and nothing else, later re-peopling it with English colonists who were assigned shops, inns and tenements. He gave many of the fine houses of the rich bourgeois to his friends.

For two centuries Calais was to be the English gate into France—both entrepôt and bridgehead. A commentator has written, 'The vital importance of Calais to the English is perhaps best realized if one were to imagine France in possession of Dover throughout the war, and the advantage this would have given her.' The English soon felt passionately about Calais; as Philip Contamine, the modern French historian, says, 'For two centuries it remained a little piece of England on the continent,' and it was even part of the diocese of Canterbury.

Yet the town's acquisition should not be seen in isolation, as the Crécy-Calais campaign was only one of the three interdependent operations of Edward III's grand strategy. In the south-west the Earl of Derby was able to hold on to most of his gains; he had been besieged at Aiguillon, but the Duke of Normandy raised the siege as soon as he heard of his father's defeat and took his army north of the Loire. One of the reasons which may have made Philip abandon Calais was news of another English victory, in Brittany at La Roche Derrien where an English garrison was besieged. On 27 June 1347 Sir Thomas Dagworth wiped out the forces of Charles of Blois, who was captured and sent to join the King of Scots in the Tower of London. Only in Flanders did the English position grow weaker, the new Count (the strongly pro-French Louis de Mâle) managing to win over the towns.

The Papacy deplored the misery caused by Edward's campaigns. In 1347 Clement VI remonstrated with the King, writing to him of 'the sadness of the poor, the children, the orphans, the widows, the wretched people who are plundered and enduring hunger, the destruction of churches and monasteries, the sacrilege in the theft of vessels and ornaments of Divine worship, the imprisonment and robbery of nuns'.

At the Pope's intervention England and France agreed to a truce, in September 1347. King Philip was in a desperate position. Not only had his armies been routed but he was without money. Yet he had to rebuild his strength without delay in case of another invasion. This proud and haughty man abased himself before the Estates when they met in Paris in November. Their spokesman told him, 'You, by bad counsel, have lost everything and gained nothing,' adding that the King had been 'sent back scurvily' from Crécy and Calais. They would not grant him any money. With great difficulty Philip's officials managed to extract a little from the local assemblies and the clergy. Even now, after so many years of frustration and humiliation, he still planned to invade England.

Edward III basked in the adulation of his subjects. The Parliament Roll records how both Lords and Commons approved motions thanking God for their King's victories and agreeing that the monies which they had voted him had been well spent. The 'realm of England hath been nobly amended, honoured and enriched to a degree never seen in the time of any other King'.

It was probably in June 1348 that Edward formally

founded the Order of the Garter at Windsor, based on an association of knights on the model of the Round Table some years before. It seems that the legend is true, that the first Garter was dropped by the beautiful Countess of Salisbury while dancing and that the King—who was in love with her—fastened it round his own knee, saying '*Honi soit qui mal y pense*' to save her from embarrassment. (The blue, different from today's Garter blue, was no doubt derived from the royal blue of the French arms.) Membership of the Order was to be the crown of a successful military career throughout the Hundred Years War; it is noticeable how many leading commanders received the Garter right up to the very end of the War, both English and Guyennois— with some exaggeration it may be compared to the Companionship of the Bath (CB) during the Peninsular War.

The incident of the Countess of Salisbury and her garter is said to have taken place at a triumphant banquet at Calais, in celebration of its capture. The King nearly lost his new town when its governor, an Italian mercenary, offered to sell it to the French. Unfortunately for the latter Edward got wind of the plot, persuaded the governor to co-operate, and with the Prince of Wales crossed the Channel so secretly that no one knew he was in Calais. When the French arrived to take possession they were ambushed and all taken prisoner. With his accustomed style King Edward, 'bareheaded save for a chaplet of fine pearls', entertained his captives to a sumptuous dinner on New Year's Eve.

In 1350 Edward won yet another victory. The Count of Flanders had allowed the Castilians to assemble a fleet at Sluys, from where they wrought havoc on English merchant shipping and menaced the sea-link with Guyenne. Edward gathered his ships at Sandwich in August and, accompanied by his third son John of Gaunt (who was only ten), sailed to meet the enemy. The Castilian fleet of forty vessels was commanded by Don Carlos de la Cerda—a prince of the royal house of Castile. In a famous passage Froissart describes how Edward appeared to those on board the cog *Thomas*, the same vessel in which he had fought at Sluys ten years earlier. 'The King stood at his ship's prow, clad in a jacket of black velvet, and on his head a hat of black beaver that became him right well; and he was then (as I was told by such as were with him that day) as merry as ever he was seen.' He made his minstrels play on their trumpets a German dance which had just been brought to England by Sir John Chandos, and commanded Chandos to sing with the minstrels, laughing at the result. From time to time he looked up at the mast, for he had put a man in the crow's nest to warn him when the Castilians were sighted. On seeing the enemy Edward cried, 'Ho! I see a ship coming and methinks it is a ship of Spain!' When he saw the whole Castilian fleet he said, 'I see so many, God help me! that I may not tell them.' By then it was evening—'about the hour of vespers'. The King 'sent for wine and drank thereof, he and all his knights; then he laced on his helm'.

The battle which ensued—off Winchelsea, but known as Les-Espagnols-sur-Mer—was a far more dangerous and close-fought business than Sluys. The advantage of galleys over cogs has already been emphasized, and the Castilians were armed with stone-throwing catapults, giant crossbows and cannon. They also had the wind in their favour. Both the King and the Prince of Wales had their ships sunk beneath them and only survived by boarding enemy vessels. After a ferocious combat which continued till nightfall, fourteen Castilian galleys—some say more—were captured and their crews thrown overboard, the remaining enemy vessels fleeing. England rejoiced at the news, especially the coastal counties of the south.

But France had already suffered a far worse disaster, the Black Death—bubonic plague—which had broken out in Marseilles and spread all over France during 1348 and 1349. According to one chronicler, the death-toll in Paris alone reached 80,000. People said that the end of the world had come. The King, who obviously believed that God was punishing France for her sins, imposed a somewhat unusual sanitary precaution: he issued an edict against blasphemy. For the first offence a man was to lose a lip, for the second the other lip and for the third the tongue itself. There can have been few unhappier monarchs than Philip VI in the last years of his reign.

However, the plague also crossed the Channel. It appeared in Dorset in August 1348, spreading all over England where it raged until the end of 1349. It is generally believed that about a third of the entire population died. Land was abandoned, rents fell off or were unpaid. In consequence the yield from taxes declined drastically. The resulting shortage of both men and money had a dampening effect, to say the least, on any thoughts of invasion or large-scale military operations by the English and French monarchies.

On 22 August 1350 King Philip of France died at Nogent-le-roi. 'On the following Thursday his body was buried at Saint-Denis, on the left side of the great altar, his bowels were interred at the Jacobins, at Paris, and his heart at the convent of the Carthusians at Bourgfontaines in Valois.' He has gone down to history as a lamentable failure. France has never forgiven him for Crécy, while historians blame him for weakening the French monarchy by granting too many privileges and exemptions for ready money. Yet Crécy was a single tactical error. He raised vast armies and kept them in the field by triumphing over an almost inoperable fiscal system, and in his bargains with the local assemblies he made them realize that the English threatened the entire kingdom. Although he lost Calais, he left France a far larger country: in 1349 he bought the town of Montpelier from the King of Majorca, while the same year, after long negotiation, he succeeded in buying the Dauphiné from its last Count or *Dauphin* in the name of his grandson, the future Charles V. This was the biggest acquisition of territory since the reign of St Louis—the frontiers of France had at last reached the Alps. Moreover this grandson, who was to prove one of the greatest of all French kings, would follow many of the policies of Philip VI.

Although Edward III was to take the field again, the victory of Les-Espagnols-sur-Mer marks the end of the period when he was the dominant protagonist in the Hundred Years War. He had shown himself to be a superb soldier and had humiliated his Valois rival. He was no nearer his ambition of gaining the crown of France, but he remained as determined as ever to take their kingdom from the Valois—or a large part of it—and he was ready to wait for the right moment to restart the War, even if someone else was to lead his armies.

3

Poitiers
and the Black Prince
1350–1360

Give me an armour of eternal steel!
I go to conquer Kings . . .

The Raigne of King Edward III

We took our road through the land of Toulouse,
where many goodly towns and strongholds were
burnt and destroyed, for the land was rich and
plenteous.

The Black Prince in 1355

The next stage of the Hundred Years War, from 1350 to 1364, saw the emergence of Philip's son, King John II of France, and of the Black Prince, Edward III's son, who eventually took up permanent residence in Guyenne. Edward of Woodstock, Prince of Wales, and traditionally known as the Black Prince (from the colour of his armour), is one of the great heroes of English history. As with most heroes the reality was a little different from the legend, but unquestionably he was a son after Edward III's heart. In 1350 the Prince was twenty and shared to the full his father's appetite for military glory. However, he had to contain his warlike spirit in patience for some time, as the conflict of the early 1350s was largely limited to negotiation.

Few negotiators can have been as inept as 'Jean le Bon',

probably the most stupid of all French kings. Born in 1319, the former Duke of Normandy was by now verging on medieval middle age, a big handsome man with a thick red beard. His ill-merited soubriquet was bestowed on him for prowess in the tournament and pigheaded bravery on the battlefield, but his marked characteristics were blind rage and a tendency to panic. John II's only other outstanding quality seems to have been a certain charm of manner—when he was on his best behaviour.

Although Edward III had abated none of his ambitions, the years from 1350 to 1355 were (save in Brittany) a low-key period of the War. Either the English King had taken the exact measure of his new opponent and hoped to man-œuvre him into concessions, or else he was waiting for England to recover from the ravages of the Black Death. Professor Perroy considers that 'Edward III was not un-aware of the weaknesses and the panic fear of the new King of France. He took pleasure in prolonging the threat, con-tinually postponed, of a fresh landing.' All one can say is, however, that apart from a series of truces there is little evidence of constructive diplomatic activity until 1353. Edward then took advantage of Papal mediation to offer to abandon his claim to the French crown in return for Guyenne 'as his ancestors had held it' (i.e. with Poitou and the Limousin) and Normandy, together with the suzerainty of Flanders—though he hinted that he was generously pre-pared to forgo Normandy. The following year he actually increased these demands to include Calais, Anjou and Maine. Almost incredibly King John agreed to them in a provisional treaty at Guines in April 1354. But then John refused to hand over the stipulated territories—possibly he had been merely playing for time.

Meanwhile English intervention in Brittany had been most successful. Their garrisons were mostly in the Celtic west of the duchy, in ports like Brest, Quimperlé and Vannes, though there were some in the French-speaking east, as at Ploermel. The King's Lieutenant in Brittany, Sir Thomas Dagworth, and his garrison captains launched raid after raid. In 1352 Sir Thomas was ambushed and murdered by a Breton traitor but his successor, Sir Walter Bentley, was quite as vigorous and the same year, using bowmen, won an important victory at Mauron.

The warfare in Brittany was on a comparatively small scale but, to judge from the chronicles, it obviously made a considerable noise among the fighting classes. For contemporaries, if not for history, one of the most important events of the Hundred Years War was the 'Combat of the Thirty' —'a magnificent but murderous kind of tourney' as Perroy calls it—which tells us a good deal about the mentality of the officer class of 1351. That year the English garrison at Ploermel was attacked by a French force under Robert de Beaumanoir. To avoid a siege the garrison commander, Sir Richard Bamborough, suggested a combat on the open plain before Ploermel between thirty men-at-arms from each side. Bamborough told his knights (who included Bretons and German mercenaries as well as English) to fight in such a way 'that people will speak of it in future times in halls, in palaces, in public places and elsewhere throughout the world'. They all fought on foot, with swords and halberds, until four of the French and two of the English had been killed and everyone was exhausted. A breathing-space was called but when Beaumanoir, badly wounded, staggered off to find some water, an Englishman mocked at him— 'Beaumanoir, drink thy blood and thy thirst will go off.' The combat recommenced. It seemed impossible to break the English, who fought in a tight formation, shoulder to shoulder. At last a French knight stole away, quietly mounted his great warhorse and then returned at the charge, knocking his opponents off their feet. The French pounced on the English, killing nine including Bamborough, and taking the rest prisoner. Among the latter were Robert Knollys with his half-brother Hugh Calveley, a pair of whom more will be heard.

Less chivalrous activities in Brittany had continued to make the War popular with all classes of Englishmen. These were the various methods of making money out of the

local population. The most profitable was of course ransom
—selling a prisoner his freedom. A prince or great nobleman
commanded an enormous price, but the market was not
restricted to magnates ; a fat burgess or an important cleric
could be an almost equally enviable prize. Indeed there was
a famous scandal during the siege of Calais when a certain
John Ballard was rumoured to have captured the Archdeacon of Paris and smuggled him back to London, where
he was supposed to have fetched a mere £50. For ransoming
was often more like the kidnap racket of modern times, and
small tradesmen and farmers had their price ; even plough-
men fetched a few pence. Sometimes fortunes were made—
—Sir John Harleston's *share* in a French knight taken
during Edward's march through Normandy amounted to
no less than £1,500. Nor was the business confined to the
upper classes ; the humblest archer, a serf at home perhaps,
might suddenly find himself a rich man.

Even Edward himself engaged in the ransom trade,
acting as a kind of broker. He bought particularly valuable
prisoners from their captors at a reduced price, hoping to
recover the full asking-price from the prisoner's relatives or
representatives. The King possessed the administrative
machinery for such transactions so it was often well worth
the captor's while to sell to him ; in 1347 Sir Thomas
Dagworth sold Charles of Blois to the King for 25,000
gold crowns (nearly £5,000) and no doubt Edward made a
good profit. Other magnates also acted as ransom brokers,
purchasing high-ranking prisoners as a speculation ; sometimes, like any other marketable commodity, the prisoners
changed hands several times. Calais was to become the
centre of this trade. Payment was not necessarily in money
but could be in kind—horses, clothing, wine, weapons.

The garrisons in Brittany also engaged in a more sinister
trade—that of the *pâtis* or protection-racket. Every village
and hamlet had to pay the troops from the local stronghold
dues in money, livestock, food and wine ; failure to pay was
punished by arbitrary executions and burnings. Travellers
had to pay dearly for safe conducts, road-blocks and

toll-gates being set up. Profits from the *pâtis* were pooled; the soldiers paid one-third of their booty to the garrison commander, who remitted one-third to the King, together with a third of his own profits. In 1359–1360 £10,785— an average of £41 per parish—was collected from the parishes controlled by the garrisons of Ploermel, Bécherel and Vannes. Such extortion caused armed risings, while sometimes the inhabitants fled from their villages. In a report in 1352 Sir Walter Bentley said that in areas where strongholds had recently been taken over from the Blois party, the peasants would soon be too frightened of the English soldiers to plough their fields; he explained that many of his troops were men of low degree instead of knights or squires and had only come to the wars for the sake of personal gain, and that they were growing rich from despoiling the inhabitants, townsmen as well as peasants. The English soldiers were hated with a bitter hatred; when the French recaptured the town of La Roche Derrien in 1347 the locals threw themselves on the garrison and 'killed them with sticks and stones like dogs'. In time the *pâtis* would be extended to all English-occupied France.

The English now regarded France as a kind of El Dorado. The whole of England was flooded with French plunder. The chronicler Walsingham says that in 1348: 'There were few women who did not possess something from Caen, Calais or another town over the seas, such as clothing, furs and cushions. Table cloths and linen were seen in everybody's houses. Married women were decked in the trimmings of French matrons and if the latter bemoaned their loss the former exulted at their gain.' Even the troops' wages were good; a mounted archer got 6d a day, the rate for a master craftsman at home, the foot archer 3d a day when a good ploughman was lucky to make 2d. Furthermore, the indentures of the men-at-arms and archers who volunteered guaranteed them a share of booty. In Dr Fowler's words, however: 'It was not the certainty of profit that lured men to service in the war, but the chance, often no more than one in a hundred, of hitting the jackpot.'

Although it meant heavy taxes again, there were many who waited hopefully for the King to recommence hostilities.

Edward III knew all about this enthusiasm and just how to exploit it. He had already shown himself to be a surprisingly sophisticated publicist, making full use of the primitive mass-media available. The reading of Philip's invasion *ordonnance* in every parish church has been mentioned, but this was only one instance. Edward's use of proclamations, to be read out at market-places or at county courts, was so thorough that it has been likened to 'a kind of news service'; these proclamations explained in simple terms such great matters as the invasion of Normandy, the victory at Crécy and the taking of Calais, while the slightest threat of invasion was always fully exploited. In addition, the King made shrewd use of the clergy, asking the bishops for public prayers for the War, prayers which must have been said in many parishes. In 1346 the Dominican friars, who were generally credited with being the best preachers, were given the task of explaining to the King's subjects why he was claiming the French throne and why he had gone to war. In consequence information about the campaigns of the 1330s and the victories of the 1340s had been surprisingly widespread.

If Edward was now even poorer than he had been before the Black Death, he had at least acquired a better understanding of what he could afford. Since 1345 his Treasurer had been the brilliant William Edington, Bishop of Winchester, who in 1356 was to become his Chancellor as well. Edington's policy was to centralize all government finance under the Exchequer; only by pooling the entire revenue could he hope to pay for the King's campaigns. Parliament was prepared to co-operate. As that great English historian Professor McKisack explains, when dealing with Parliament Edward's approach was 'to present the war as a joint stock enterprise undertaken for the defence of the realm and of his legitimate claim to the throne of France', while keeping it informed about what was happening abroad and consulting it on matters of foreign policy. Edington's skilful management made it possible for Edward to manage without asking too much in taxation.

Furthermore the English had found a new ally in France, the young King of Navarre. Charles the Bad was more than just the monarch of a tiny transmontane kingdom; not only did he possess several counties in Normandy and rich estates near Paris, but if anything he had a better claim to the throne of France than Edward III. His mother was the daughter of Louis X (d. 1316), and therefore even nearer in line of succession than her aunt Isabel, though her uncles had been able to set aside her claims—largely on account of her mother's reputation for promiscuity. Nevertheless, if her son Charles had been of age in 1328 he might well have been preferred as King of France to Philip of Valois. In consequence this personable, smooth-talking and amoral young man—eighteen in 1350—was consumed by a sense of burning injustice. To make matters worse, in addition to losing the throne he had been despoiled of the great counties of Champagne and Angoulême, and when to cut his losses he married King John's daughter, her dowry was never paid. Charles decided that his best course was to play Plantagenet against Valois by offering to help Edward, and then persuading John to buy a Navarrese alliance. He seems to have had what amounted to almost a mania for intrigue.

However, the King of Navarre's first move—in 1354—was far from subtle. He had long nursed a bitter hatred for the Constable of France, Don Carlos de la Cerda (the Castilian Admiral at Les-Espagnols-sur-Mer) to whom King John had given Angoulême; the Constable was now lured into Charles's Norman territories, and then ambushed and hacked to death. 'Know that it was I who with God's help killed Carlos of Spain,' Navarre declaimed in delight, although he then 'excused himself to the King of France'. While John was infuriated by the murder of his favourite, he was so terrified by the rumours that his dangerous young cousin was corresponding with Edward III that he not only pretended to forgive Navarre but tried to buy him off with a large slice of the Cotentin. Charles was in no way mollified.

The knowledge of his active discontent encouraged the English to recommence hostilities.

Edward again adopted a policy of attacking on three fronts at the same time. Originally he intended to lead one army himself into Picardy, while Lancaster (now a Duke) launched a joint Anglo-Navarrese campaign in Normandy and the Prince of Wales raided from Guyenne. In the event, although the King took an army to Calais in October 1355 he returned to England within a month. The operation's chief campaign turned out to be a *chevauchée* by the Black Prince, who had been appointed Lieutenant in Guyenne and who had arrived at Bordeaux in September. In October 1355 the Prince rode out of the ducal capital with an army of probably no more than 2,600 men-at-arms and archers all told, but everyone on horseback, to spend the next two months killing and burning in Languedoc almost as far as Montpelier and the Mediterranean seaboard. He stormed Narbonne and Carcassonne—where he found useful supplies of food and wine—and burnt a large part of both towns to the ground, though he did not succeed in taking their citadels in which the citizens had taken refuge. Castle-naudry, Limoux and many other little towns suffered almost as much, while during the Prince's 600-mile march count-less villages and hamlets went up in flames, together with their mills, their châteaux and their churches. One of the Prince's secretaries wrote, 'Since this war began, there was never such loss nor destruction as hath been in this raid,' while the Prince himself commented smugly on the 'many goodly towns and strongholds burnt and destroyed'. It was not gratuituous cruelty or wanton lust for devastation. The object of every *chevauchée* was to underline the enemy's weak-ness and deprive him of his taxes by destroying the lands and property on which they were levied. Chivalry had noth-ing to do with it—that was reserved for battles—and on this occasion, meeting almost no opposition, the Anglo-Gascon raiders behaved in a notably unchivalrous manner. Accord-ing to Froissart, the troops preferred silver-plate and money but nothing of value was ignored, especially carpets, and the

army returned with a baggage-train groaning with plunder
—once back at Bordeaux, 'they spent foolishly all the gold
and silver they had won'. The devastated regions took years
to recover, despite a programme of reconstruction which
included tax exemption, gifts of royal timber and the con-
scription of masons and carpenters.

During such a *chevauchée* the English killed every human
being they could catch (apart from those worth good money),
so people unable to reach a town or castle had to hide. Some
took refuge in caves or elsewhere underground—many
castles and fortified churches had a network of cellars and
tunnels dug beneath them. Others fled to the forest where
they built huts, though the English searched the woods
systematically. The peasants who dwelt in the *plat pays*—
the flat, open plains which are the typical terrain of so much
of France—were particularly at risk.

The rest of France was so shaken by the news from
Languedoc that when the Estates met at Paris in October
1355 they agreed to taxes—including the extension of the
gabelle on salt throughout the entire realm—which would
enable John to maintain 30,000 troops for a year, although
they tried to keep control of tax collection. In the event the
exhausted taxpayers refused to pay. Nevertheless the desperate King summoned a great army, which began to assemble
at Chartres in the spring of the following year.

Meanwhile Charles the Bad had not been idle, extracting
even more concessions from John by spreading rumours that
he meant to join Edward in England. But the King of
Navarre pushed his luck too far. He ingratiated himself
with the Dauphin who, fascinated by his charming cousin,
spent so much time with him that the boy's father began to
suspect that the pair were plotting to depose him. In April
1356, in a frenzy of paranoia, King John galloped to
Rouen, burst into the hall where Navarre and the Dauphin
were dining, arrested the entire party and had four beheaded,
including the Count d'Harcourt and three other Norman
lords. King Charles of Navarre was incarcerated in a dun-
geon in the Louvre.

Edward was far from discouraged by King John's preparations, even if he may have guessed that the Frenchman was determined to avenge Crécy. Towards the end of the summer he sent the Duke of Lancaster from Brittany with an army of perhaps 6,000 men to raise Navarre's supporters in Normandy and then to attack in Anjou, his ultimate orders being to link up with the scarcely larger force of the Prince of Wales. The latter set out from Bergerac on 4 August 1356 on a long *chevauchée* north-east through the Limousin and Berry, besieging and capturing— by the use of Greek fire or flaming naphtha—the castle of Romorantin, where a French detachment who had tried to ambush him had taken refuge. He then swung north-westward and advanced on Tours where he began to burn the suburbs. By now he had become the main target of the French. King Edward had hoped to distract King John, but he had again been forced to return to England after only a day or two in France by the news that the Scots had taken Berwick. Similarly, although Lancaster had led the French army a dance, he failed to cross the Loire and join forces with the Prince.

Even if the Duke of Lancaster had succeeded in linking up with the Black Prince their combined army would still have been hopelessly outnumbered. Neither had any intention of seeking battle, but only meant to wage the *chevauchée*. In the early days of September, when he was before Tours, Prince Edward suddenly learnt that an army of 40,000 men was in hot pursuit of him and his plunder-laden troops. He made a run for it, retreating as fast as he could down the road to Bordeaux.

However, King John managed to outflank the Prince and reached Poitiers first, cutting the road to Bordeaux. He had with him perhaps 16–20,000 soldiers, most of them men-at-arms, though there were also a number of light troops including 2,000 crossbowmen. The two commanders only realized how near they were to each other when on 17 September the English advance guard suddenly collided with the rear of the French army at La Chabotrie. After a brief skirmish, the Prince marched on to camp at a village then called Maupertuis, which was some seven miles southeast of Poitiers.

The Black Prince was desperately anxious not to fight, for his men, laden with plunder, were obviously exhausted by their retreat. But the escape to the south was barred by the little river Miosson. Any attempt to ford it meant the possibility of annihilation by a well-timed enemy attack. Luckily he had the benefit of the advice of that gifted veteran, Sir John Chandos, who was a soldier of genius. Accordingly he unwillingly made ready for battle, taking command of the main division and keeping Chandos by his side where the latter seems to have acted as a chief-of-staff. The other divisions were commanded by the Earls of Salisbury and Warwick, the last being in charge of the Guyennois contingent. Each of the three divisions consisted of about 1,200 men-at-arms on foot, rather fewer archers, some dismounted Gascon lancers, and a handful of Welsh knifemen. Although the exact topography is obscure, the terrain was beyond question ideally suited for such a combination—rolling ground covered with undergrowth, hedges, vines and patches of marsh. The front was guarded by a ditch and a long and stout hedge at the top of a gentle slope, the left by a thick wood, and the rear and left by the river. Though the English were able to use a slight hillock to watch the French, they themselves were to a large extent hidden from the enemy's view—part of the Prince's division was in a thicket, while the horses were tethered well out of sight.

King John made ready to attack at dawn next day. But it was Sunday and the Papal envoy, the Cardinal de Perigord, persuaded the King to let him try and negotiate. The Cardinal spent the entire day riding hopefully between the two armies. The Black Prince offered to return the towns and castles he had captured during his *chevauchée* together with all his prisoners, and to swear not to take up arms against the French King for seven years. He also offered a large sum of money. But John would accept nothing else than the unconditional surrender of the Prince and a hundred English knights—'the which the Prince would in no wise agree unto'. Meanwhile the English spent the holy day frantically improving their defences, making 'great dykes and hedges about their archers'. Even so, the Prince still hoped to avoid a battle and to escape to Bordeaux.

What happened remains a matter of controversy. However, it seems that next morning the English began to steal away, leaving the rearguard under Salisbury to cover their retreat. King John had not yet finished drawing up his troops. His plan was to send a small advance force of 300 mounted men-at-arms to charge through the one gap in the hedge where four knights could ride abreast, and to deal with the dreaded archers before he mounted his main attack. His first division, or 'battle', consisting of his foot soldiers and some German mercenaries who retained their mounts, were to follow. Then would come the second division under the Dauphin (4,000 men), the third under the Duke of Orleans (3,000) and the fourth under the King himself (6,000); the men-at-arms in these last three divisions were all to march on foot in their heavy armour, apparently at the suggestion of a Scots knight, William Douglas.

When at about 10.00 a.m. John realized that the English were trying to escape, his divisions had not yet formed up. Nevertheless he launched his 300 carefully chosen mounted knights, under Marshals de Clermont and d'Audrehem, at the hedge which protected the English front. The archers, safe behind the hedge, shot steadily at the Marshals' battle, which had split in two, 'and did slay and hurt horses and knights, so that the horses, when they felt the sharp arrows, they would in no wise go forward but drew back and reared up and took on so fiercely that many of them fell on their masters'; many of the Marshals' men were slain as they lay on the ground by Salisbury's knights, who came out from behind the hedge. Clermont was killed and d'Audrehem taken prisoner, while William Douglas fled. The Germans and footmen who followed them belatedly were disorganized by the broken ground but reached the hedge where the English managed to hold them. By this time the Black

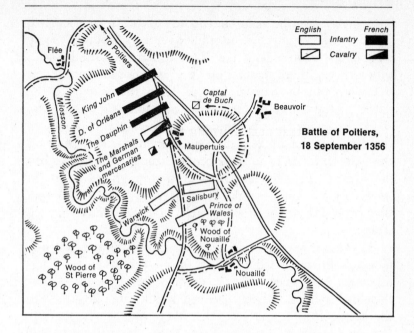

English   French
Infantry
Cavalry

Flée

To Poitiers

King John

Miosson

D. of Orléans

The Dauphin

The Marshals
and German
mercenaries

Capital
de Buch

Beauvoir

Maupertuis

**Battle of Poitiers,
18 September 1356**

Salisbury

Warwick

Prince of
Wales

Wood of
Nouaillé

Wood of
St Pierre

Nouaillé

Prince had seen what was happening and brought his troops
back to relieve Salisbury. The Germans were finally driven
off when a body of archers came out from far along the
hedge and, protected from heavy troops by standing in
marshy ground, shot murderously into the enemy flank.

The bulk of the enemy still remained, 13,000 dismounted
men-at-arms. The first of their three divisions, that of the
Dauphin, advanced towards the hedge, toiling on foot up the
slope, through the scrub and brambles. Nevertheless they
reached the English line, crossed the ditch and tried to
break through the hedge 'with a clamour that rose to the
skies of "St George!" or "St Denis!".' The French attacked
with such ferocity that the Prince had to bring up to the
hedge everything he had, with the exception of a final
reserve of 400 crack men-at-arms. At last the Dauphin's
troops reeled back from the hedge in full retreat.

The English were in scarcely better case. 'Some of our
troops laid their wounded under bushes and hedges out of
the way, others having broken their own weapons took

spears and swords from the bodies of the men they had killed, while archers even pulled arrows out of enemy wounded who were only half dead.' Apart from the Prince's tiny reserve, 'there was not one who was not unwounded or not worn out by hard fighting'. Then they saw that the battle of the Duke of Orleans (King John's brother) was about to attack. But to the astonishment—and relief—of the English the Duke's division turned and marched off the field with the Dauphin's broken troops. If Orleans had not despaired, the English—even though they might have repelled him—would have been so worn down that they would have been overwhelmed by the final French attack.

As the last enemy division trudged towards the hedge—6,000 fresh troops led by King John—the exhausted English wondered where they would find the strength to meet this final assault. An experienced knight standing next to the Black Prince muttered that there was no hope. The Prince angrily shouted at him, 'You lie, you miserable coward—while I am alive it is blasphemy to say we are beaten!' None the less the rank and file felt they were doomed. The English archers, 'moved to fury because they were desperate', shot better than ever but the French managed to ward off the arrows by holding shields over their heads. The Prince brought in his last reserve, the 400 men-at-arms, shouting to Chandos, 'John, get forward—you shall not see me turn my back this day, but I will be ever with the foremost.' He ordered his standard-bearer, Walter of Wodeland, to bear his banner straight towards King John and then, 'courageous and cruel as a lion' charged at the King. 'The Prince of Wales suddenly gave a roar and attacked the Frenchmen with his keen sword, breaking spears, warding off blows, slaying those who sprang at him, helping up those who had fallen.' The battle was now on the open ground in front of the hedge from behind which the archers, who had used up their last arrows, came out with swords and axes to help their men-at-arms. This was the fiercest fighting of the entire day—the clash with which the two sides met, the hammering of weapons on helmets, could be heard in Poitiers seven miles away.

Suddenly the banner of St George was seen behind the French. The Prince had sent the Captal de Buch with sixty men-at-arms and a hundred archers down a hidden track, through a hollow, which came out behind the enemy. The French, not realizing how small was the Captal's force, began to falter, whereupon the Prince led a final charge. (They were still on foot and *not* on horseback, whatever Froissart may say—there would simply not have been time to bring up the horses and remount.) The French formation was broken, 'the banners began to totter, the standard-bearers fell . . . dying men slipped on each other's blood'. Although the Prince, hacking his way in the direction of King John, met with 'valiant resistance from very brave men', the rest of the French were leaving the field.

By about 3.00 p.m. King John, wielding a large battle-axe to considerable effect, was left fighting alone with his fourteen-year-old son Philip. He was recognized and sur-rounded by a great crowd of soldiers anxious to take so fabulous a ransom. Although he surrendered to a knight of Artois he was still in peril, for the brawling mob of Gascons and Englishmen began to fight for him. Finally he and his son were rescued by the Earl of Warwick and Lord Cobham who took him to the Prince.

The latter had already stopped fighting, as Chandos had told him that the battle was over. Sir John advised the Prince to set up his banner on a bush as a rallying-point for his scattered troops—'I can see no more banners nor pennons of the French party, wherefore, Sir, rest and refresh you for ye be sore chafed.' Trumpets sounded. Then the Prince took off his helmet and his gentlemen helped him off with his armour. A red tent was erected and drink was served to the Prince and his friends.

Meanwhile 'the chase endured to the gates of Poitiers', so Froissart tells us. 'There were many slain and beaten down, horse and man, for they of Poitiers closed their gates and would suffer none to enter; wherefore in the street

1 Foot

before the gate was horrible murder.' It was reported by the Black Prince that at the end of the day nearly 2,500 French men-at-arms had fallen, including many great lords. 'There was slain all the flower of France,' says Froissart. The English losses were obviously much smaller, but there is no reliable record—some English knights, pursuing too impetuously, were taken prisoner.

As many French were captured as were killed, among them seventeen counts together with other lords. 'You might see many an archer, many a knight, many a squire, running in every direction to take prisoners,' writes the Chandos herald who was there, while Froissart says: 'There were divers English archers that had four, five or six prisoners.' Indeed there were so many that it was impossible to keep them under guard and the English had to release some solely in return for a promise that they would come to Bordeaux with their ransoms before Christmas. Fortunes were made. The Earl of Warwick who rounded up the Archbishop of Sens did particularly well, later obtaining £8,000 for him; he also made a large sum out of the Bishop of Le Mans in whom he had a three-quarters share. The squire who actually captured the Bishop, Robert Clinton, was able to sell his own small share to King Edward for £1,000. Edward purchased three of the Black Prince's personal prisoners for £20,000, while the Prince bought another fourteen on his father's behalf for £66,000.

'All such as were there with the Prince were made rich,' Froissart informs us, 'as well as by ransoming of prisoners as by winning of gold, silver, plate, jewels.' There was so much that valuable armours were ignored. Many of the splendid pavilions of the French lords were still standing at their camp, where looters reaped a rich harvest. Some

---

Sir George Felbrygg, one of the squires-at-arms (or bodyguard) of King Edward III. His son, Sir Simon Felbrygg, was to become banner-bearer to King Richard II. From a brass of 1400 in the parish church of Playford, Suffolk.

Cheshire archers found a silver ship—no doubt a *nef* or large salt-cellar—which belonged to King John and sold it to their Prince. The latter also acquired John's jewel-casket.

Nevertheless, it must be appreciated that Poitiers was a very near thing. Victory might easily have gone to the French. Even with the masterminding by that brilliant chief-of-staff Sir John Chandos, the English defence would have been overwhelmed but for Orleans's cowardly refusal to attack.

The unlucky King of France gave his enemy an opportunity to demonstrate his chivalry. On the evening of the battle, the Black Prince entertained John and his son to dinner, together with the leading noblemen among the prisoners, and personally served the King on his knees. (English monarchs were always served like this, down to the time of Charles I.) The food came from the French provision wagons, as the English had had none for nearly three days. The Prince told his royal captive : 'Sir, for God's sake make none evil nor heavy cheer,' assuring him that King Edward would treat him with the utmost consideration. He also congratulated John on his bravery, saying that he had fought better than anyone, that even in defeat he had brought honour upon himself. This must have been small consolation to John II as he rode to Bordeaux with the English, who were 'laded with gold, silver and prisoners'. Nor, for all his captor's beautiful manners, did the King ever see his jewels again.

Across the Channel 'there was great joy when they heard tidings of the battle of Poitiers, of the discomfiting of the Frenchmen and taking of the King ; great solemnities were made in all churches and great fires and wakes throughout all England.' Next spring the Black Prince brought John and his son home to London in triumph. On 24 May 1357 the captive French King rode into London on a white thoroughbred, accompanied by the Prince who tactfully rode a little black pony. John was given the palace of the Savoy for his lodging, where there 'came to see him the King and

the Queen oftentimes and made him great feast and cheer'.
Edward III took a strong liking to his unfortunate cousin
and brought him to Windsor where he 'went a-hunting and
a-hawking thereabout at his pleasure'. John can hardly have
been cheered to meet the King of Scots, David II, who had
been a prisoner for eleven years.

Meanwhile there was chaos in France, where the central
government collapsed. It was all too much for the Dauphin
Charles, a sickly boy of eighteen whose very real talents had
not yet emerged. He was quite overwhelmed by his father's
misfortunes and by the difficulties of his position. Not only
did the King of Navarre's followers rise in Normandy, but
all over France the Free Companies or *routiers*—bands of
English and Gascon deserters and even Frenchmen—
seized castles and set themselves up as robber barons,
terrorizing large tracts of country and levying the *pâtis*.

When the Estates met at Paris only a few weeks after
Poitiers they were in an angry mood. They demanded a
complete reform of the administration, economies to reduce
taxation and the dismissal of royal advisers, and insisted that
the Dauphin must submit to the direction of a standing
council of knights, clergy and bourgeois. The bourgeois had
a formidable leader in Etienne Marcel, a rich cloth-dealer
who was Provost of the Merchants (the nearest thing to a
Lord Mayor of Paris). What made them more dangerous
was that they were allied with Navarre's followers, who
wanted their unsavoury King to be Regent. Gradually the
Dauphin lost control of the situation. Navarre escaped from
prison at the end of 1357 and came to Paris where he forced
the Dauphin to pardon him. The King of Navarre addressed
an assembly on the subject of his wrongs: 'His language
was so pleasant that he was greatly praised and so little by
little he entered into the favour of them of Paris, so that he
was better beloved there than the Regent [i.e. the Dauphin].'
However, Navarre shrewdly refused to stay in the capital
where Marcel's party grew more obstreperous every day. In
February 1358 they broke into the Dauphin's chamber to
murder the Marshals of Champagne and Normandy, 'so

near him that his clothes were all bloody with their blood and he himself in great peril'. The mob also made him put on a red and blue bonnet—the colours of Paris.

In May 1358 came the *jacquerie*. Unlike the lords in their castles or the bourgeois in their walled towns, the peasants had been unable to defend themselves from the English. During the day they only dared work in the fields if there was a lookout in the church tower to warn them of approaching troops ; at night they hid in caves, marshes or the forest. In *L'Arbre des Batailles*, Honoré Bonet writes how the soldiers take 'excessive payments and ransoms . . . especially from the poor labourers who cultivate lands and vineyards', how 'my heart is full of grief to see and hear of the great martyrdom that they inflict without pity or mercy on the poor labourers'. Even their own *seigneurs* persecuted them, seizing their crops and animals to pay ransoms and to make up for the decline in revenues caused by the Black Death. Finally the wretched toilers of the Beauvaisis took up knives and clubs and turned upon the lords who had failed to protect them. Dreadful stories circulated—of a lady who was raped by a dozen men and then forced to eat her roasted husband's flesh before being tortured to 'an evil death' with all her children. Soon there were thousands of *jacques* north of the Seine, plundering and burning castles and manor houses. Etienne Marcel hoped to employ them as an auxiliary army and sent troops to their aid, politically a disastrous move. The shrewder King of Navarre gathered troops and then massacred the ill-armed mob near Meaux, thereby winning boundless popularity with the French nobility.

The Dauphin had fled from Paris in March. But the bourgeois were turning against Etienne Marcel, who at the end of July was cut down with an axe by one of his own supporters. The Dauphin returned, riding in amid the cheers of the fickle Parisians. Nevertheless Navarre was still at large, and defeated a royal army at Mauconseil the following month.

Meanwhile French envoys had been negotiating with the

The Palace of the Savoy. 'Henry, Duke of Lancaster, repaired or rather new built it, with the charges of fifty-two thousand marks [roughly £34,000] which money he had gathered together at the town of Bergerac.' (Stowe)

Edward, Prince of Wales—the Black Prince (1330–1376)

'In war, was never lion rag'd more fierce,
In peace was never gentle lamb more mild,
Than was that young and princely gentleman.'

English to obtain the release of King John. In January 1358, by the first Treaty of London, the Dauphin agreed to surrender the sovereignty of Guyenne, together with the Limousin, Poitou, the Saintonge, Ponthieu and other regions—also in full sovereignty—which comprised at least a third of the entire realm of France. In addition John's ransom was set at four million gold crowns. Edward in return was to renounce his claims to the French throne. However, although these were Edward's own proposals, he was so encouraged by the Dauphin's difficulties that he decided he wanted more—Anjou, Maine and Normandy, the Pas-de-Calais, together with the overlordship of Brittany. But the Estates declared that this second Treaty of London was 'neither bearable nor feasible'. In fact Edward had probably never expected that these new demands would be met, and had made them simply as an excuse for further military intervention.

The English King now prepared to take the field himself, for the final campaign. Understandably he had no difficulty in raising an army of 30,000 men, all avid for plunder and encouraged by the wonderful victory at Poitiers. Most of his nobles accompanied him, and four of his sons, all recruiting large companies under the indenture system. Famous commanders were flooded with applications: so great was the reputation of Sir John Chandos that his company was superior to that of some earls, although he was only a knight. The army included 6,000 men-at-arms and countless wagons carrying kitchens, tents, mills, forges and even collapsible leather boats. Unfortunately instead of invading in the spring, the King did not land at Calais until 28 October.

The object of this campaign was to mount a mighty *chevauchée* which would culminate in Edward's coronation as King of France at Rheims—the traditional place of consecration. After being joined by some German mercenaries and by many *routiers* (including Robert Knollys), Edward marched out of Calais on All Saints Day 1359, proceeding by way of Artois, the Thiérache and Champagne to Rheims, burning and slaying in the now customary

manner. But Rheims knew he was coming and the Arch-
bishop-Duke brought in provisions for a long siege. The
English arrived before its strong walls in December in
dreadful weather, and had to camp in snow.

Among those who rode with Edward was Geoffrey
Chaucer, probably as a man-at-arms. He had had the misfortune to be taken prisoner on a raid into Brittany and the
King was kind enough to contribute £16 towards his ransom.
Obviously the poet had a grim time. Later he wrote: 'There
is ful many a man that crieth "Werre! Werre!" that wot ful
litel what werre amounteth.'

In January 1360, after cruel suffering by men and horses,
Edward despaired of taking Rheims. He set off for upper
Burgundy where, after frightful devastation—at Tonnerre
the English drank 3,000 butts of wine—the Duke was only
too glad to buy him off for 200,000 gold *moutons* (£33,000).
The King then struck at Paris, laying waste the Nivernais en
route. He camped at Bourg-la-Reine but did not feel strong
enough to assault the capital. A Carmelite friar, Jean de
Venette, who was in Paris at the time, recorded how everyone fled from the suburbs to take refuge behind the city
walls. 'On Good Friday and Holy Saturday the English set
fire to Montlhéry and to Longjumeau and to many other
towns round about. The smoke and flames rising from the
towns to the sky were visible at Paris from innumerable
places.'

(Ironically an incident had just occurred on the other side
of the Channel which shocked all England. On 15 March
1360 some French ships attacked Winchelsea and burnt the
town. Although the raiders spent only a single night on
English soil, it was the first time such a thing had happened
for twenty years. The English people were so terrified by
this one small experience of what they had been inflicting
on the French for decades that panic swept the entire
country.)

Edward hoped that the French would come out from
Paris to attack him. He sent heralds with a challenge to the
Dauphin, who wisely refused it. Sir Walter Manny rode up

to the walls and threw a javelin ; even this elegant provocation failed. So, after spending a fortnight in the region of
Paris, the English moved into the plain of the Beauce to
inflict further misery. Near Chartres they were struck by a
freak hail storm which threw the whole army into confusion.
They called the day 'Black Monday'.

Shortly afterwards the Abbot of Cluny arrived with peace
proposals. Lancaster pointed out that while the King had
fought a wonderful war, and though his men were profiting
from it, it was far too expensive for his resources and would
probably continue for the rest of his life. He advised Edward
to accept the proposals—'for, my lord, we could lose more in
one day than we have gained in twenty years'. The King
agreed ; it had been his longest campaign and, in terms of
strategy, was a failure. The fact that the Dauphin had made
peace with Navarre and was beginning to improve his
position generally may also have had something to do with
Edward's decision.

On 1 May 1360 negotiations began at the little hamlet of
Brétigny near Chartres and within a week the Black Prince
and the Dauphin had reached an agreement. King John's
ransom was to be cut to three million gold crowns
(£500,000), while the English would reduce their territorial
demands to those of the first Treaty of London—Guyenne
in full sovereignty, together with the Limousin, Poitou, the
Angoumois, the Saintonge, Rouergue, Ponthieu and many
other districts, all in full sovereignty. On 24 October the
Treaty of Brétigny was ratified at Calais. It was agreed that
Edward would renounce his claim to the French throne and
John his sovereignty over the ceded areas only when the
latter had been transferred to the English. In the event,
Edward stopped calling himself King of France, but on both
sides no one bothered about formal renunciation.

The Dauphin signed the treaty in good faith, for France
was exhausted. It seems unlikely that he had any secret
reservations (as used to be suggested by some historians)
and the transfer of territory began in autumn 1361. By
spring the following year all save a few areas were in English

hands. Edward was sovereign ruler not only of an independent Guyenne but of Aquitaine, a huge state which comprised one-third of France. While it would be wrong to detect any spirit of modern nationalism, undoubtedly the inhabitants of some of the ceded territories were most reluctant to change sovereigns—perhaps partly because of the injuries inflicted on them by the English, partly for fear of losing rights and privileges. But only at La Rochelle was there noticeable resentment; one Rochellois said that his fellow citizens 'would obey with their lips but not with their hearts', and others declared they were ready to pay half their wealth in taxes annually rather than be ruled by England. However, there was no real opposition and no bloodshed. In the event little changed, most mayors being confirmed in office; a number of Englishmen were put into the more important seneschalcies and castellanies but the greater part of the administration was left to Frenchmen. The ruler of the new state was not the King of England but the Black Prince at Bordeaux, whom Edward made Duke of Aquitaine.

In October 1360, when 400,000 gold crowns had been paid, two-thirds of the first instalment of his ransom, Edward III allowed John II to go home, though he had to leave three of his sons as hostages. (The sum was raised partly by crippling consumer taxes, on salt, wine and all other forms of merchandise, and by selling the hand of John's eleven-year-old daughter Isabel to the son of the ill-famed Duke of Milan, Gian Galeazzo Visconti—'the King of France sold his own flesh and blood'.) Unfortunately one of John's sons, the Duke of Anjou, broke parole to rejoin a beautiful young wife and refused to return. The chivalrous King John therefore went back to London in 1364, to meet with a princely reception. In fact it was so princely that it has been suggested that the parties and banquets were too much for him. John II died at his palace of the Savoy on 8 April 1364, aged only forty-four. After a magnificent requiem at St Paul's his remains were returned to France for interment at Saint-Denis.

If Edward III had not won the crown of France, it must none the less have seemed to contemporaries that he had carried off a very great prize. Beyond question the Brétigny settlement was a remarkable achievement. And it was amazing that a poor little country like England, formerly considered to be of no account militarily, could bring so rich and powerful a neighbour to her knees.

For the French of course it was a disaster. Edward's triumph meant more than just 'the abasement of the French monarchy' and some lost battles. Prior Jean de Venette tells us what it meant to him. 'The loss by fire of the village where I was born, Venette near Compiègne, is to be lamented, together with that of many others near by.' He tells how there was no one to prune the vines or stop them rotting, no one to sow or plough the fields, no sheep or cattle even for the wolves, and how the roads were deserted. 'Houses and churches no longer presented a smiling appearance with newly thatched roofs but rather the lamentable spectacle of scattered smoking ruins amid nettles and thistles springing up on every side. The pleasant sound of bells was heard indeed, not as a summons to divine worship but as a warning of hostile intention, so that men might seek out hiding places while the enemy were still on the way. What more can I say?'

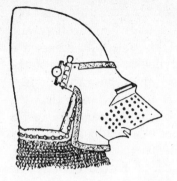

4

Charles the Wise
1360–1380

Ah, France, why shouldst thou be thus obstinate
Against the kind embracement of thy friends?

The Raigne of King Edward III

Merde pour le Roy d'Angleterre

Song of the Hundred Years War

The reign of Charles V is the story of the defeat of
Edward III and the Black Prince. The English lost everything they had gained at Brétigny, though they retained
Guyenne and Calais. For the first time the Plantagenets
faced an enemy who was their superior.

Charles was one of the truly great French rulers. In
appearance he was unprepossessing with a thin, bony face,
which however had a certain wry humour. (For some years
the Louvre *metro* was graced by a copy of a contemporary
statue of Charles V in the guise of St Louis, portraying a
man of considerable charm.) He had a wretchedly frail
physique, being afflicted by ulcers and a poor circulation
and debilitated by an undiagnosed disease which frequently
sent him exhausted to his bed. Even had he wanted, he

could never have been a man of action. In fact he was both pious and bookish with a keen interest in theology and history, a genuine intellectual of his time who amassed a library of nearly 1,200 chained books in a tower of the Louvre. Indeed the name *Carolus Sapiens* bestowed on him by chroniclers meant Charles the Erudite rather than the Wise. Although no less magnificent and grandiose in his concept of kingship than his father—he held a surprisingly splendid court—Charles V's unusual talents combined to give him a curiously legal approach to matters of state; he had all the lawyer's passion for correct procedure and care for detail.

The new King of France was not at first ready to confront the English or to overthrow the Brétigny settlement, which had at least bought him time. He had first to deal with four other problems—the war in Brittany, the King of Navarre, the Flemish succession, and the Free Companies (*routiers*).

After twenty years of bloody warfare the Montfort and Blois factions were still fighting for the Duchy of Brittany, a situation which the English continued to exploit with their accustomed rapacity. Duke John IV had returned to the land of his ancestors in 1362 and in September 1364 (under the able direction of Sir John Chandos and Sir Hugh Calveley) finally defeated and killed his rival, Charles of Blois, at Auray. Though the French candidate had lost, there was now at least peace and a stable situation, and Duke John paid homage to King Charles in 1365.

The King of Navarre was altogether a more serious matter, as his lands near Paris enabled him to blockade the capital. At the beginning of 1364 he had again risen in revolt, enraged by King John's bestowal of the Duchy of Burgundy on his son Philip; Navarre had been deprived of yet another inheritance, for his claim to Burgundy through his grandmother was better than that of his Valois cousins. He raised his followers in Normandy and recruited men from the Free Companies together with Gascon mercenaries under the redoubtable Captal de Buch. However, the latter's forces were completely routed at Cocherel in May 1364 and the French then thrust deep into Normandy, overrunning the Navarrese strongholds. Charles the Bad made peace the following year and surrendered all his estates near Paris. Henceforward, although still an irreconcilable enemy, he was no longer a real danger.

Flanders once again was threatening to fall under English control. Count Louis had decided that Margaret, his daughter and heiress, should marry an English prince, Edmund, Earl of Cambridge; and King Edward offered to endow his son with all his possessions in northern France. Charles V, much alarmed, managed to obtain a Papal ban on the projected marriage, on grounds of consanguinity; after years of diplomatic manœuvre the French King finally succeeded in obtaining Margaret's hand for his brother, Philip of Burgundy. If later the Valois were to regret bitterly this union of two vast fiefs, it was at least better than the establishment of a northern Guyenne.

The *routiers* of the Free Companies were the most difficult problem of all. There were so many of them, veteran soldiers who were unwilling to return to a life of poverty or even serfdom. Often they had served under the Black Prince and had taken to living off the country after being discharged. So professional were they that every company had a proper command structure with a staff which included secretaries and *butiniers* to collect and share out the loot; some had their own uniform, like the *bandes blanches* of the terrible Archpriest Arnaud de Cervole. Among them were Bretons, Spaniards, even Germans, and of course Englishmen, but the majority were Gascons. However, most of the captains were English, like Sir John Hawkwood, Sir Robert Knollys, Sir Hugh Calveley, Sir John Cresswell, and many more.

The *routiers* 'wasted all the country without cause, and robbed without sparing all that ever they could get, and violated and defiled women, old and young, without pity, and slew men, women and children without mercy'. Captives were tortured as a matter of routine, in the hope that they might reveal hoards of treasure, or even just grain. The *routiers'* lives were as uncertain as they were violent; the Archpriest amassed a fortune but was lynched by his own troops, while a Gascon captain, Seguin de Badefol, accustomed to returning to Guyenne 'with great pillage and treasure', was poisoned by the King of Navarre for foolishly asking for arrears of pay. English captains seem to have been luckier though they were quite as rapacious, with a taste for monasteries with good cellars; Sir John Harleston is said to have given a party to his *routiers* at which they drank out of a hundred chalices looted from the churches of Champagne. Significantly the French called all men of the Free Companies English, whatever their origin—Philippe de Mézières said that such Englishmen were the scourge of God.

Routiers were much in evidence after Brétigny, 'Englishmen, Gascons and Almains, who said they must needs live' and refused to evacuate the fortresses from which they levied their protection rackets, moving on and seizing new castles when an area had been milked dry. They were simply practising those English inventions, the *chevauchée* and the *pâtis*. The companies became still more dangerous when they formed themselves into bigger units—the Grand Companies, in which they were grouped by nationality in *routes*. In 1361 a Grand Company rode down the Rhône valley to Avignon and more or less held the Pope to ransom, while another peculiarly vicious band, the *Tard-Venus* or 'Latecomers' terrorized Lyons. In 1363, at Brignais, the Archpriest defeated a large army under the Duke of Bourbon, who died of his wounds.

Charles had neither the troops nor the money to exterminate these pests. Time and again local authorities had to buy them off. The King did at least try and persuade them to seek their fortunes elsewhere. He employed an obscure little Breton hedge-squire, the Sieur Bertrand du Guesclin, who had himself ridden with the *routiers*, to talk them into going on Crusade to help the Hungarians who were threatened by the Turks, but the plan failed. A golden opportunity came in 1365 when the Castilian pretender, Henry of Trastámara, asked Charles for help against his half-brother King Pedro the Cruel. A delighted Charles sent du Guesclin over the Pyrenees with every *routier* he could find. They met with gratifying success, establishing Henry on the throne of Castile, but two years later he was defeated at Nájera by the Black Prince and the *routiers* poured back into France.

Pedro the Cruel had sought the help of the Prince of Aquitaine as a fellow Biscayan ruler, offering lavish payment and the province of Guipuzcoa. The Prince responded enthusiastically, leading an army of English, Guyennois, Navarrese, exiled Castilians and 'rutters'—the contemporary English term for *routiers*—down to the Ebro where on 2 April 1367 he won his crushing victory at Nájera—'a marvellous dangerous battle and many a man slain and sore hurt'—and restored Pedro to his throne. It was more than just a chivalrous adventure : a friendly Castile would not allow France to use Castilian galleys against England. Unfortunately, true to his knight-errant's code, the Prince refused to hand over to Pedro the key men of the Trastámara faction whom he had captured, and in 1369 Pedro was again overthrown and killed by his half-brother, who understandably was no friend to the English. Worst of all, Pedro had been unable to pay the Black Prince the 600,000 florins he had promised him and on which the latter was counting to pay for the campaign ; his principality would now have to foot the bill. (Prince Edward's sole tangible gain was a great 'ruby'—actually a garnet—once the property of the Sultan of Granada and still a famous English Crown Jewel.)

From the beginning the Black Prince's reign in Aquitaine had not been altogether happy. He and his Princess held great state at Bordeaux and at Angoulême—'so great, that in all Christendom was none like'. (He had made a love match in 1361 with his beautiful Plantagenet cousin, Joan of Kent, who was over thirty, twice married—one husband was still alive—and penniless. An annulment had been obtained from the Pope.) While an ecstatic Chandos herald might write that at Prince Edward's court 'there abode all nobleness, all joy and jollity, largesse, gentleness and honour, and all his subjects and all men loved him right dearly', there was considerable local grumbling. Too many Englishmen had followed the Prince to Aquitaine and too many were given the best jobs. The Guyennois disliked having an energetic ruler of '*si hauteyn et de si graunt port*' on the spot instead of far away over the sea, and were irritated by administrative reforms and a vastly increased bureaucracy. For the Guyennois the new administration took away the whole charm of English rule, which had been that they were left in peace. Worst of all were the new taxes. The Prince's stately court, his feasting and his jousting, had to be paid for and three years running (in 1364, 1365 and 1366) he imposed a ferocious *fouage* or hearth tax throughout his domain. When King Pedro could not pay him he demanded yet another *fouage*, for five years. The English Chancellor of Aquitaine, John Harewell, persuaded most of the Aquitainian lords to agree to it at an assembly at Niort, though they did so with the utmost reluctance. Chandos warned the Prince to drop it but he would not, so Sir John retired to his Norman estates. Not only in the new territories but in the heart of English Guyenne men thought of transferring their allegiance.

In 1368 some of the highest lords of Guyenne, led by the Count of Armagnac (who in any case was on bad terms with the Prince) and Armand-Amanieu of Albret, refused to allow the hearth tax to be levied on their lands. Armagnac and Albret, who were in Paris for the latter's wedding to the French King's sister, suddenly decided to appeal to Charles V against the Prince's excessive taxation. To allow their appeal would be to claim sovereignty over Aquitaine, a clear violation of the Treaty of Brétigny. But the French had never formally renounced suzerainty. Charles, who possessed such a taste for the law that Edward III sneered he was no better than a lawyer, at once realized that by a shrewd use of legal processes he could undermine the entire English position in France.

King Charles had been preparing for war for a long time. He had retained and extended the harsh consumer taxes— the *aide*, *taille* and *gabelle*—imposed for his father's ransom, and while he still owed nearly half of the ransom, his war treasurers were seeing that his troops were paid more regularly than hitherto. No more ransom money was sent to the English, and the income from special taxes was ten times that from the irregular war taxation which the English Parliament allowed Edward III. Over a number of years the French King issued imaginative edicts dealing with military matters, and eventually he had a permanent force— it can hardly be called a standing army—of 3,000–6,000 men-at-arms and 800 crossbowmen, paid for by the new revenues. There were also attempts to impose a primitive command structure; men-at-arms were grouped in companies of a hundred under captains, who in turn were under lieutenants and marshals. The machinery of muster and review which controlled soldiers' pay was tightened up to stop commanders claiming money for non-existent troops. Townsmen were ordered to practise archery so that they could help in defending their own walls, while château owners were commanded to keep their fortifications in good repair, the castles being regularly inspected and their lords being given money to maintain proper garrisons. Some frontier châteaux were taken over by the King and those which were indefensible were demolished. The arsenal at the Louvre was restocked. New warships were laid down in the Clos des Galées at Rouen.

Although he never once went on campaign, Charles masterminded all military operations throughout his reign. His strategy was a combination of scorched earth and guerrilla raids, and his troops were forbidden to engage in full-scale battle with the English. He recruited new commanders, obscure men who had proved themselves as captains of frontier garrisons or as *routiers*. He wanted guerrilla leaders, not paladins. Soon he had a formidable band—Olivier de Clisson, Boucicault, Amaury de Craon, the Bègue de Vilaines, the Admiral Jean de Vienne and, above all, Bertrand du Guesclin whom he made Constable of France.

Nothing shows Charles's resourcefulness more than his

use of du Guesclin. Perroy considers him to have been 'incapable of winning a battle or of being successful in a siege of any scope, just good enough to put new life into pillaging *routiers* who recognized their master in him, swollen with self-importance'. This is not quite fair. Admittedly du Guesclin was a rotten general, but in the end he learnt to understand his King's Fabian tactics, recognizing that there was no other way of defeating the English combination of archers and dismounted men-at-arms in a direct confrontation. He became a commander who, if he could not win battles, could win campaigns. Charles deliberately metamorphosed the ugly, ungifted plebeian little man into a folk-hero, ransoming him at exaggerated prices, making him a Count and finally burying him with the Kings of France at Saint-Denis.

Throughout 1368 Charles's agents collected nearly 900 appeals against the Black Prince in Aquitaine, appeals by magnates and squires, by towns, by bishops and abbots. All this was done in secret, until at the very end of the year the French King announced publicly that he was entitled to receive such appeals. In January 1369 he sent a summons to the Black Prince at Bordeaux to answer them. 'We command you to come to our city of Paris and there to show and present yourself before us in our chamber of peers.' The Prince, visibly astonished, shook his head and then glared at the French envoys. 'Sirs, we will gladly go to Paris,' he replied grimly, 'but I assure you that it shall be with helmet on our head and 60,000 men.' However though Prince Edward might be able to send an army he could not now ride with it; since his Spanish campaign he had suffered from dysentery and mysterious fevers and was now swollen with dropsy—he could only travel by litter. Illness was affecting both his temper and his judgement.

Edward III, shrewder than his son, saw impending disaster and told him to withdraw the hearth tax. The English King implored Charles not to receive appeals from Aquitaine and suggested that both sides make the formal renunciations stipulated ten years earlier at Brétigny.

Charles took no notice and sent a letter of formal defiance to King Edward; it was delivered—so Froissart claims—by a scullion, which infuriated him. War was declared in June 1369. In November the French King announced that he had confiscated Aquitaine.

Before the English knew what was happening the French had also overrun Abbeville and the county of Ponthieu. Fighting broke out in Pérrigord, in Quercy and in the Agenais, while all the Rouergue was lost. At the end of 1369 the English suffered a truly disastrous casualty; the Prince had hastily recalled Sir John Chandos, who returned to be killed at an obscure siege on New Year's Eve. Even his enemies mourned him—Charles V said that had Chandos lived he would have found a way of making a lasting peace.

The English resorted to old, tried tactics. King Edward's third son John of Gaunt—now Duke of Lancaster—led a *chevauchée* into Normandy in midsummer 1369, before the harvest. It was indistinguishable from a Grand Company's campaign as the English government was too short of money to pay the troops properly and made arrangements to pay them out of booty, appointing special receivers for the purpose. Indeed many of Gaunt's men were *routiers*, together with large numbers of the worst criminals in England who had been promised pardons. The following year Sir Robert Knollys—who had once boasted that he fought neither for the King of England nor for the King of France, but for himself—was actually put in command of another and larger *chevauchée*. Many English lords in the army were horrified at having to serve under 'the old bandit' [*vetus vispilio*] and went off on their own. Sir Robert struck boldly into the Ile de France devastating the country up to the very gates of Paris; King Charles could see the smoke going up from burning villages at his palace, the Hôtel de Saint-Pol, but would not let his troops offer battle. Eventually, as in 1360, the English left in disgust.

Generally the French refused to fight a pitched battle even when odds were in their favour. The Constable's tactics were those of raid, ambush, night attack and general harassment. He concentrated on isolated towns and fortresses where garrisons were small, savaging foraging parties and wagon-trains, cutting communications, and wearing down enemy morale by constant surprises. At sieges he offered good terms and even money to bring about a quick surrender, and he kept his word. His overall strategy was to encourage the French of Aquitaine to rise and he used persuasion, bribery and threats to make them do so. If they were frightened of English reprisals, he told them to stay behind their walls till the English had gone, emerging only to attack stragglers, and he promised them armed assistance.

One town which found such tactics less than successful was Limoges which, led by its Bishop, Jehan de Cros, turned against the English in 1370. The Black Prince was particularly angry because he had thought that the Bishop, who was his son's godfather, was a friend, and swore 'by his father's soul' that he would make the people of Limoges pay dearly. For an entire October the English mined the walls. (A medieval siege-mine was a tunnel beneath the foundations which was supported by wooden props ; when it was ready the props were fired, to bring the wall above crashing down.) The defenders counter-mined without success, and the attackers' mine suddenly demolished a large section of the wall, the rubble filling the moat. The English poured into the town before the garrison realized that a breach had been made. Prince Edward was carried in on his litter, ordering his men to give no quarter. 'It was great pity to see the men, women and children kneel down on their knees before the Prince for mercy, but he was so inflamed with ire that he took no heed to them.' More than 3,000 civilians were massacred. The three leaders of the garrison survived, but only because they found themselves in single combat with John of Gaunt, his brother Cambridge and the Earl of Pembroke who accepted their surrender. Gaunt also saved the Bishop's life. But the fate of Limoges did not deter other towns from rising against the English.

The siege was almost the Black Prince's last campaign

'for always his sickness increased'. He was also demoralized by the death of his eldest son. On the advice of his surgeon the Prince returned to England in January 1371, leaving John of Gaunt in charge. At home he recovered a little and next year sailed on an expedition, but was blown back by bad weather. In October 1372 he finally resigned his Principality of Aquitaine, retiring to his castle at Berkhamsted where, apart from a few rare public appearances, he spent his time as a bedridden invalid. The 'flower of the chivalry of England' died in April 1376. His monument may still be seen at Canterbury Cathedral—he wears armour and is much as he must have appeared at Poitiers. He left a remarkable legend. Shakespeare wrote of him, in King Richard II :

> In war, was never lion rag'd more fierce,
> In peace was never gentle lamb more mild,
> Than was that young and princely gentleman.

England's new royal paladin was John of Gaunt—John, King of Castile and Duke of Lancaster to give him his full style and titles. He was probably the mightiest subject England has ever seen. The Duchy of Lancaster was an independent palatinate within whose boundaries the King's writ did not run. In addition Gaunt possessed countless rich estates and properties throughout England, ranging from a vast sheep ranch in the Peak District to his splendid palace of the Savoy just outside the City. His revenues and his retinue were scarcely surpassed by those of his father. Moreover, as the husband of Pedro the Cruel's daughter he was rightful King of Castile. Yet although vigorous and ambitious, he was not of the same stuff as his father and eldest brother and turned out a curiously ineffectual figure—not a man to roll back the French advance.

King Charles's reconquest had continued. Although the Mayor of Poitiers supported the English, its people opened the gates to du Guesclin in 1372 and the rest of Poitou soon followed its capital. In June the same year, off La Rochelle, a Castilian fleet defeated an English fleet under the Earl of Pembroke—the new Governor of Aquitaine—sending the ship carrying his troops' pay to the bottom and taking the Earl back to Spain as a prisoner. In consequence the Mayor of La Rochelle overpowered the English garrison and admitted du Guesclin. The Constable also took Usson in the Auvergne, while the whole of the Angoumois and the Saintonge went over to the French. There were not enough English troops to provide adequate garrisons and the enemy seemed to be everywhere. The English strongholds in Normandy and Brittany were falling and even Guernsey was invaded by a French force under Evan of Wales (a member of the former ruling family of Gwynedd).

King Edward, old, wifeless, in the hands of a greedy mistress—Alice Perrers—and possibly drinking too much, made a final effort. At the end of August 1372 a fleet of 400 ships carrying 4,000 men-at-arms, 10,000 archers and the ailing Black Prince left Sandwich, the King on board the *Grace-Dieu*. For six weeks the English armada sailed into contrary winds, beaten and buffeted and blown off course time and again, until the sailors despaired and put back to port. The abortive expedition cost the enormous sum of £900,000. 'God and St George help us!' cried old Edward. 'There was never so evil a King in France as there is now, nor ever one who gave me such trouble.'

The following year the Archbishop of Canterbury asked for prayers for another *chevauchée*, which was the only answer the English had to the new French tactics. In mid-summer 1373 John of Gaunt led 3,000 men-at-arms and 8,000 archers out of Calais on one of the most daring raids of this sort, going through Picardy, Champagne, Burgundy, the Bourbonnais, the Auvergne and the Limousin, cutting a hideous swath of fire and destruction down central France. After a terrible passage through the mountains of the Auvergne in the depths of winter, Gaunt reached Bordeaux and safety with 6,000 starving troops, having lost most of the rest and all his horses from cold and hunger. It was a brilliant feat—he had covered over 600 miles in five months—but he had not succeeded in capturing a single town or found anyone to fight him.

By the end of 1373 Aquitaine no longer existed. Even Guyenne was diminished; during the year the Duke of Anjou had taken Bazas on the English side of the Garonne, and even La Réole, the key to Bordeaux. The d'Albret, ancient vassals of the Plantagenets, had gone over to the Valois, driving a salient into the duchy which was now smaller than when Edward III had begun the war in 1337. Furthermore, most of Brittany had been occupied by the French, including every English stronghold, and its Duke had had to take refuge in England. In the north only Calais and a garrison in Normandy held out.

But by 1374 both sides were growing weary, especially in Aquitaine. Edward III was drink-sodden and used up, an old man with a long white beard. For these last years of the reign John of Gaunt stood behind the throne, but his ministers were unpopular and he himself seems to have been incapable of organizing a concerted war effort—there was no overall strategy as in the 1340s or 1350s. The treasury was empty; even before the War had recommenced in 1369 the vast sums paid for King John's ransom had been spent, while the English economy—and therefore royal revenues— had not recovered from the Black Death. *Chevauchées* and all the tactics once so successful had failed totally. Gaunt, still recovering from his unpleasant experiences in the Auvergne mountains, was only too ready for a truce. From this year on, on the other hand, Charles V's health grew progressively worse, gout being added to all his other afflictions. The Constable du Guesclin saw little hope of overrunning the heart of Guyenne. In January 1374 at Périgueux, he and Gaunt agreed to a truce covering all Aquitaine. In June 1375 a further truce was negotiated, to last for two years and covering not merely Aquitaine but all France. Pope Gregory XI, a Limousin from a province which had suffered severely, did his best to secure a lasting peace. From 1375–1377 a surprisingly modern-sounding peace conference sat permanently at Bruges, with Cardinals as negotiators and attended by both Gaunt and the Duke of Burgundy. A territorial compromise was reached, but neither side would give way on the old question of the sovereignty of Guyenne. Even so, the Duke of Burgundy gave a banquet for the participants when the conference ended.

On 21 June 1377 King Edward III died at the notable—for the time—old age of sixty-five. Sadly, on account of that most unpopular of mistresses, Alice Perrers, he was little mourned by his subjects although he had been a great King. However Charles V, who if no knight-errant did not lack chivalry, pronounced that Edward was worthy to rank with the world's greatest heroes and said 'how nobly and valiantly he had reigned'. He summoned the lords of France to attend a requiem for the English King at the Sainte-Chapelle. Edward was succeeded by the Black Prince's ten-year-old son, Richard of Bordeaux.

Nevertheless the war began in June 1377, and this time took a new turn. While only five English 'King's Ships' were still operating, the French had been steadily building up their navy at the Clos des Galées; by the late 1370s they had at least twenty-five galleys. The English had to hire Genoese warships, though they were able to obtain oared sailing-barges known as 'balingers' from the Cinque Ports. What made the French naval effort so formidable was their excellent Admiral, Jean de Vienne, whose aim was to control the Channel and prevent English reinforcements reaching Guyenne and Brittany. The same month that King Edward died nearly fifty ships carrying 4,000 troops crossed the Channel. Rye was sacked, after which the French penetrated as far inland as Lewes which they burnt; they then sailed on to burn Plymouth. In August they returned and burnt Hastings, but were beaten off at Southampton and Poole. Pinpricks by comparison with what had been done in France, such raids caused uproar in England. But though there were further raids—Winchelsea and Gravesend suffered in 1380—these hit-and-run tactics failed to cut England's sea communications which were buttressed by a string of fortresses on the French coast from Calais to Bayonne.

Also in 1377 the Duke of Anjou and the Constable again invaded Guyenne. The Seneschal, Sir Thomas Felton, was defeated and taken prisoner at Eymet in September, and Bergerac fell. But the Guyennois held firm, staying loyal to the Plantagenets. It is illuminating to remember Froissart's considered opinion of the 'Gascons' : *'ils ne sont point estables'* —not a stable people, but preferring the English to the French and inclined to think that the English would always win. Indeed the Captal de Buch KG, that doughty squire from the sandy Landes, preferred to die in captivity rather than transfer his allegiance, although he was offered large sums of money. In 1379 a really capable Lieutenant arrived at Bordeaux, Lord Neville of Raby KG, from County Durham, who took the offensive, raiding in the style of the French Constable and sailing up the Gironde to recapture Mortagne. He is said to have retaken over eighty towns, fortresses and castles during his lieutenancy which lasted hardly more than a year.

The French were being contained on other fronts too. Although they had conquered Brittany they failed to take the port of Brest, which was relieved by a fleet under the Earl of Buckingham (Edward III's youngest son, the future Duke of Gloucester). Then King Charles made the mistake of trying to confiscate Brittany from Duke John in the way that he had confiscated Aquitaine. The Bretons rallied *en masse* to their Duke—they had no desire to be united to the kingdom of France. Accompanied by Sir Robert Knollys, John returned to be received with joy, and he speedily recovered the west, eventually regaining the whole of his duchy. He ceded Brest to his English allies.

From Calais in 1377 the Deputy Sir Hugh Calveley raided Boulogne, burning ships and plundering. When the fortress of Marke in the Calais march fell to the French he retook it the same day. In 1378 the King of Navarre returned to the scene : he seems to have offered John of Gaunt the County of Evreux in return for the hand of his daughter Catherine. He also had an interesting scheme for poisoning Charles V (he was credited with having recently rid himself of an irritating cardinal by this method), a plot which was discovered when two of his agents were arrested. The Constable at once invaded Navarre's last possessions in Normandy. But before fleeing to his Pyrenean kingdom, Charles the Bad managed to sell Cherbourg to the English, who rushed in a garrison.

In Normandy, Brittany and the Pas-de-Calais the ordinary people had continued to suffer from English garrisons. In 1371 that of Saint-Sauveur-le-Vicomte in the Contentin held 263 parishes in thrall, extracting over £13 from each. The English were greedier in Brittany; at Brest in 1384 they were to mulct every one of 160 parishes of nearly £40, and they had been equally rapacious at Vannes, Ploermel and Bécherel. During the peace which followed Brétigny, and in the midst of all the reverses of the French reconquest, English troops, as well as blackmailing miserable peasants, also contrived to make a fat profit from ransoms. Sometimes enormous sums were realized. In 1365 Sir Matthew Gurney obtained nearly £5,000 for Jean de Laval, and in 1375 Lord Basset of Drayton got £2,000 for a prisoner. There were other ways in which a soldier might make money in addition to ransoms and loot. In 1375 the English garrison at Saint-Sauveur-le-Vicomte were paid £9,000 to surrender their fortress and march off peacefully. (Cherbourg replaced Saint-Sauveur-le-Vicomte as the scourge of Normandy.)

So long as men gave good service to the English King's armies, the most deplorable conduct was tolerated. Sir Robert Knollys, said by Jean le Bel to have been one of the first *routiers*, was the principal captain of the Grand Company in 1358 and made 100,000 gold crowns (nearly £17,000) during that one year alone, when he controlled forty castles in the Loire valley—where the peasants were credited with throwing themselves into the river out of terror at the mere mention of his name—sacked the suburbs of Orleans, and threatened the Pope himself at Avignon. Charred gables were called 'Knollys's mitres'. Yet Edward III was so pleased with the damage inflicted by Sir Robert on the

French that he gave him an official pardon. Later he became one of the King's principal generals, leading as has been seen the *chevauchée* of 1370 and acting as chief-of-staff in another in 1380. (In 1370 he was paid the princely sum of 8s per day, or £146 a year.) Sir Robert amassed 'regal wealth' and built a palatial house in London as well as buying rich estates. He died full of years and honour in 1407. Even Sir John Chandos's respected friend, Sir Hugh Calveley, led 2,000 *routiers* to ravage Armagnac in the late 1360s; like Knollys, who was his half-brother, Calveley had to seek pardon for felony. Later he was Deputy Lieutenant of Calais and then Governor of Brest.

In 1376 the Commons petitioned the King to give a pardon like that of Knollys' to Sir Nicholas Hawkwood, who was the most famous of all the 'rutters'. The son of an Essex tanner and said to have been a London tailor in his youth, Hawkwood was pressed into Edward's army as an ordinary archer, but by 1360 he was leading the *Tard-Venus* to blackmail the Pope. Two years later he took the notorious White Company over the Alps, to begin a long and glorious career as a *condottiere* in Italy; he ended with a bastard Visconti for his bride and a pension of over 3,000 gold ducats from the Florentine Republic.

Another instance of social mobility was that of a certain bondsman of Saul in Norfolk. Conscripted by the commissioners of array in the 1340s to serve in Brittany, by 1373 he was Sir Robert Salle, captain of the fortress of Marck near Calais; he had been knighted by King Edward and his courage was admired even by the snobbish Froissart, though his end was far from prosperous. In 1381 he was murdered in his home county by envious peasants. (A chronicler calls Sir Robert 'a hardy and vigorous knight ... but a great thief and brawler'.)

The War was long remembered as a time to rise in the world. The fifteenth-century herald, Nicholas Upton, wrote that 'in those days we saw many poor men serving in the wars of France ennobled'. Other serfs besides Robert Salle may have become gentlemen of coat-armour. Moreover as

some gentry families were killed off there was room for new men to rise up and take their places.

Many great houses were paid for by booty won in France. Cooling Castle in Kent was built out of such resources by Lord Cobham in 1374, as was Bodiam in Sussex by Sir Edward Dallingridge (Captain of Brest in 1388), and probably Bolton in Yorkshire, which cost Sir Richard Scrope, a noted captain in the War, £120,000 and took eighteen years to complete. Soldiers anxious for their salvation founded religious establishments out of their ill-gotten gains, like the church at Pontefract endowed by Sir Robert Knollys, and Sir Walter Manny's Charterhouse in London.

The English armies had earned their country a bad name, particularly the rank and file. Froissart—who, it must be remembered, was not a Frenchman but what today we would call a Belgian—considered the English 'men of a haughty disposition, hot tempered and quickly moved to anger, difficult to pacify and to bring to sweet reason. They take delight in battles and slaughter. They are extremely covetous of the possessions of others, and are incapable by nature of joining in friendship or alliance with a foreign nation. There are no more untrustworthy people under the sun than the middle classes in England.' However 'the gentlefolk are upright and loyal by nature, while the ordinary people are cruel, perfidious and disloyal . . . they will not allow them [the upper classes] to have anything—even an egg or a chicken—without paying for it.'

But in war the English nobility showed themselves no less avaricious than their inferiors. It was not only the adventurers who made fortunes, as has been seen. So did—in the words of their inspired historian, the late K. B. McFarlane—'that maligned body of far-from-average men, the landed aristocracy of medieval England'. The same writer claims that 'there is no truth in the theory that the aristocracy

A knight of the Dallingridge family and his wife, c. 1390. This is probably Sir Edward Dallingridge, Captain of Brest in 1388, who built Bodiam. (From a brass at Fletching, Sussex)

started the war and left the mercenaries to finish it off', listing a host of noblemen who played a crucial part and in consequence amassed huge sums of money. In the Good Parliament of 1375 William Lord Latimer KG (who had fought at Crécy) was accused of having made £83,000 out of his captaincy of Bécherel—he undoubtedly managed to buy twelve English manors to add to his estates. Richard Fitzalan KG, Earl of Arundel and Surrey—popularly known as 'Copped Hat'—left £60,000 in coin and bullion alone when he died in 1376 ; he was both an imaginative investor and a money-lender on a large scale, though in the view of McFarlane (the leading authority on the medieval English nobility) the original source of Arundel's wealth was almost certainly the War. The Beauchamp Earls of Warwick were another noble family which did well out of the fourteenth-century campaigns in France, as did the great house of Stafford. Royal rewards for service in the field enabled the Cobhams to enter the peerage. Everyone, adventurer or magnate, *routier* or pressed archer, had good reason to keep the War going.

Here one should emphasize that, although everyone had hopes, not every soldier actually made a fortune out of the Hundred Years War. At the Count of Foix's castle at Orthez 'a squire of Gascony called the Bascot of Mauléon, a man of fifty years of age, an expert man of arms' was only too keen to tell Froissart his story while they sat by the fire waiting for midnight and for the Count to begin supper. The Bascot (Bastard) was a by-blow of a family of petty nobles and had had to support himself entirely by soldiering. 'The first time I bore arms was under the Captal de Buch at the battle of Poitiers,' said the Bascot. 'I had that day three prisoners, a knight and two squires, of whom I had one with another 400,000 francs.' He then went to Prussia to fight at the side of the Teutonic Knights, returning to put down the *jacquerie* ; and he was with King Edward during the Rheims campaign. After Brétigny he became Captain of a Free Company, riding with Hawkwood to Avignon to demand money from the Pope. He was in Brittany under

Sir Hugh Calveley, taking prisoners at the battle of Auray 'by whom I had 2,000 francs', and he accompanied the Black Prince to Spain. During the renewed war between France and England he kept the main chance in mind, capturing a castle near Albi which had since been worth '100,000 francs' to him (presumably by extorting money from the surrounding countryside), though 'I abide still good English and shall do while I live'. Yet although the Bascot travelled 'as though he had been a great baron' and ate off silver, he admitted he had known 'as much loss as profit', that at times he had been so miserably poor—'so overthrown and pulled down'—that he could not afford even a horse. For all his campaigns and silver plate, he was ending as a mere household man of the Count of Foix. Many English men-at-arms must have been disappointed in the same way.

In 1378 a new Pope was elected, the Italian Urban VI. The Papacy had returned to Rome in 1369 and Urban decided upon radical reforms which would diminish French influence. A group of cardinals were so alarmed that they declared Urban's election invalid and chose another Pontiff, Clement VII. Charles was delighted and invited Clement to reinstall the Papacy at Avignon. Western Christendom was to be divided by the Great Schism for nearly half a century. Only the Scots and the Neapolitans joined the French in recognizing Clement, most countries trying to remain neutral. Naturally the English gave Urban enthusiastic support. Hitherto the Papacy had played a most valuable part in negotiating truces and attempting to make peace—now there was no international body to perform this work of mediation.

Charles V, iller than ever and approaching the end of his painful life, was so worn out and so depressed by his recent lack of success that he sued for peace. He offered the English all Aquitaine south of the Dordogne, together with Angoulême and a marriage between his daughter and Richard II; the project collapsed when one of Urban's cardinals arranged another match for the young English King. The French

Seal of the Black Prince after the Treaty of Brétigny in 1360, when the English ruled a third of France. The inscription reads: 'Seal of Edward, the King of England's eldest son, Prince of Aquitaine and Wales, Duke of Cornwall and Earl of Chester.'

were increasingly restive under Charles's ferocious taxation, which was essential for the war effort. There were revolts in Languedoc during which tax collectors were lynched. The risings were crushed but the King's nerve was shaken and he abolished the most important levy, the hearth tax, thereby seriously diminishing the regular revenue which was vital for war.

The English were nothing if not persevering. The Earl of Arundel, Marshal of the West, attacked Harfleur at

Whitsun 1378, but met with such a warm reception that he had to beat a hasty retreat back to his ships. The same year he and Gaunt besieged Saint-Malo with no better success. In July 1380 the Earl's brother, Sir John Arundel who was Marshal of England, led a nasty little raid on Brittany which demonstrated both the savagery of the English and their self-righteous hatred of the Pope at Avignon. His troops stormed a convent and raped and tortured the nuns, carrying off some of the unfortunate women to amuse them for the rest of the raid. God, however, does not seem to have appreciated this fine theological distinction between schismatic and orthodox nuns, and a terrible storm sent Sir John to the bottom on the way home, with twenty ships and a thousand men. Only Sir Hugh Calveley and seven others were washed ashore alive.

In the same month the Earl of Buckingham and Sir Robert Knollys marched out of Calais on yet another *chevauchée*. They made for Brittany by a circular route which went through the Beauce and Vendôme before linking up with Duke John's troops at Rennes. They did the usual fearful damage without being offered battle, and achieved nothing.

It was also in July 1380 that Bertrand du Guesclin fell ill and died while he was besieging a castle in the Auvergne. His master survived him less than three months, dying on 16 September at Vincennes from a heart attack. He was only forty-three. Yet even though he had failed to drive the English out of his country, Charles V had won back the greater part of that which had been conquered by Edward III.

5

Richard II: A Lost Peace
1380–1399

For ye [Richard] be always inclined to the pleasure
of the Frenchmen and to take with them peace, to the
confusion and dishonour of the realm of England.

Froissart

For the people of England . . . said how Richard of
Bordeaux would destroy them all if he be let alone.
His heart is so French that he cannot hide it, but
a day will come to pay for all.

Froissart

In 1380 the Kings of England and France were both minors.
Richard II, born at Bordeaux in 1367, grew up to be
fastidious and overbearing, with a streak of megalomania
and a neurotic flair for making enemies. Charles VI, a year
younger, took after his grandfather John II in combining
an excessive love of pleasure with a pugnacious and un-
balanced temperament. Both these monarchs were sur-
rounded by greedy, opinionated uncles. In England the
enormously rich and powerful John of Gaunt so obviously
thought that he deserved a throne himself that some contemporaries suspected him of seeking to supplant young
Richard; the Earl of Cambridge was a timid nonentity—'a
prince that loved his ease and little business'—but the
youngest uncle Thomas of Woodstock, Earl of Buckingham

and future Duke of Gloucester, was as ambitious as he was violent-tempered and would later intrigue murderously against his nephew's government. The three English royal Dukes reluctantly acquiesced in the realm being ruled by a council chosen by Parliament. In France, on the other hand, Philip the Bold of Burgundy soon governed the kingdom as he pleased, the Duke of Anjou becoming more interested in pursuing a claim to the Neapolitan throne, while the Duke of Berry was immersed in a lavish patronage of the arts.

The War in these years was an international struggle which was not restricted to England and France. At the beginning of Richard II's reign the English Parliament spoke fearfully of all the wars in 'France, Spain, Ireland, Aquitaine, Brittany and others'—which would soon extend to Flanders, Scotland and even Portugal. The conflict was further complicated by the schism between Rome and Avignon ; there was no longer an impartial Pope to mediate. Moreover by now it was the French rather than the English who were the aggressors in Guyenne and at sea, and England went in fear of invasion.

The most urgent tasks of Richard II's Council were to find ships to fight the combined French and Castilian fleet which was raiding the south coast, and to maintain the garrisons on the French coast which kept open the sea-route to Guyenne. The latter were Calais, Cherbourg, Brest and Bayonne, the 'barbicans of the realm', and in 1377 their yearly maintenance cost no less than £46,000. The Commons complained that it was not their duty to find money for foreign wars, and by 1380 the Crown Jewels were in pawn, several large loans for defence could not be serviced and the royal treasury was completely exhausted ; none of the troops in the French garrisons had been paid for twenty weeks, while the Earl of Buckingham's army in Brittany was six months in arrears. Reluctantly Parliament agreed to a graded poll tax on every soul in the kingdom save paupers 'as well for the safety of the realm as for the keeping of the sea'.

A tax of a groat (4d) a head was a cruel burden on serfs

Beverstone Castle, Gloucestershire. 'A castle builded by one of the Berkeleys of spoil that he won in France . . . a pile at that time very pretty.' (Leland)

Bodiam Castle, Sussex. Said to have been built from the proceeds of French plunder by Sir Edward Dallingridge, Captain of Brest.

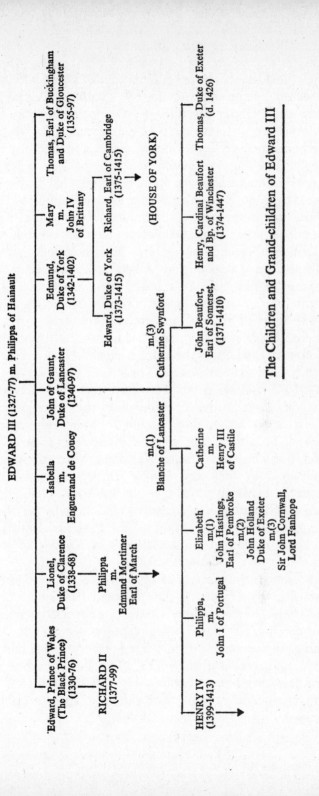

EDWARD III (1327-77) m. Philippa of Hainault

Edward, Prince of Wales (The Black Prince) (1330-76)

RICHARD II (1377-99)

Isabella m. Enguerrand de Coucy

Lionel, Duke of Clarence (1338-68)

Philippa m. Edmund Mortimer Earl of March

John of Gaunt, Duke of Lancaster (1340-97)

m.(1) Blanche of Lancaster

m.(3) Catherine Swynford

HENRY IV (1399-1413)

Philippa, m. John I of Portugal

Elizabeth
m.(1) John Hastings, Earl of Pembroke
m.(2) John Holland Duke of Exeter
m.(3) Sir John Cornwall, Lord Fanhope

Catherine m. Henry III of Castile

John Beaufort, Earl of Somerset, (1371-1410)

Henry, Cardinal Beaufort and Bp. of Winchester (1374-1447)

Thomas, Duke of Exeter (d. 1426)

Edmund, Duke of York (1342-1402)

Edward, Duke of York (1373-1415)

Richard, Earl of Cambridge (1375-1415)

(HOUSE OF YORK)

Mary m. John IV of Brittany

Thomas, Earl of Buckingham and Duke of Gloucester (1355-97)

The Children and Grand-children of Edward III

who toiled on the land without wages. They were already unsettled by the depopulation of the Black Death; it had made their labour saleable, yet they were unable to leave their masters' manors for paid employment. In May 1381 the bondsmen of Kent, Sussex, Essex and Bedford rose in revolt, marching on London under the banner of St George and bringing their bows. (It is revealing that in Kent they would take no one living within twelve leagues of the sea, whose job it was to guard the coast.) En route the 'true commons' killed any tax collectors they could catch, sacked manor houses and monasteries and molested the Queen Mother. In London they killed some Flemings and a number of rich citizens, released prisoners from the gaols, burnt John of Gaunt's Palace of the Savoy and the Priory of the Knights of St John, and stormed the Tower of London where they hacked off the heads of the Archbishop of Canterbury, who was the Lord Chancellor, and of the Prior of St John who was the Treasurer. Froissart says that 'England was at a point to have been lost beyond recovery' but adds disdainfully, 'three fourths of these people could not tell what to ask or demand but followed each other like beasts'. They forced the young King to meet them at Smithfield, but when their leader Wat Tyler was cut down before their eyes by the Lord Mayor 'these ungracious people' scattered in panic and the rising was over. Hangings continued all through the summer. Undoubtedly war taxation was the spark which had set off the Peasants' Revolt.

Taxation caused similar risings in France. Anjou was President of the Council until his departure for Naples in 1382 and during his brief régime re-introduced the taxes abolished by Charles V. The enraged Parisians broke into the arsenal, seized weapons and made themselves masters of the capital, hunting down the tax collectors; there were risings of the same sort in other northern towns and a full-scale insurrection in the south. Only Philip of Burgundy's firmness saved the situation. He quickly gathered troops and crushed the mobs. For the next six years he ruled France.

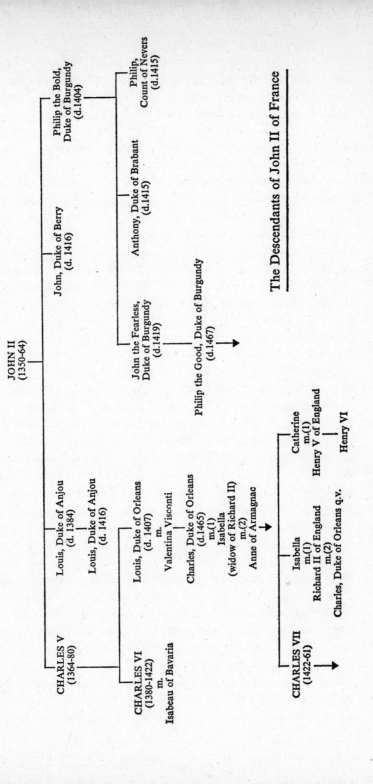

The Descendants of John II of France

Economic troubles were crippling England's ability to fight, let alone to conquer. The wool trade had been throttled by excessive taxation, while people were paying nearly double for their wine; many vineyards in Guyenne had been abandoned because of French devastation, and shipments between Bordeaux and Southampton were much more expensive as vessels had to sail in armed convoys to protect themselves. In 1381, 1382 and 1383 Parliament again refused to grant taxes for war. In consequence the garrisons suffered—during this time the Captain of Cherbourg's pay was reduced from £10,000 to £2,000—and the troops had to live almost entirely off ransoms and the *pâtis*.

Meanwhile the Duke of Burgundy was closing his grip on Flanders. Since 1379 his father-in-law Count Louis de Mâle had been fighting the weavers of Ghent, and in 1382 they defeated him; soon their *ruwaert* (or regent) Philip van Artevelde, the son of Edward III's old friend, had over-run the entire country. Louis appealed to his son-in-law for help, Artevelde to the English. King Richard prepared to lead an army to Flanders but the Commons refused to grant the money. At Roosebeke in November 1382 the French overwhelmed the Flemish pikemen 'and slew them without pity, as though they had been but dogs': Artevelde was among the slain. Count Louis himself died the year after, and henceforward Philip of Burgundy was Count of Flanders.

The impecunious English government found an ally in Pope Urban VI, who, alarmed at the success of the French 'Clementists', wrote to the English bishops ordering a tax on clerical wealth to subsidize a crusade against the Anti-Pope's supporters. They preached with such eloquence that many Englishmen believed they could not enter paradise unless they contributed to so holy a cause; in the diocese of London alone 'there was gathered a tun full of gold and silver'. The 'Crusade' was led by a young Bishop, Henry Despenser of Norwich, who had a taste for war and flew a splendid personal banner. He landed at Calais in April 1383 with perhaps 2,000 men, including Sir Hugh Calveley. They advanced along the Flemish coast, taking several towns and besieging Ypres, although Flanders was impeccably Urbanist. When a large French army advanced to meet them, they retreated with inglorious haste, to be besieged in their turn at Gravelines from where they had to be rescued by the Bretons. The Bishop returned to England and was impeached for his pains.

There was now a new Chancellor, Sir Michael de la Pole —son of the great Hull merchant—and a new policy of appeasement. Pole saw that the monarchy was sinking further and further into debt because of the War, that in consequence it might lose control of central government which would pass to Parliament. He was right about the cost of war, but his attempts to secure peace were to prove disastrous; at home he divided the English into a war party and a peace party, while abroad he abandoned England's most loyal allies.

When Ghent asked for an English Prince of the Blood to come and be her *ruwaert*, Pole merely sent Sir John Bourchier with a derisory force of 400 men. Ghent gave in to Philip of Burgundy at the end of 1385 and the Duke soon controlled most of the Low Countries, acquiring the reversion of Brabant, a territory as big as Flanders, by marrying his younger son to its heiress. England now had to fear economic blockade and the disruption of the wool trade. Pole then infuriated Duke John IV of Brittany—Edward III's protégé—by releasing the Blois claimant to the duchy from captivity in England; in 1386 John's troops invested the English garrison at Brest. By then the policy of détente had not only cost England all her allies in Flanders and Brittany, but was encouraging her enemies to attack her. A Franco-Scottish army had already raided northern England and there was obviously worse in store.

Pole, now Earl of Suffolk, still did not appreciate the extent of the danger. He allowed John of Gaunt to lead an expedition to Castile, in pursuit of the crown which he claimed by right of his second wife, Pedro the Cruel's daughter. Gaunt's departure in July 1386 was sheer madness, as England was facing the greatest invasion threat of the century. A French army 30,000 strong had gathered in and around Sluys; men came from all over France—'Let us now invade these miserable English folk who have caused such mischief and destruction in France, and avenge ourselves for our fathers and mothers and friends whom they have killed.' Vast amounts of food, munitions and horses were collected at special depots; there was even a collapsible wooden fortress made in sections, with keep, watchtowers and curtain walls, to be used in establishing a bridgehead. To transport this enormous concentration of men and material, an armada of 1,200 cogs, galleys and sailing-barges assembled in the harbour at Sluys.

When the English realized the threat they were terrified. The people of London, 'as though maddened by wine', demolished the suburbs to make the City defensible, although the French had not even landed; many went on a spending spree, wasting 'thousands of pounds', so certain were they that England was lost. The troops called up by the commissioners of array were not paid and roamed through the countryside robbing and looting to such an extent that they were forbidden to go within fifty miles of London; many northern units were disbanded and sent home as soon as they reached the south, though the French were expected hourly. England was in uproar.

Nevertheless the English Council had an excellent plan of defence. The King's Ships were to lie in the Thames until the enemy troops had been lured inland and then attack their fleet to cut off any hope of escape. Meanwhile small English forces scattered along the coast were to retreat before the French until they could rejoin the main English army near London.

However, the invasion was delayed until the autumn because of the illness of Philip of Burgundy. When the time came the sailing-masters told the French high command that the weather was by now too unreliable. 'Most dread and powerful lords: of a truth, the sea is foul and the nights be too long, too dark, too cold, too wet and too windy. We are short of victuals, while we must have a full moon and a favourable wind with us. Moreover the English coast and the English havens are dangerous. Too many of our ships are old and too many are small and might be swamped by those that are large. And the sea is at its worst between 29 September and 25 November.' In mid-November 1386 the French decided to call off the invasion.

No doubt had the French managed to land they would have perpetrated atrocities like those of the English in France. Some historians emphasize that French troops behaved just as badly to their own people as the English, and in this context it has been argued that late medieval France was not a nation but a collection of nations. However, there is plenty of evidence to show that Frenchmen of every region blamed the anarchy and bloodshed of the War exclusively on the English; it is significant that throughout France the *routiers* were known as 'the English', although there were many Frenchmen among them. This hatred gave rise to such strange legends as the story that the English had tails (probably due to Welsh footmen hanging their long knives from the back of their belts).

The War played an important role in the growth of English nationalism. As the English began to regard the French as their natural prey, they developed feelings of hatred and contempt; in a poem Eustache Deschamps (who died in 1410) credits an English soldier with the words: 'Dog of a Frenchman, you do nought but drink wine.' As with the French, a common hatred came to override local loyalties.

Even so, some of the noblest English minds of the time rejected the War. In *De Officio Regis* the Lollard heresiarch John Wyclif condemned all warfare as contrary to God's Commandment to love one's neighbour; he also questioned any man's right to claim a kingdom and to hazard lives in pursuit of such a claim. The Dominican John Bromyard, by no means a heretic, was concerned in his *Summa Predicantium* (Points for Preachers) with the corruption caused by warfare—the greed, contempt for life and lack of scruple which it engendered, especially among ill-paid troops.

Hatred of the French was much in evidence at the Parliament of October 1386, which met when England still thought itself threatened by invasion. The absence of the moderating influence of John of Gaunt, away in Castile, was only too apparent. The King's uncle Buckingham, now Duke of Gloucester, led the opposition to the Chancellor, Suffolk. Richard reacted with characteristic arrogance, saying that his people were in rebellion and he would ask 'our cousin, the King of France' to help put them down. This provoked the retort that if a monarch 'rashly in his insane counsels exercise his own peculiar desire', it was lawful for lords and magnates 'to pluck down the King from his royal throne and to raise to the throne some very near kinsman of the royal house'. Gloucester, who seems to have meant himself by this, also reminded his nephew of Edward II's fate. He warned Richard that: 'The King of France is your chief enemy and the mortal foe of your realm. And if he should set foot on your land, he would rather work to despoil you, seize your kingdom, and drive you from your throne, than lend you helping hands ... Recall to your memory therefore how your grandfather King Edward III and your father Prince Edward worked untirely all their lives, in sweat and toil, in heat and cold, for the conquest of the realm of France, which was their hereditary right and is yours by succession after them.' Gloucester continued, saying how innumerable Englishmen, lords and commons, 'have suffered death and mortal peril in that war', and 'how the commons of the realm have ceaselessly poured out countless treasures' to wage it.

Obviously the Duke had plenty of support—if the English disliked paying for war, they liked the prospect of invasion even less. Reluctantly Richard yielded, dismissing Suffolk who was impeached for crimes 'committed to the grave prejudice and injury of the King and kingdom'. A new Council was appointed, dominated by the fire-breathing Gloucester and his chief ally, the Earl of Arundel—Richard's detested former governor—and embarked on a year's campaigning against France. In March 1387, at Cadsand off Margate, Arundel and only sixty ships attacked a Flemish wine-fleet which was sailing from La Rochelle to Sluys. The Earl captured fifty Flemish ships with 19,000 tuns of excellent wine which was immediately sent back to England and sold at a token price, to the joy of the public and brief popularity of the new Council—'The praises of the Earl grew immensely among the commons'. However, Arundel went on to raid the Flemish coast and missed the opportunity of occupying Sluys which would have put all maritime Flanders at his mercy. He then went to Brittany, to relieve Brest and to try to effect a reconciliation with Duke John, suggesting an Anglo-Breton attack on France. But John remained hostile and Arundel was forced to return to England.

In August 1387 Richard II announced his intention of ruling in his own name and appointed a Council from his favourites. Gloucester and Arundel thereupon raised an army and defeated the favourites at Radcot Bridge. Next year the Lords Appellant (accusers), among them Gloucester and Arundel, condemned them to death in the Merciless Parliament, despite Richard's pleading. Gloucester and Arundel then mounted a supreme effort against the French, having at last obtained a promise of assistance from Brittany. But John of Gaunt, who had returned from Castile and was Lieutenant in Guyenne, refused to attack in the south-west, which so alarmed the Duke of Brittany that he too decided not to fight. Unaware of their defection, Arundel sailed in June 1388, but all he could do was raid the Isle of Oléron and the region round La Rochelle; he was unable to advance inland because the Bretons would not supply him with horses. Even this petty skirmishing was only done by ignoring the Council's order to return. The campaign's dismal failure, together with astronomical demands for fresh subsidies, finally antagonized the Commons, while a crushing defeat inflicted by the Scots on the Percys at Otterburn in August terrified all northern England. Gaunt and other magnates grew more disposed again to make peace.

Across the Channel Charles VI was maturing, in his own way—growing into a lover of luxury and magnificence like his grandfather John II. He was encouraged in his taste for pleasure by his beautiful, sluttish wife, Isabeau of Bavaria. In November 1388 he dismissed his uncles from his Council, much to their anger, and reinstated his father's ministers (who were popularly known as the Marmosets, their old gnarled faces being said to resemble doorknockers of that name). There were some extremely able and cool-headed men among the Marmosets and they decided on peace.

Overruling Gloucester and Arundel, the English Council began to negotiate. In May 1389 Richard II was able to assume power and govern for himself, and he too wanted peace. The King had little taste for battles; the Monk of Evesham says specifically that he was 'timid and unsuccessful in foreign war'. Richard also seems to have genuinely admired the French; as an aesthete he may well have respected the most civilized society in northern Europe. Furthermore his treasurers must have shown him the enormous cost of the War, and how much this exceeded ordinary royal revenues and made him dependent on the Lords and Commons.

On 18 June 1389 French and English envoys signed a truce at Leulinghen near Calais. Henceforward Richard did his best to keep the peace. Cherbourg was sold back to the new King of Navarre in 1393 (who promptly resold it to the French), Brest to the Bretons in 1396. Both sides tried to find a lasting settlement. King Charles and his lords wanted one so that they could go on crusade against the Turks. Even Philip of Burgundy was enthusiastic, as he was well aware of what a price his subjects set on good commercial relations with England.

But there was still an English war party. On hearing that France was ready to cede lands in Aquitaine for English territories elsewhere, Gloucester protested: 'The French want to pay us out of what is already ours. They know this: we hold charters sealed by King John and all his children, that all Aquitaine was given over to us to hold in sovereignty, so that which they have since retaken they have obtained by fraud and trickery; for they are constantly plotting both night and day to deceive us. If Calais and the other lands which they are demanding were given back to them, they would be masters of all their maritime frontiers, and all our conquests would be lost. So I shall never agree to peace for as long as I live.' Arundel likewise declared that he would never change his views.

But Richard was determined and saw Guyenne as the key. John of Gaunt had by now abandoned all hope of Castile but he still wanted a throne. One way of establishing peace between France and England would be to settle Guyenne on Gaunt and his heirs, separating the duchy from the English crown. Even Gloucester supported the idea if only to keep Gaunt abroad, after which Gloucester 'would have shifted well enough in England'—at least that was Froissart's impression. In 1390 Richard created Gaunt Duke of Guyenne for life and in 1394 gave him the succession as well. But the Guyennois had unhappy memories of the Black Prince and were also afraid that Gaunt's heirs might marry into the Valois and that the duchy would be absorbed by France. They rose in rebellion and Gaunt was unable to bring them to heel. In 1398 the English and French reluctantly settled for a truce of twenty-eight years.

Richard had gone ahead with his marriage to Charles VI's nine-year-old daughter Isabel in 1396, accepting a dowry of nearly £170,000. At the wedding near Calais, an earlier Field of Cloth of Gold, he was obviously deeply moved by his meeting with Charles, so much so that he made the disastrous mistake of promising to persuade the English Church to submit to Avignon and to try to make the Urbanist Pope at Rome abdicate. It is probable that historians have underestimated the shock and horror which this caused Richard's subjects. Some English clergy murmured, 'Our King is become French; he intendeth to do nothing but dishonour and destroy us, but he shall not!' Ordinary Londoners grumbled how Richard 'had a French heart'.

Froissart, who obviously disliked Gloucester, had to admit that he was extremely popular. The irrepressible

Duke 'whose heart was by no means inclined to the French'
continued to wage a private war. When news reached England in 1396 of the slaughter of the largely French crusade
at Nicopolis by the Turks, Gloucester was delighted, com-
menting that it served 'those rare boasting Frenchmen' right ;
he added that were he King he would attack France at once
now that she had lost so many of her best troops. Many
Englishmen shared the Duke's opinions. They had been
fighting France for over half a century ; almost every summer
ships filled with eager young soldiers had sailed from Sandwich to Calais or from Southampton to Bordeaux. War was
still the nobility's ideal profession ; the English aristocracy
saw a command in France much as their successors regarded
an embassy or a seat in the cabinet. Moreover, men of all
classes from Gloucester to the humblest bondman, regarded
service in France as a potential source of income : if the War
had cost the English monarchy ruinous sums, it had made a
great deal of money for the English people, for many of
whom peace meant more than just unemployment. In
modern terms, refusing to continue the War was as though
a government were to decide to abolish football pools and
horse-racing.

Richard II finally destroyed the leaders of the war party
in 1397. The Duke of Gloucester gave the King his opportunity during a banquet at Westminster in June. Some of
the garrison of Brest, which had just been sold to Brittany,
were present and in his cups the Duke asked his nephew
what they were going to live on, adding that they had never
been properly paid. The King answered that they were
living at his expense at four pleasant villages near London
and would certainly receive their arrears. Gloucester ex-
ploded. 'Sire, you ought first to hazard your life in capturing

The *routier* Sir Nicholas Dagworth. Captain of Flavigny in Burgundy in
1359, he led a 'free company' of mercenaries into Spain in 1367. Ironically,
he negotiated a truce with the French for Richard II in 1388. From a brass
of 1402 in the parish church at Blickling, Norfolk.

a city from your enemies before you think of giving up any city which your ancestors have conquered.' Richard was furious and the Duke realized he had gone too far. In August Gloucester, Arundel and their friends met secretly at Arundel Castle in Sussex to discuss how to seize power and imprison the King. They were soon betrayed and arrested. Arundel was beheaded while Thomas of Gloucester, despite begging for mercy 'as lowly and meekly as a man may' was smothered in a feather-bed in his prison at Calais. (Though Froissart heard that he was strangled with a towel.)

Richard had now become almost insanely tyrannical, flouting the established laws and customs of the realm. 'The King did what he would in England and none dared speak against him.' A figure even more tragic than that portrayed by Shakespeare, not only did he lose a kingdom but he lost it from wanting to possess it more completely. He finally overreached himself by exiling Henry of Bolingbroke, Gaunt's son and heir, and then when Gaunt died in 1398, making Bolingbroke's banishment lifelong and confiscating all his estates. This and other blatant injustices, such as making anyone he disliked pay a crippling sum for a pardon, outraged the English magnates. In 1399 Bolingbroke returned to England while Richard was away in Ireland and found so much support that he was able to depose the King, who, a modern biographer suggests, became 'a mumbling neurotic sinking rapidly into a state of complete melancholia'. Bolingbroke ascended the throne as Henry IV, the first of the Lancastrian dynasty. Richard died a few months later, probably of self-starvation—'some had on him pity and some none, but said he had long deserved death,' observes Froissart. Whatever his faults Richard II had been genuine in his attempts to make peace with France, and his failure meant the revival of the War.

6

Burgundy and Armagnac: England's Opportunity 1399–1413

The Duke of Burgundy . . . was sore abashed and said 'Out, harrow! What mischief is this? The King [of France] is not in his right mind, God help him. Fly away, nephew, fly away, for the King would slay you.'

Froissart

Normandy would still be French, the noble blood of France would not have been spilt nor the lords of the Kingdom taken away into exile, nor the battle lost, nor would so many good men have been killed on that frightful day at Agincourt where the King lost so many of his true and loyal friends, had it not been for the pride of this wretched name Armagnac.

The Bourgeois of Paris

Events across the Channel were also conspiring to prevent a lasting peace between France and England. The growing rivalry among the Valois Princes of the Blood was to end by plunging their country into a French Wars of the Roses, and in consequence France would be unable to defend herself against invasion. It was to provide England with her greatest opportunity.

In 1392 Charles VI had gone mad while riding through a forest, slaying four of his entourage and even trying to kill his nephew. Later he would run howling like a wolf down the corridors of the royal palaces; one of his phobias was to think himself made of glass and suspect anyone who came near of trying to shatter him. He recovered, but not for long, lucid spells alternating with increasingly lengthy bouts of madness—'far out of the way, no medicine could help him,' explains Froissart. (The cause may have been the recently diagnosed disease of porphyria, which was later to be responsible for George III's insanity.)

When the King was crazy France was ruled by Burgundy, who annually diverted one-eighth to one-sixth of the royal revenues to his own treasury. When Charles was sane his brother Louis, Duke of Orleans, held power, no less of a bloodsucker than his uncle Philip. Louis hoped to use French resources to forward his ambitions in Italy, where he had a claim to Milan through his wife Valentina, the daughter and heiress of Gian Galeazzo Visconti (and a lady 'of high mind, envious and covetous of the delights and state of this world'). He imposed savage new taxes and was also suspected of practising magic, becoming even more disliked than Burgundy. Frenchmen began to divide into two factions. Few can have realized that this was the birth of a dreadful civil war which would last for thirty years and put France at the mercy of the English. However, fighting did not break out for almost another two decades.

The French were stunned by the news of King Richard's deposition. Henry IV hastily sent commissioners to confirm the truce and Charles VI's government agreed, although the new English King owed a good deal of his home support to his repudiation of Richard's policy of peace. Having bought time, Henry refused to send little Queen Isabel home. She was only restored to her family at the end of July 1400, without her jewels or her dowry; he explained that he was keeping them because King John's ransom had not been paid in full.

In fact Henry was desperately short of money. During Richard II's reign the average annual revenue from customs duties on exported wool had been £46,000, but by 1403 it had fallen to £26,000; later it rose but only to an average of £36,000. Calais cost the exchequer £17,000 a year and Henry could not pay its garrison; eventually the troops mutinied and had to be bought off with loans from various rich merchants. Moreover the King was plagued by revolts

by great magnates and by a full-scale national rising in
Wales. Henry IV was therefore in no position to go campaigning in France, though everyone knew that he hoped to
do so one day.

Louis of Orleans believed that the time was now ripe to
conquer Guyenne. In 1402 the title of Duke of Guyenne
was bestowed on Charles VI's baby son, a gross provocation
as Henry IV had already given it to the Prince of Wales. In
1404, with the approval of the French Council, Louis of
Orleans began a systematic campaign against the duchy and
took several castles. Henry thought of going to the aid of the
Guyennois in person, but was only able to send Lord Berke-
ley with a small force. In 1405 the situation worsened, the
Constable Charles d'Albret overrunning the north-eastern
borders, the Count of Clermont attacking over the Dordogne, and the Count of Armagnac advancing from south
of the Garonne to menace Bordeaux. In 1406 the Mayor,
Sir Thomas Swynborne, prepared the ducal capital for a
siege after the enemy had reached Fronsac, Libourne and
Saint-Emilion, almost on the outskirts of Bordeaux (and to
the grave detriment of the vineyards). The Archbishop of
Bordeaux wrote desperately to Henry 'we are in peril of
being lost', and in a later letter reproached the King for
abandoning them. Somehow the Bordelais beat off the
attack, defeating the French in a river battle on the Gironde
in December 1406. The other Guyennois cities were also
loyal to the Lancastrians ; even when occupied by the French
Bergerac appealed to the English for protection. When in
1407 Orleans failed to take Blaye (the last stronghold on the
Gironde before Bordeaux), he and his troops, already disheartened by disease and unending rain, withdrew in
despair. Guyenne was left in peace to make a full recovery.

The French offensive had not been confined to Guyenne.
Privateers roamed the Channel and the Count of Saint-Pol
raided the Isle of Wight in 1404, demanding tribute in the
name of Richard II's Queen though with scant success. An
attack on Dartmouth was also unsuccessful while an attempt
to take Calais failed disastrously. In July 1404 Charles VI

concluded an alliance with Owain Glyndŵr whom he recognized as Prince of Wales ; but a French expedition of 1,000 men-at-arms and 500 crossbowmen was prevented from sailing by bad weather. The force which eventually landed at Milford Haven the following year was too small to be of much use to the Welsh ; in any case Owain's rising was already doomed. In 1407 dramatic developments in France precluded any further interference in the affairs of Wales, let alone of England.

In 1400 the French monarchy had once again appeared to be the strongest power in western Europe. It was France who mounted the Crusade of Nicopolis in 1396 to aid the Hungarians against the Turkish onslaught and, though the crusaders met with a terrible defeat, even to mount such an operation was a remarkable achievement. Furthermore France still possessed her own Pope at Avignon. She had tamed Brittany and absorbed Flanders and dominated the Low Countries. She had also acquired the overlordship of Genoa and was now engaged on an ambitious Italian policy which might well gain her Milan.

This appearance of strength was the hollowest of façades, and owed more to the splendour of the French court and of the French Princes than to reality. For the realm was divided into great *apanages* as, unlike England, French duchies and counties were territorial entities, sometimes whole provinces, which went with the title and constituted semi-independent palatinates. (The only remotely comparable parallel in England was the Duchy of Lancaster.) The greedy Valois magnates who held them were usually content to live in semi-regal splendour in their beautiful châteaux, even if the countryside around them was still ravaged by *routiers*. There were two exceptions, the Dukes of Burgundy and Orleans.

Sir John de la Pole, nephew of Richard II's Lord Chancellor and father-in-law to the Lollard heretic Sir John Oldcastle, with his wife Joan, daughter of Lord Cobham. From a brass of 1380 in the parish church at Chrishall, Essex.

Philip the Bold of Burgundy had died in April 1404, to be succeeded by his son John the Fearless—so called from gallant behaviour during the Crusade of Nicopolis. He was a taciturn little man, hard, energetic and charmless and, to judge from a famous contemporary portrait, singularly ugly, with an excessively long nose, an undershot jaw and a crooked mouth. In character, in Perroy's view, he was even more ambitious than his father and 'harsh, cynical, crafty, imperious, gloomy and a killjoy'. No one could have been more different from his refined and graceful, if scandalous cousin of Orleans.

Both Dukes were equally determined to rule France. They were opposed to each other in almost every important matter of policy. While John of Burgundy supported the Pope of Rome to please his Flemish subjects, Louis of Orleans upheld the Pope at Avignon; John opposed war with England because of the danger to Flemish trade, but Louis was hot against the English. Council meetings were wrecked by the Dukes' loud arguments and recriminations, while their followers—who constituted two political parties—brawled in the streets. When the Orleanists adopted the badge of a wooden club to signify Louis's intention of beating down opposition, John made his Burgundians sport a carpenter's plane to show that he would cut the cudgel down to size. However on 20 November 1407 Duke John and Duke Louis took Communion together, in token of reconciliation. Only three days later, on a pitch-black Wednesday night and after visiting the Queen, Louis of Orleans was ambushed as he went down the rue Vieille-du-Temple; his hand was chopped off (to stop it raising the Devil) and his brains were scattered in the road. The Duke of Burgundy wept at his cousin's funeral—'never was a more treacherous murder,' he groaned—but two days later, realizing that the assassins were about to be discovered, he blurted out to an uncle, 'I did it; the Devil tempted me.' He fled from Paris and rode hard for Flanders.

France, and especially Paris, divided into two armed camps—Burgundians and Armagnacs. The latter took their name from their leader, Bernard, Count of Armagnac, whose daughter had married Louis's son, Charles of Orleans. The Burgundians drew their strength from the Parisian bourgeoisie and academics, while the Armagnacs were what might be called the party of the establishment and included the greater royal officials, a few of the richer bourgeoisie, most of the nobles outside John's territories and the other Princes of the Blood. In 1408, having hired a theologian from the Sorbonne to justify his cousin's assassination—on the grounds that he had been a tyrant—John returned to Paris and extracted a pardon from the King. He then set up as a champion of reform, promising to reduce the high taxes imposed by Louis, and secured the execution of the Chancellor of the royal finances. By 1411, after purging the administration and by well-placed gifts, especially to the important Guild of Butchers, Burgundy had won control of Paris. The Armagnacs assembled an army and with the Duke of Berry (Charles V's last surviving brother) blockaded the capital.

John of Burgundy then had recourse to Henry IV, offering the hand of his daughter for the Prince of Wales, four towns in Flanders (including Sluys) and help in conquering Normandy, in return for troops. In October 1411, 800 English men-at-arms and 2,000 archers marched out from Calais under the Earl of Arundel. Henry had meant to lead them himself, but was prevented by chronic ill-health. The English expedition soon joined John and 3,000 Parisian militia at Meulan. The combined force stormed the Armagnac strongpoint at Saint-Cloud and broke the blockade. Arundel and his men then went home.

Led by old Berry, the Armagnacs now made their own bid for English aid. In May 1412, in return for the use of 1,000 men-at-arms and 3,000 archers for three months, they offered the eventual cession of all Aquitaine as it had been in 1369, with the immediate surrender of twenty fortresses on the Guyenne border. In August Henry's second son, the Duke of Clarence, landed in the Cotentin and marched down towards Blois. Here, however, he received news that

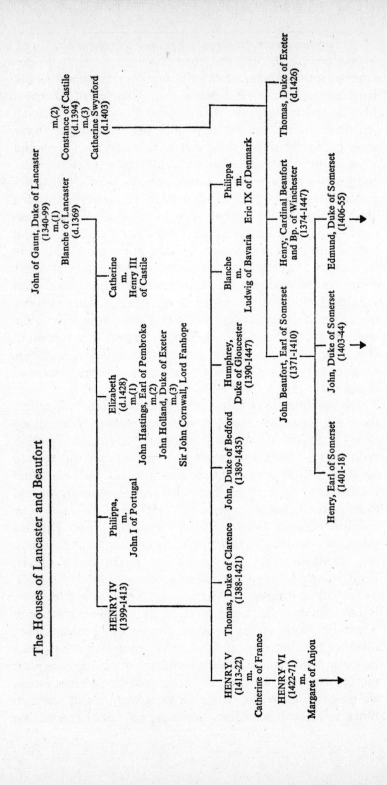

The Houses of Lancaster and Beaufort

Burgundian troops had invaded Berry's territory and forced
the Armagnacs to surrender, and that all the French Princes
including Burgundy were declining any sort of military
assistance from England. Undeterred, Thomas of Clarence
crossed the Loire and went through the wild and marshy
Sologne and down the Indre valley. The English were only
bought off by the Princes with a promise of 210,000 gold
crowns (over £34,000), 75,000 of which were to be paid
immediately, together with seven important hostages as
surety for the balance. The English leaders also extracted
individual payments. Clarence asked for 120,000 crowns
and received 40,000 and a gold crucifix worth 15,000 (with
a ruby as the wound in the side and three diamonds as the
nails in the hands and feet). His cousin the Duke of York
wanted 40,000 crowns and was given 5,000 together with a
gold cross of Damascus work valued at 40,000. Sir John
Cornwall, King Henry's brother-in-law was paid in full—
21,375 gold crowns. (It must have been this money which
paid for Sir John's new house at Ampthill in Bedfordshire;
it was built 'of such spoils as it is said that he won in France',
recorded Leland.) Nothing could have been better calculated
to excite the greed of the English aristocracy and put them
in mind of those wonderful sums extorted from the French
by their fathers and grandfathers. Clarence and his army
then went on to winter in Bordeaux, burning and slaying en
route in the good old style.

Meanwhile in northern France the Calais garrison had
taken advantage of Clarence's *chevauchée* to attack and
capture Balinghem. It provided yet another fortress in the
March of Calais to add to the ring of strongpoints which
defended the precious English bastion.

Even John of Burgundy now became nervous about the
possibility of a full-scale English invasion. He summoned
the Estates to meet in Paris to grant new taxes to pay for
defence. When the Estates began to criticize his government, John retaliated by unleashing his Paris butchers who,
led by their leader Caboche, began a reign of terror which
lasted for several weeks and was aimed as much against the

rich as the Armagnacs. So murderous were their excesses that many bourgeois turned against Duke John and invited the Dauphin and Princes to come and save them. In August 1413, after a vain attempt to kidnap Charles VI, John the Fearless of Burgundy had to abandon Paris to the Armagnacs and Count Bernard's ferocious Gascons, and went home to spend the next few years in his own semi-kingdom. Already he and the Armagnacs had ruined France. For on 20 March Henry IV had breathed his last in the Jerusalem Chamber at Westminster Abbey and there was a new King of England—Henry V.

7

Henry V and Agincourt
1413–1422

And the flesh'd soldier—rough and hard of heart—
In liberty of bloody hand, shall range
With conscience wide as hell; mowing like grass
Your fresh-fair virgins, and your flowering infants.
What is it then to me, if impious war—
Array'd in flames, like to the prince of fiends—
Do, with his smirch'd complexion, all fell feats
Enlink'd to waste and desolation?

King Henry V

Owre Kynge went forth to Normandy,
With grace and myght of chivalry;
The God for hym wrought marvelously,
Wherefore Englonde may calle, and cry
                              Deo gratias:
Deo gratias Anglia redde pro victoria.

The Agincourt Carol

In the national legend Henry V remains the most heroic of English Kings. He is the glorious conqueror who broke the French chivalry at Agincourt and won the throne of France for his son's inheritance. In reality he displayed a number of markedly unheroic qualities and, in a gentlemanly, medieval sort of way, he had more than a little in common with Napoleon and even Hitler.

Henry of Monmouth, son of Henry IV and grandson of John of Gaunt, was twenty-five years old when he ascended the throne in March 1413. Even if some of what Shakespeare says about a riotous youth seems to be justified, the young King was already experienced in statecraft; he had put down the Welsh rising with considerable bloodshed, and had acted as President of the Council during his father's illness. He was tall and muscular, wearing his armour as though it were a light cloak. Under a brown pudding-basin crop—the military haircut of the day—he had brown eyes and a long nose in a long, high-coloured face. In manner he was aloof but courteous. He had no mistresses, at least not when he was King. Indeed a Frenchman who saw Henry at Winchester in the spring of 1415 thought he looked more like a churchman than a soldier, and undoubtedly he had a churchman's tastes; he liked books and often wrote his own letters, he was a patron of sacred music, and he took a keen interest in theology and ecclesiastical affairs. Furthermore before his accession he played an active role in suppressing heresy; on one occasion he personally superintended the burning of a Lollard blacksmith in a barrel. When the man began to scream Henry had him pulled out and offered him a pension if he would recant—the man (who had denied transubstantiation) refused and was promptly put back in the flaming barrel.

Ruthless authority and cold cruelty were marked characteristics of this frugal, puritanical Plantagenet, yet he also possessed what is nowadays called charisma and could inspire genuine devotion. Shakespeare discerned grandeur and perhaps megalomania. A Victorian historian summed up Henry as 'hard, domineering, over-ambitious, bigoted, sanctimonious, priggish', but added 'take him for all in all, he was indisputably the greatest Englishman of his day'. Yet there was something else which was not English. A modern historian (E. F. Jacob) sees an Italianate quality about Henry V, something of an Este or a Gonzaga, while Perroy considers that he 'belongs to the age of the Italian tyrants'.

Henry's brutal single-mindedness hints at inner tensions. Perhaps these derived from an unwilling or unconscious recognition of how very questionable was his right to the throne; he was only descended from a third son of Edward III, while the Earls of March were descended from a second son through the female line. One Lord March had actually been proclaimed heir presumptive by

Richard II, and descent from the March heiress would one day be the basis of the claims of the House of York. Everyone in England knew that the Plantagenet title to France came through a female line. Although Henry was confident enough to release the current Earl of March from prison and to rebury King Richard in his magnificent tomb at Westminster, this element of doubt and insecurity may well have induced what was at times an almost hysterical insistence on his rights—even, most illogically of all, in France—together with a fanatical conviction that God was on his side.

In any case it was inevitable that Henry V would cross the Channel and attack the Valois. Only domestic troubles followed by ill-health had stopped his father doing so. But now the Welsh were broken and the new King was confident he could quell any trouble in England; he had little difficulty in smashing Sir John Oldcastle's pitiful Lollard conspiracy before it got under way. He discounted invasion by the Scots whose young ruler, James I, was an unwilling guest in the Tower of London. Probably Henry hoped that a renewal of the War would unite England. Above all, France continued to be in disarray, torn between the rival factions of Armagnac and Burgundy. It was an opportunity which no ambitious English King could afford to miss.

By 1413 the Armagnacs, led by the Count of Armagnac and the Constable Charles d'Albret, had won control of most of France including the capital. Duke John of Burgundy sulked in his own domains, while elsewhere his French supporters were being persecuted and murdered. A Burgundian army failed to retake Paris early in 1414, whereupon the Armagnacs announced their intention of invading Burgundy and deposing the Duke. Both sides negotiated with King Henry.

Duke John's agents arrived in England in the spring of 1414. He wanted only 2,000 English troops, promising that when he had defeated the Armagnacs Henry would be given the Gascon lands of their leaders together with the Angoumois. But in the autumn the English horrified the Duke by asking for all the territories they had received at

Brétigny, with Berry in addition, and for the recognition of Henry as King of France.

All this time Henry had also been negotiating with the Armagnacs, asking for Charles VI's daughter as his bride with a dowry of ten million crowns; his envoys argued fluently in favour of succession to the French crown through the female line. From the beginning the English King demanded more than the Brétigny settlement, stepping up his terms at each meeting. Far from offering tennis balls as Shakespeare suggests, the Armagnacs were only too willing to supply a French Princess and were even prepared to restore Aquitaine as it had been in 1369—though not its sovereignty—besides paying the remainder of King John's ransom. But Henry insisted on sovereignty and on having Normandy. The Armagnac envoys made a last try, until at Winchester in midsummer 1414 the Chancellor, Bishop Beaufort, told them that unless his master received not merely Aquitaine and Normandy but Anjou, Touraine, Poitou, Maine and Ponthieu as well he would come and take them himself at the point of the sword. The envoys went home reluctantly, no doubt infuriated by Henry's insistence that they were responsible for the ensuing war: they knew very well that he had been arming since the year before.

As with Edward III, finance was Henry V's biggest problem. It has already been seen that normal royal revenues in the preceding reign were far less than in Edward's time. Nothing testifies more to the enthusiasm of the English for the War than the readiness with which Henry's subjects lent him money. In November 1414, in response to an appeal by Bishop Beaufort, Parliament voted the King a most generous subsidy. It was still not enough, so commissioners were dispatched throughout England to borrow money, a practice which continued for the rest of the reign. Loans without interest were raised from prelates and abbeys, from nobility and gentry, from city corporations and individual burgesses; Dick Whittington, the rich London merchant, eventually contributed no less than £2,000, while some small tradesmen advanced sums as small as 10d.

Unlike Edward III's loans, most of Henry V's were repaid.

Henry's army was recruited by the indenture system, captains being commissioned to hire men-at-arms and archers in specified numbers and at a stipulated rate. The first pay-packets were usually advanced by the captain, after which he was refunded by the exchequer who then supplied money for future payments ; generally the rate was the same as in Edward's day. The bowmen's equipment remained what it had been for a century, but the armour of the men-at-arms was very different from that worn at Crécy and Poitiers. For the last fifty years plate had been replacing mail to protect the wearer against arrows. It was still surprisingly flexible as a man-at-arms fought more on foot than on horseback. But it was undeniably very heavy, weighing up to 66lbs. English noblemen often imported these elaborate armours from Milan or Nuremburg. The wearers fought with weapons which smashed rather than cut or thrust—maces, battle-hammers and pole-axes. They no longer carried shields as they needed both hands for such tools.

In all Henry raised an army of about 8,000 archers and 2,000 men-at-arms, besides some unarmoured lancers and knifemen. They were supported by a large artillery train with sixty-five gunners, which had been in preparation for the last two years. Provisions, munitions, horses and ships were assembled on the same massive scale as the previous century. The King had a flair for logistics and personally supervised the operation ; to ensure fresh meat he had cattle and sheep driven to the ports on the hoof. Ships were supplied by the Cinque Ports or else hired or impounded, and eventually a fleet of 1,500 vessels assembled in the Solent. The flagship, the *Trinité Royale*, was no less than 540 tons and was manned by a crew of 300. Henry spent many weeks on the coast at Porchester Castle, organizing the entire embarkation with meticulous attention to detail and seemingly inexhaustible energy.

During this time the Earl of March suddenly revealed a conspiracy to murder the King and replace him by the Earl himself, who was the son of Richard II's heir presumptive.

The 'three corrupted men' in this 'Southampton Plot' were Henry's first cousin, the Earl of Cambridge, with Sir Thomas Grey, and the royal Treasurer Lord Scrope of Masham; the Percys and the Lollard Sir John Oldcastle were also involved. In less than a week the three ringleaders had been beheaded. There was no further trouble.

On Sunday 11 August 1415, a bright sunny day, Henry V and his armada set sail. There was only a slight breeze so the voyage across the Channel took three days. Instead of landing at Calais as expected, the English landed in Normandy at the Chef-de-Caux on the Seine estuary, just outside the rich port of Harfleur. The King had told very few even of his closest advisers of the carefully chosen destination; Harfleur was to be the base from which he would conquer Normandy and strike down the river at Paris. It would be another Calais but with shorter supply lines more suited to campaigning in the French heartland. However, Harfleur was not easy to capture. It had dauntingly strong walls with twenty-six towers and three mighty barbicans—fortified gateways, strengthened by drawbridges and portcullises—together with a deep moat. Its garrison, commanded by the tough and able Sieur d'Estouteville, numbered several hundred men-at-arms. When Henry called on them to surrender to the rightful Duke of Normandy, he received a sarcastic answer—'You gave us nothing to look after, so we've nothing to give you back.'

The English built a ditch and a stockade all round the town, their ships guarding the estuary effectively cutting Harfleur off from any hope of reinforcements or revictualling. They began to mine the walls, but grew discouraged by the French skill at detecting their tunnels and countermining. Henry had to rely on his artillery. This included cast-iron cannon twelve feet long and over two feet in calibre, firing stone balls which weighed nearly half a ton

Sir Simon Felbrygg, KG, Richard II's banner-bearer, who served with John of Gaunt at the relief of Brest; and his wife Margaret, daughter of Przimislaus, Duke of Teschen, and sometime maid-of-honour to King Richard's queen, Anne of Bohemia. Brass of 1416 at Felbrigg, Norfolk.

and were capable of demolishing the strongest masonry—
though sometimes they splintered, producing a primitive
but viciously effective shrapnel. The trouble was to get them
into position as the Harfleur garrison had guns too, mounted
on the walls. The English built earthworks and dug trenches
and slowly edged their cannon forward on clumsy wheeled
platforms protected by thick wooden screens. They suffered
considerably, but eventually positioned their guns which
began to batter away at the walls; often the King was up all
night directing them. Sections of the walls began to collapse,
crashing to the ground with a terrifying roar. Yet after a
month the English had still failed to take what was only a
small town, and partly because of the sweltering heat of high
summer, partly because many of them had to sleep on
marshy ground and partly through drinking bad wine and
cider and contaminated water, dysentery and probably
malaria broke out. Many died, including the Earls of
Arundel, March and Suffolk and the Bishop of Norwich.
'In this siege many men died of cold in nights and fruit
eating; else of stink of carrions,' says the chronicler Capgrave. But on 17 September a barbican fell to the English.

Inside the town the bombardment had demolished
buildings and caused severe casualties, while food was
exhausted; no reply to desperate appeals for help had been
received from the Dauphin and his advisers. On 18 September the garrison asked for a truce until 6 October, when they
would surrender if they had not been relieved. Henry would
only allow them until 22 September. No help came and on
that day, a Sunday, Harfleur surrendered. After walking
barefoot to the principal church to give thanks, the King
expelled the inhabitants: 'they put out alle the French
people both man woman and chylde and stuffed the town
with English men.' The rich bourgeois were sent back to
England to be ransomed, while 2,000 of the 'poorer sort'
had to find their way to Rouen. Only a few of the very
poorest were allowed to stay and these had to take an oath
of allegiance.

Although Henry had gained a useful new base in France,

King Henry V (1387–1422)

'Unto the French the dreadful judgement day
So dreadful will not be as was his sight.'

John, Duke of Bedford,
Regent of France (1389–1435)

'Give me my steeled coat,
I'll fight for France.'

King Henry VI (1421–1471)

'Pale ashes of the House of Lancaster!
Thou bloodless remnant of that royal blood!'

he had suffered disastrous losses ; about a third of his army were dead, either killed during the siege or from disease, while many of those still on their feet were ill. Besides sending his sick home, he had to leave a garrison. On 3 September he had written in a letter to Bordeaux that he intended to go down the Seine, past Rouen and Paris and then march to Guyenne, a journey of several hundred miles. His advisers convinced him that such a raid was now out of the question but failed to persuade him to return to England. The King insisted on a *chevauchée*—he would march the 160 miles to Calais. It was an odd decision ; perhaps he meant to demonstrate the inability of the French to harm their rightful sovereign chosen by God. On 6 October his troops began to leave Harfleur, the King and the Duke of Gloucester commanding the main army, Sir John Cornwall the advance guard and the Duke of York and the Earl of Oxford the rearguard. They abandoned their artillery and baggage-train, carrying provisions for only eight days, and they took these only because they expected to march through a devastated countryside. They did not foresee any opposition. Henry's plan was simply to march north-east until the Somme was reached and then south-east down the river to the first undefended ford and, after crossing it, to make straight for Calais.

The Dauphin's forces had decided to intercept the English. An army many times larger assembled, gradually joined by such magnates as the Dukes of Orleans, Bourbon, Alençon, and Brittany, and even by John of Burgundy's younger brothers, the Duke of Brabant and the Count of Nevers. The Dauphin himself was not allowed to take part. All brought splendidly equipped men-at-arms. It seems likely that Marshal Boucicault and his advance guard had linked up with the Constable d'Albret and the main body at Rouen even before Henry had left Harfleur. It was all too easy for them to follow the English whose path was marked by blazing farmhouses—King Henry once observed that war without fire was like 'sausages without mustard'.

We know a good deal about Henry's *chevauchée* from the

narrative of a chaplain who rode with his army. As they marched through the pelting rain the English did not at first realize that they were being pursued, but at ford after ford along the Somme they found their way barred by troops. Blanche Taque, Edward III's ford, was defended by Boucicault in person. Furthermore the river was in flood. On 19 October Henry at last managed to cross, almost at the source of the Somme, by the two fords of Béthencourt and Voyennes near Peronne ; archers went over first at Béthencourt through water waist-deep, the men rebuilding the causeway which had been destroyed by the French ; while a similar operation was carried out at Voyennes. Enemy horsemen attacked but were beaten off, the crossings being completed shortly after dark. On 20 October French heralds arrived at Henry's camp, bearing a challenge. 'Our lords', they told him, 'have heard how you intend with your army to conquer the towns, castles and cities of the realm of France and to depopulate French cities. And because of this, and for the sake of their country and their oaths, many of our lords are assembled to defend their rights ; and they inform you by us that before you come to Calais they will meet you to fight with you and be revenged of your conduct.' Henry replied simply : 'Be all things according to the will of God.' Adding that whatever happened he would march to Calais, he sent them away with a hundred gold crowns each. Accepting that he had been outmanœuvred, the King at once ordered his men to take up positions—obviously he expected to be attacked at any moment. But there was still no sign of the French army.

Next morning the English trudged on through a torrential downpour which was blown into their eyes by a driving wind. For several days they continued their march without serious incident, covering as much as eighteen miles a day, all of it beneath the unrelenting rain. On 24 October the Duke of York's scouts saw through the drizzle the French army advancing on their right like 'an innumerable host of locusts', in a direction which meant that they would soon intercept the English line of advance. Henry took up battle positions along a ridge, and the French, who had now sighted their quarry, also took up positions. The enemy appeared to have learnt a good deal since Crécy and would not attack such a strong position so late in the day. Nonetheless, they continued to advance so that by nightfall they had effectively blocked the English road to Calais.

All hope of retreat had gone. The English plodded on up the muddy road to the little village of Maisoncelles. The King himself slept near the village of Blangy, no doubt under cover. His men had to sleep in the open beneath the drenching rain, the luckier finding some wretched shelter beneath trees or bushes. There were now less than 6,000 of them—about 5,000 archers and perhaps 800 men-at-arms. Many were still suffering from dysentery while even the strongest had been weakened not only by their miserable march through the wet but by lack of nourishment, being reduced to a little cold food supplemented by nuts and raw vegetables taken from the fields. They seem to have had few fires that night. The archers must have been especially tired as unlike the men-at-arms many of them had no horses and had to carry their weapons, which included quivers holding fifty arrows and wooden stakes for defence. All were terrified by the enormous size of the force facing them. Even Henry was shaken and released his prisoners, sending a message to the enemy commanders in which he offered to return Harfleur and pay for any damage he had done if he were allowed safe passage to Calais ; but the French terms were too steep —renunciation of his claims in France to everything save Guyenne.

The King ordered his troops to be silent during the night, threatening knights with the confiscation of horse and armour, lower ranks with the amputation of an ear. Understandably an eerie quiet prevailed throughout the English camp, interrupted only by armourers hammering and sharpening, and by the whispers of men being shriven by their chaplains. The French took it for a good sign, believing that the English thought themselves already beaten. Many of the latter must surely have felt like this, hearing all the

confident noise and bustle from the enemy camp where there were between 40,000 and 50,000 men-at-arms. Meanwhile Henry sent out scouts to examine the ground.

By dawn both armies were preparing for battle. The rain had at last stopped, but the ploughed land underfoot was nothing but slippery mud—in some places knee-deep. The King drew up his bedraggled troops in a field of newly sown wheat (in a formation similar to that used by Edward III at Crécy). He himself commanded the centre, the Duke of York the right, and Lord Camoys KG the left; there were three 'battles' of dismounted men-at-arms, the gaps between the battles being filled by projecting wedges of archers; while the main body of bowmen formed horns on the wings, standing slightly forward so they could shoot inwards if the French attacked the centre. There was no reserve, but at least the English flanks were protected by woods.

The French position, directly north of the English, also lay between these two small woods, one of which was close to the little village of Tramecourt, the other to that of Agincourt. It was a badly chosen position; not only was it too narrow but the ploughed fields in front had been churned up by horses' hooves. The actual formation consisted of two long lines of dismounted men-at-arms carrying sawn-off lances, while behind them and on the wings were the remaining men-at-arms who were still on horseback. The artillery was on the wings too, but was hampered by the confusion among the men-at-arms who found their heavy armour a terrible hindrance on the sodden ground. Marshal Boucicault and the Constable d'Albret were nominally in command, though in practice there was no proper command-structure or leadership of any sort. However, for the moment the French had the sense to wait for the English to attack.

King Henry heard three Masses and took communion before addressing his men. He told them 'he was come into France to recover his lawful inheritance', and that the

Sir Hugh Halsham, who fought at Agincourt in Lord Arundel's retinue; and his wife, Joyce Culpeper. Brass of 1441 at West Grinstead, Sussex.

French had promised to cut three fingers off every English archer's right hand so 'they might never presume again to shoot at man or horse'. Although he rode only a little grey pony he must have been an impressive figure, in his gold-plated helmet with its golden crown of pearls, rubies and sapphires. His army shouted to him, 'Sir, we pray God give you a good life and the victory over your enemies.' Undoubtedly they admired him and believed in his genius, and were confident that he would rescue them from this terrifying situation.

The King must have prayed for the French to attack so that he could use his bowmen. But for several hours the French stayed calmly in their positions. At about nine o'clock Henry therefore told Sir Thomas Erpingham, 'a grey-headed old knight', to take the archers on the wings forward within range of the enemy. When this had been done the King gave the order for the rest of his little army to move forward—'Banners advance! In the name of Jesus, Mary and St George!' After making the sign of the Cross and kissing the earth, the English marched forward solidly over the dirty ground in good order. Most of the bowmen 'had no armour but were only wearing doublets, their hose rolled up to their knees, with hatchets and axes or in some cases large swords hanging from their belts; some of them went barefoot and had nothing on their heads, while others wore caps of boiled leather'. They halted at a little less than 300 yards from the enemy and, after sticking their pointed stakes in the ground in front of them, began to shoot. The French put their heads down, the English arrows falling so thick and fast that no one dared look up. In desperation the mounted French men-at-arms on the wings charged the archers. As always the horses suffered most from the arrows, becoming unmanageable or bolting, while those that did reach the English lines were impaled on the six-foot stakes which were set a horse's breast high.

The first line of the enemy's dismounted men-at-arms then formed themselves into a column, hoping fewer would be hit by arrows, and toiled slowly forward towards the

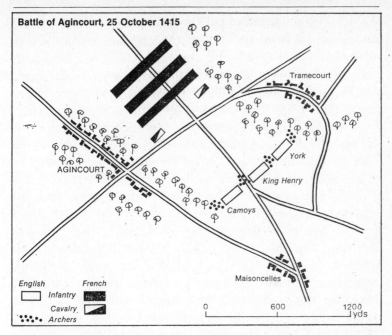

Battle of Agincourt, 25 October 1415

Tramecourt

York

King Henry

AGINCOURT

Camoys

Maisoncelles

English   French
Infantry
Cavalry
Archers

0   600   1200
                       yds

English through the thick mud which had been churned up still further by the horses. The English on the wings shot steadily into the sides of the column, inflicting many casualties, their arrows making a terrifying hiss and clatter. When the French at last reached the English lines they were in no coherent formation and too tightly packed, while the deep mud had slowed them almost to a halt. This combination of disorder and immobility would cost them the battle.

Nevertheless at the first impact the French threw back the front line of English men-at-arms at Henry's centre, almost knocking them off their feet. The King quickly ordered his archers to drop their bows and go to the men-at-arms' assistance, whereupon seizing 'swords, hatchets, mallets, axes, falcon-beaks and other weapons' they hurled themselves on the enemy. The liquid mud of the battlefield gave the advantage to the bowmen who were able to dance round the ponderous Frenchmen, whom they stabbed through the joints of their armour or bowled over. Some of the latter lay writhing on their backs like capsized crabs until their visors were knocked open and daggers thrust into their faces ; most drowned in the mud or died of suffocation, pressed down by the bodies of their comrades on top of them.

The enemy's second line of men-at-arms, also in column, came on in equal disorder to meet with the same reception from the English, who were now standing on piles of French corpses. Their leader, the Duke of Alençon, fought like a lion, striking down the Duke of Gloucester and beating the King to his knees—he actually hacked a *fleuret* from his crown—but was eventually overwhelmed. He surrendered to Henry, taking off his helmet, but was at once cut down with an axe by a berserk English knight. The Duke of Brabant, who had arrived late without his surcoat and donned a herald's tabard instead, was disarmed ; not being recognized, he had his throat cut. After only half an hour both the first and the second French columns had been annihilated ; in some places the heaped bodies were higher than a man's head. The English turned them over, searching for loot and any valuable prisoners still alive, who were sent to the rear. Henry and his commanders soon made the men return to their positions. There was still a threat from the remaining French troops.

While the King was waiting for a third enemy assault, a cry went up that the French had received reinforcements. At the same moment he learnt that hundreds of peasants were attacking his baggage. Henry immediately ordered the execution of all prisoners save the most distinguished. The men guarding them were most reluctant to lose so many valuable ransoms, so the King detailed 200 archers to do the job, the Frenchmen being (in the words of a Tudor historian) 'sticked with daggers, brained with poleaxes, slain with mauls'—to make quite sure, they were also 'paunched in fell and cruel wise'. One group was burnt to death by setting fire to the hut where they were confined. English writers attempt to whitewash this piece of *Schrechlichkeit* by Henry, usually with reference to 'the standards of the day', but in fact by medieval criteria it was a particularly nasty atrocity to murder unarmed noblemen who had surrendered in the confident expectation of being ransomed.

In fact the third enemy assault never materialized. Although they still outnumbered the English, the remaining French men-at-arms were so horrified by the butchery in front of them that they refused to attack and rode off the battlefield. In less than four hours the English, against all expectation, had defeated an army many times larger. The French had lost about 10,000 men, among them such great lords as the Dukes of Alençon, Bar and Brabant, the Constable d'Albret (though his fellow commander Marshal Boucicault survived as a prisoner), the Count of Nevers with six other counts, 120 barons and 1,500 knights. The English had lost perhaps 300 men, the only persons of note among them being Henry's cousin, the fat Duke of York— he had fallen over and been suffocated by bodies falling on top of him—and the Earl of Suffolk together with half a dozen knights. Many were badly wounded however, notably Henry's brother the Duke of Gloucester—'in the hammes'.

The chivalry of the Black Prince was not for King Henry. That night his high-ranking prisoners had to wait on him at table. The troops took another hopeful look at the French casualties still lying all over the field; anyone who was rich and could walk was rounded up, but the poor and the badly wounded had their throats slit. Next day, laden with plunder from the corpses, the English recommenced their march to Calais, dragging 1,500 prisoners along with them. The rain began again. Wetter and hungrier than ever, the little army reached Calais on 29 October. Here, although the King was fêted rapturously, his men were hardly treated as conquering heroes. Some were even refused entry, while the Calais people charged them such exorbitant prices for food and drink that they were soon cheated out of their loot and rich captives. (Henry kept the great prisoners for himself—he wanted every penny of their ransoms.)

The troops were too exhausted for any further campaigning, so in mid-November the King sailed for England. On

23 November he entered London to receive an ecstatic welcome. There were pageants and tableaux, orations, dancing in the streets and carols—including the famous Agincourt Carol—while the drinking fountains ran with wine. The euphoria was such that Henry was to have little trouble in raising fresh loans for more campaigns during the next few years. Meanwhile he gave thanks at St Paul's.

In reality, as Perroy emphasizes, the Agincourt campaign decided nothing—it was just another *chevauchée*. Nevertheless it is hardly surprising that Henry was determined to follow it up. He made the most of Harfleur, the sole tangible gain, every inducement including free housing being offered to merchants and artisans in the hope that they would settle there and make it a Norman Calais.

In 1416 the Holy Roman Emperor Sigismund arrived in England to stay at Westminster, his object being to make peace between England and France in the interests of church unity. His real business was to heal the Papal schism, which ended with the election of Pope Martin V in 1417. However, he concluded a treaty of mutual help and alliance with Henry. This so impressed Duke John of Burgundy that he decided to ally with the English himself, and in October of that year he travelled to Calais to meet Henry. The Duke promised to become the Englishman's vassal, acknowledging him as King of France and promising to help him depose Charles VI.

Henry V did not restrict himself to diplomacy. He began to build up a formidable navy and by the end of 1417 there were thirty-four King's Ships, compared with six in 1413. Some were surprisingly big, such as the *Holy Ghost* of 740 tons. In 1430 a Florentine sea-captain saw Henry's great cog, the *Grace Dieu*, at Southampton. He reported: '... truly I have never seen so large and splendid a construction. I had the mast measured on the first deck and it was about 21 feet in circumference and 195½ feet high. From the galley of the prow to the water was about 50 feet and they say that when she is at sea another corridor is raised above this. She was

about 176½ feet long and about 96 feet in the beam.' The
fleet included seven captured Genoese carracks and about
fifteen ballingers—oared sailing-barges—as well as the cogs.
Henry also ordered another large ship to be built at Bayonne.
He engaged a rich merchant, William Soper, to help him
construct a naval base at Southampton, like the French
Clos des Galées at Rouen, with a dock and a storehouse. At
Hamble nearby there were other storehouses and wooden
fortifications behind which the ships could shelter. The
Keeper of the King's Ships was responsible for building
and refitting, and also for supplying equipment and paying
crews, and even for providing vessels for patrols and
transport.

The benefits of Henry's maritime policy were quickly
apparent. When the French blockaded Harfleur in the
summer of 1416, the Duke of Bedford inflicted a crushing
defeat on the Franco-Genoese fleet, capturing several enemy
vessels and relieving the beleaguered port. The following
year, off the Chef-de-Caux, the Earl of Huntingdon destroyed what remained of the French navy, taking four
carracks and the enemy commander, the Bastard of Bourbon.
Henceforward English patrols sailed the Channel un-
challenged, giving Henry the command of the sea-routes
necessary for his campaigns.

By 1417 the King had obtained fresh subsidies from
Parliament besides borrowing money, and was ready to
renew the struggle. Among many preparations for war was
a quaint but eminently practical instruction to the sheriffs
in February 1417, which ordered them to have six wing-
feathers plucked from every goose and sent to London for
the fletchers to flight arrows. The expedition, which sailed
in July, was about the same size as that of 1415, 10,000
soldiers carried in something like 1,500 ships. However, this
time Henry had a different objective—he intended to conquer and subdue France, region by region, with a war of
slow, thorough sieges, and he would begin with Normandy.
As before he concealed both his aims and his destination.
Instead of disembarking at Calais or Harfleur, on 1 August

the English landed at the mouth of the river Touques, between the modern resorts of Deauville and Trouville.

There was no one to oppose him. The civil war was raging as fiercely as ever and the new Constable, the Count of Armagnac, dared not leave Paris because of a Burgundian army waiting outside. If the English could conquer lower Normandy they would not only acquire a useful supply-base, rich in provisions and forage, but they would cut the Normans off from any hope of relief from Anjou or Brittany, and be able to besiege Rouen, the ducal capital, at their leisure. By 18 August Henry had invested Caen (which had probably not forgotten the sack by his great-grandfather over seventy years before). The city was protected on three sides by the river Orne and two tributaries, and it had strong new walls and a great citadel. The English stormed two abbeys in the suburbs and mounted artillery on their tall towers. The English guns pounded the fortifications with stone shot and with hollow iron balls filled with flaming tow—an early species of shell. Henry's cannon were surprisingly effective, if erratic; their chief weakness seems to have been unreliable powder.

Soon the walls were breached in several places and the King called on the French to give up or to expect no quarter. They refused to surrender, so on 4 September Henry led an assault on the east side. At the same time his brother Clarence attacked from the west over the river. One of the King's knights, young Sir Edmund Springhouse, fell off the wall into the ditch whereupon the French threw flaming straw on top of him and burnt him alive, an atrocity which enraged the English. Clarence and the Earl of Warwick won the day, storming in over the river wall and cutting their way through to Henry's side. The victors herded the inhabitants—men, women and children—into the market-place where they proceeded to butcher them, killing at least 2,000. The city was then sacked, those who had escaped the massacre in the market-place suffering all the horrors of plunder and rape. A fortnight later the garrison in the citadel surrendered. Henry had by then done much to restore order and had given instructions for the ruined buildings to be rebuilt. He established himself in the citadel which became a favourite residence and where, characteristically, he installed a well furnished chapel. He also gave a number of the city's best houses to his troops.

The chronicler Basin tells us of the terror inspired by Henry and the English among the Normans, which explains something of the King's success; the entire population of Lisieux fled, leaving only two old cripples behind. Bayeux quickly surrendered to the Duke of Gloucester, with almost no resistance. In October Henry captured Argentan and Alençon. The reputedly impregnable fortress of Falaise took a little longer, but finally surrendered to its besiegers in February 1418. By the spring all lower Normandy and the Cotentin, from Evreux up to Cherbourg, had been overrun. The conquered territory was given four new *baillis*—Sir Roland Lenthall at Alençon, Sir John Popham at Caen, Sir John Radcliffe at Evreux and Sir John Assheton in the Cotentin. These English *gauleiters* were assisted by mainly Norman *vicomtes* and at once began to force the local population to accept Henry's rule; on payment of 10d any Norman who took the oath of loyalty was given a certificate of allegiance. Caen became the centre of this new administration, which was provided with an English chancellor and an English president of the *chambre des comptes*, and where a mint issued coins in Henry's name. Many Norman *seigneurs* abandoned their castles and manors, fleeing rather than recognize Henry as their Duke and King. The clergy were less squeamish and provided a useful supply of bureaucrats.

Meanwhile Henry, after spending a pious Lent at Bayeux, made ready to conquer the rest of Normandy. In June he took Louviers; its cannon had scored a direct hit on the royal tent during the siege so he hanged eight enemy gunners—one source says that he crucified some of them. He then besieged Pont de l'Arche, which fell on 20 July after the English had crossed the river on portable boats of skin and wickerwork. Its famous bridge straddled the Seine between Paris and Rouen which was seven miles downstream, and its capture meant that the Norman capital was cut off from receiving reinforcements or supplies from Paris. As the English already controlled the mouth of the Seine, Rouen had been effectively isolated, and on 29 July, at night, Henry pitched camp outside it.

Rouen was one of the wealthiest and most beautiful cities in France, rich from weaving and from sending its luxury goods and goldsmiths' work up-river to the capital. It contained a noble cathedral, three famous abbeys, over thirty convents and nearly forty parish churches. The King was not exaggerating when he wrote to his subjects in London that Rouen was 'the most notable place in France save Paris'. Its walls extended for five miles, strengthened by six mighty barbicans and sixty towers; one side was defended by the Seine, the three others by an unusually deep and wide ditch filled with wolf-traps. In addition, an enormous bank of earth had been built on the inside of the walls to help them resist bombardment; the ditch had been deepened and the suburbs demolished, while large stocks of food had been brought in from the countryside. There was a garrison of 4,000 men-at-arms under the redoubtable Guy le Bouteiller, while the belligerent citizens—who seem to have been armed chiefly with crossbows—were led by a brave *bailli*, Guillaume Houdetot. There was an abundance of artillery— three cannon in every tower, each stretch of wall between them mounting another cannon supported by eight small guns. The city felt so confident that it had given refuge to many refugees from lower Normandy, admitting thousands of useless mouths. Indeed there were many more besieged than there were besiegers.

However, Henry V was equally confident. He built four fortified camps, one on each side of the city and linked by trenches, and blocked the river upstream with a great chain. Downstream he made a bridge of boats which had been hauled overland. His army was soon reinforced by 3,000 troops under Gloucester and by 1,500 Irish kern—knife and javelin men led by Fra' Thomas Butler, Prior of the

Knights of St John in Ireland.* The scorched-earth tactics of the French made supplies scarce, but Henry overcame the problem by bringing food across the Channel and up the Seine; one consignment from London included thirty barrels of sweet wine and a thousand pipes of ale.

Henry set up his headquarters in the local charterhouse, far enough outside the walls to have escaped demolition. Here he waited while he starved the enemy into submission. He had gibbets constructed in view of the walls on which he hanged prisoners; the French retaliated by building a gibbet of their own on the battlements and stringing up an English captive. From the walls the Vicar-General of Rouen, Robert de Linet excommunicated King Henry. (Henry was so infuriated that when he took Rouen he put Linet in chains where he stayed for the rest of his life.) The beleaguered city counted on help from Burgundians or Armagnacs, and in November a rumour reached Rouen that an army was on its way. The rumour proved false: the Burgundians had now reoccupied Paris, after a popular revolt had driven out the Armagnacs and lynched the Constable, and they were too intent on holding it to worry about what was happening in Normandy.

By mid-October Rouen was eating horseflesh. Towards Christmas it was reduced to cats, dogs, rats and even mice. 'And then they took to eating rotten food and any vegetable peelings they could find—they even ate dock roots,' says

* The Prior and many of his men were killed. The kern had made a strong impression by their outlandish dress and their ferocity, riding back from raids with severed heads and even babies dangling from their bareback ponies. There were other Irishmen who, led by the Butler family, made a small but effective contribution to the Lancastrian war effort in France. The fourth Earl of Ormonde—Fra' Thomas was his bastard son—had been on Clarence's *chevauchée* in 1412 and also took part in the siege of Rouen. Two more of his sons, Sir John and Sir James Butler (later the fifth Earl) were to be noted captains under Bedford and Old Talbot in the 1430s and 1440s. Besides a long-haired, moustachioed, saffron-cloaked, barefooted 'tail' of javelin men and axe- and claymore-wielding gallowglasses, these Anglo-Irish chieftains would have brought more conventionally armed *daoine uaisle* (gentlemen) recruited from their relations.

John Page, an English soldier who was present. 'And now the people in the city began to die. Every day many died and could find no burial.' The defenders took ruthless action—'All the poor folk of that city were expelled from every gate, many hundreds at a time.' No less than 12,000 were driven forth, including old men and nursing mothers. Henry refused to let them pass, so they had to stay in the ditch in the depths of winter and starve. It rained unceasingly. Even the English troops felt sorry for them. 'Our soldiers gave them some of their own bread although they had fought us so bitterly.' On Christmas Day the King made one of his few magnanimous gestures and sent food and drink into the ditch by two priests, who were the only men that the defenders would admit. But the day's truce was soon over and those in the ditch began to die miserably. 'There' relates John Page, 'one might see wandering here and there children of two or three years old begging for bread as their parents were dead. These wretched people had only sodden soil under them and they lay there crying for food—some starving to death, some unable to open their eyes and no longer breathing, others cowering on their knees as thin as twigs. A woman was there clutching her dead child to her breast to warm it, and a child was sucking the breast of its dead mother. There one could easily count ten or twelve dead to one alive, who had died so quietly without call or cry as though they had died in their sleep.' It was scarcely better inside the city.

On New Year's Eve 1419 a French knight shouted from a gate that the defenders wished to parley. Their envoys visited Henry at his headquarters on 2 January; after making them wait while he finished hearing Mass, he berated them for keeping him out of his own city, 'which is my rightful heritage'. He also refused to let the poor people leave the ditch—his comment was, 'Who put them there?' ('I put them not there and that wot ye.') The envoys 'treated day, they treated night, with candle and torches bright', the negotiations dragging on for ten days, Henry insisting all the time that 'Rouen is my heritage'. Eventually terms were agreed; if no relief had arrived by 19 January the city would surrender at noon on that day and pay an indemnity of 300,000 gold crowns. However, the garrison would be allowed to march off, though without their arms and on condition of not fighting against the English for a year, and so long as they took an oath of allegiance the citizens might keep their houses and goods. No relief came. The day after the surrender Henry rode in with dramatic modesty, dressed in black and accompanied by a single squire bearing a lance with a fox's brush on its tip—a favourite badge of the King. Most of the citizens who watched him were skin and bone with sunken eyes and pinched noses, and could scarcely talk or even breathe— their skin was as dull as lead. 'They looked like those effigies of dead kings that one sees on tombs.' Henry gave thanks at the cathedral with his usual ostentatious piety.

After two months at Rouen, repairing its defences and organizing the new administration, Henry was ready for a further campaign. In the meantime his captains had captured other Norman towns—Mantes, Honfleur, Dieppe, Ivry, La Roche Guyon, Fécamp. Only the impregnable abbey of Mont-Saint-Michel held out on the coast. By the end of the year the English were undisputed masters of all Normandy, including the Vexin. Furthermore, in July Henry seized Pontoise and was now within striking distance of Paris.

The English occupation of Normandy had a certain resemblance to the Norman conquest of England. Although a few became faithful servants of the Plantagenets, the native nobility were largely dispossessed, their estates being given to Englishmen. In 1418–1419 alone, six Norman counties were re-allotted. Henry's brother, heir and right-hand man, the Duke of Clarence, received three viscounties (territorial units, not just titles). The Duke of Exeter, the King's uncle, had the great county of Harcourt, with all that family's princely possessions, and the important castle of Lillebonne. The Earl of Salisbury became Count of Perche. Grants were according to rank, and these new nobles of

Normandy had to perform specified military duties in proportion to the value of the fief, such as garrisoning towns, providing troops or maintaining their châteaux as fortresses and depots. Many captains obtained castles and manors on similar conditions, though the King threatened these lesser men with death if ever they left Normandy. In addition there was a limited attempt at colonization; 10,000 English were established at Harfleur and there were smaller settlements at Caen and Honfleur, while houses were confiscated and given to Englishmen in most Norman towns. Many of these settlers married Norman girls. However, full-scale colonization was beyond the resources of so thinly populated a country as fifteenth-century England.

The new English lords benefited from more than the mere revenues of their estates. There were the salaries and profits of office, the exploitation of taxes, indemnities and money for safe conducts, together with the usual protection racket of the *pâtis*. And there were ransoms and plunder from campaigning elsewhere in France. The latter benefited every English soldier not just the magnates; the contemporary chronicler Adam of Usk tells us that after Henry's victories loot from France was on sale all over England.

The Duchy of Normandy was governed through its traditional institutions. However, the eight *baillis* were all Englishmen, though their officials were mostly Normans. The great offices of Chancellor, Treasurer-General, Seneschal and Admiral were likewise held by Englishmen. Assisted by a surprisingly loyal native bureaucracy, they were to milk Normandy dry by cruel taxation and forced loans, and by manipulating the currency (undervaluing it, calling it in and then re-coining and re-issuing it), to make the duchy pay for as much of the English war effort as possible. There was a resistance, guerrilla bands in woods and caves led by dispossessed *seigneurs* and recruited from peasants who found the *pâtis* intolerable; the English called them 'brigands' and hanged them when they caught them. Yet the duchy was held by astonishingly few troops. It is known that in 1421 Henry's garrisons amounted to about

4,500 men, later reduced to as little as 1,500, while the new English *seigneurs* maintained perhaps 2,500 further troops at scattered strongholds. These soldiers were commanded by an all powerful Lord-Lieutenant and paid by the proceeds of the *pâtis*. Despite the harshness of its régime English Normandy was to endure for thirty years, and an entire generation of Normans knew no other rule.

King Henry had a special affection for this new Guyenne, possibly because he saw himself as the heir of William the Conqueror. He was constantly referring to 'our Duchy of Normandy' with obvious pride. He tried to make himself popular with his new subjects, being careful not to over-Anglicize the administration, and he encouraged trade and commerce by issuing licences and letters of protection. He also attempted to stop his troops looting.

The possession of Normandy gave strategic advantages. Not only was it a springboard from which to control the food route of the lower Seine and throttle Paris, but occupation of its coast secured communications with Bordeaux while the Channel became a second instead of a front line of defence so that the southern English counties were safe from any threat of invasion. At the same time the loss of both the French royal docks at Rouen and the Norman ports meant the end of any French navy. Squadrons from Henry's own new fleet patrolled the Channel constantly, exploiting the situation and seizing French merchant ships.

But Henry V saw the acquisition of the duchy as only a step towards conquering his entire 'heritage'. France was ill prepared to meet such a threat, with her nobility hopelessly split between Burgundians and Armagnacs. Poor King Charles was crazier than ever. Two Dauphins had died prematurely while a third, the future Charles VII who had been born in 1399, was an unpromising youth, mentally immature and physically unprepossessing.

Horrified by the English advance, Duke John of Burgundy tried to negotiate with the Armagnacs who had the Dauphin under their thumb. Although the Burgundians had captured Paris in 1418 after an uprising in which their supporters had killed thousands of Armagnacs, a preliminary meeting at Corbeille in the summer of 1419 between Duke John and the Dauphin and his Armagnac advisers seemed to establish a measure of agreement.

In fact the Armagnacs were plotting revenge. At a second meeting on 10 September, on the bridge over the Yonne at Montereau, they hacked the Duke of Burgundy to death as he knelt in homage; it seems that the Dauphin may have given the signal for the first blow. A century later a Carthusian monk, who was showing François I the mausoleum of the Dukes at Dijon, picked up John's broken skull and commented, 'This is the hole through which the English entered France.' At the news of his father's murder, John's son and heir is said to have thrown himself on his bed, rolling his eyes and grinding his teeth with rage and grief. The breach between Burgundians and Armagnacs had now become irreparable.

The Armagnacs, who had already lost the capital, were weakened still further by widespread revulsion at the murder. Many people blamed them for all France's misfortunes. The Bourgeois of Paris wrote, 'Normandy would still be French, the noble blood of France would not have been spilt nor the lords of the Kingdom taken away into exile, nor the battle lost, nor would so many good men have been killed on that frightful day at Agincourt where the King lost so many of his true and loyal friends, had it not been for the pride of this wretched name Armagnac.' The Dauphin, who was regarded as the puppet of the Armagnacs, shared in their opprobrium. As the monk said at Dijon, this fatal division among the French was the thing which made it possible for Henry V to conquer and to hold so much of France.

Yet the accident of a simultaneous civil war between Burgundians and Armagnacs has obscured the fact that by now the Hundred Years War had become for all Englishmen and for many Frenchmen an essentially national struggle. Significantly the English ruling class had ceased to speak French as a matter of course—even the King's

first language was now English. Undoubtedly the antagon-
ism between fifteenth-century Englishmen and Frenchmen
reflected a genuinely national xenophobia. By Joan of Arc's
day at least, the French were already using the term *Godon*—
'God-damn'—to describe an Englishman. In about 1419 an
anonymous moralist writing a dialogue between 'France' and
'Truth' gives a vivid picture of how some Frenchmen felt
about the English invaders. 'The war they have waged and
still wage is false, treacherous and damnable, but then they
are an accursed race, opposed to all good and all reason,
ravening wolves, proud, arrogant hypocrites, tricksters without any conscience, tyrants and persecutors of Christians,
men who drink and gorge on human blood, with natures like
birds of prey, people who live only by plunder.' Unfortunately for France, the Burgundians and Armagnacs hated
each other more than they hated the English.

The new Duke of Burgundy, Philip the Good, was twenty-
five—fully mature by medieval standards. Although a man
of Flanders from upbringing and sympathies, luxurious and
preferring display and the joust to statecraft or campaigning,
he was no less determined to rule France than his father had
been. His solution was to partition northern France between
Burgundy and England. At first he may have believed that
the English would leave him to rule it all—if so he was
mistaken—but even with an English occupation he would
benefit substantially; he could continue to rule large areas
of France at little expense, and he might well acquire more
power by being necessary to a Lancastrian than by domina-
ting a Valois. In December 1419 he allied formally with
Henry and promised to help him conquer France.

The English and Burgundians now began to negotiate
with King Charles—or rather with Queen Isabeau—whose
shabby court was at Troyes in Champagne, where in 1417
with Burgundian support the Queen had set up a rival
government to that of the Dauphin. Henry, his brother
Clarence, and only 1,500 men marched to Troyes from
Pontoise by a circular route, praying at Saint-Denis and
parading past the walls of Paris. In Champagne he issued a

characteristic order to his troops—the local wine must be diluted with water. He reached Troyes on 20 May 1420 and a treaty which had already been drafted was concluded next day. Poor Charles VI, 'in his malady', did not seem to know who Henry was when he met him but performed obediently. By the terms of the treaty the English King became *Haeres et Regens Franciae*—Heir to the French Throne and Regent of France—Isabeau cheerfully claiming that the Dauphin was a bastard by one of her lovers. Henry was to marry Charles's daughter Catherine, the wedding taking place at Troyes within twelve days. (According to the chronicler Enguerrand de Monstrelet, the couple were enthusiastic: 'It was plainly to be seen that King Henry was desperately in love with her', while the black-haired Princess of France 'had longed passionately to be espoused to King Henry'; even so the honeymoon was spent besieging Sens.) In return Henry was to conquer all territories currently occupied by the 'pretended Dauphin' and the Armagnacs. When he became the French King he was to incorporate his Duchy of Normandy into the Kingdom of France, though while Charles VI lived Henry was to keep Normandy and receive the 'homage' of Brittany. Overjoyed, he sent the news of his 'good conclusion' to England, where there was a procession at St Paul's in thanksgiving. It was a grim irony that he would not live to wear the French crown. The Treaty of Troyes was one of the greatest humiliations in French history, comparable to that of 1940, yet as Perroy points out: 'North of the Loire no voice was raised against the treaty.'

Henry and Philip of Burgundy at once continued with the conquest of northern France, to the delight of those dispossessed by the Armagnacs. The allies besieged Montereau where Philip's father had been murdered, Henry hanging some prisoners before the walls to encourage the garrison to surrender. The town fell and Duke John's body was exhumed and taken to Dijon. The campaign's principal aim was to reduce any centres of enemy resistance between Normandy and Paris. An especially important obstacle was

Melun to which Henry and an Anglo-Burgundian army of 20,000 men laid siege in July. Although the town was garrisoned by only 700 troops, the courageous Gascon commander, Arnaud Guillaume de Barbazan, was determined to make good use of its excellent defensive position; it straddled the Seine, with its centre and citadel on an island, each of the town's three sections forming a separate walled stronghold linked to its neighbour by a bridge. The English tried mining, often knee-deep in water, but the French counter-mined and there were murderous struggles by torchlight in the tunnels, in which Henry himself took part, actually crossing swords on one occasion with Barbazan.

The English heavy guns—including one which was called *London*, a gift from loyal citizens—had no more decisive effect than the mines; the defenders swiftly plugged the breaches with barrels of earth. Dysentery broke out among the besiegers, who suffered many casualties. Henry sent a message to Barbazan to obey Charles VI, whom he had brought to the camp, but the fiery Gascon retorted that while he might be loyal to his sovereign he would never recognize any English King. Provisions failed at last, and on 18 November Melun was forced to surrender after a siege of eighteen weeks. Henry wanted to hang Barbazan, but the Gascon escaped by appealing to the laws of chivalry; he could not be executed because, having fought the King hand-to-hand, he was a brother-in-arms. Henry contented himself with putting Barbazan in an iron cage. However, Henry did succeed in hanging a score of Scottish soldiers on the thin pretext that they were traitors to their King who was his captive and theoretical ally. The Bourgeois of Paris tells us that while the English army was at Melun it devastated the country round about for more than twenty leagues.

On 1 September 1420 Henry V, Philip of Burgundy and Charles VI made a ceremonial entry into Paris to begin an English occupation which would last for fifteen years. The Parisians cheered Charles's 'true son' and priests chanted *Te Deums* in the streets, while the States-General ratified the Treaty of Troyes and the *Parlement* declared the Dauphin

incapable of succeeding to the throne because of his 'horrible
and dreadful crimes'. Monstrelet relates how Henry lodged
at the Louvre for Christmas with great splendour, in contrast
to Charles's dismal court at the Hôtel de Saint-Pol where
the mad and now dirty and unkempt old King was 'poorly
and meanly served', deserted by all save a few broken-down
servants and some hangers-on of low degree. His courtiers
were all at the Louvre. It was a hard winter and since food
was scarce and expensive—the price of bread had doubled—
the ordinary Parisians suffered accordingly. The city
rubbish-tips were filled with the bodies of children who had
died looking for something to eat among the refuse. The
Bourgeois of Paris says that people began to devour swill
which pigs disdained, while wolves swam the Seine to
disinter and gnaw newly-buried corpses. Amid this misery
the arrogance of the English invaders was peculiarly repel-
lent. A Burgundian chronicler, Georges Chastellain, lamented that they had turned Paris into a new London 'as much
by their language as by their rude and proud manner of
conversation and behaviour. And they went with their heads
high, like a stag . . .' In particular the Burgundian nobles
disliked King Henry's cold and haughty manner; he re-
buked the Marshal of France, Jehan de L'Isle-Adam, for
daring to look him in the face when answering a question.

Leaving behind the Duke of Exeter and an English
garrison of 500 men, Henry and his Queen soon rode out of
Paris, to spend Epiphany at Rouen and to demand more
money from the Norman Estates. At the end of January
they travelled to Calais and embarked for Dover.

The King had been out of England for three and a half
years, and he received a rapturous welcome wherever he
went, with the customary pageants and conduits flowing
with wine. On 23 February 1421 the Archbishop of Canterbury crowned Queen Catherine in Westminster Abbey.
Afterwards the royal couple went on progress, travelling to
St Albans, Bristol, through Herefordshire to Shrewsbury,
Coventry and Leicester. In the North they visited York and
Lincoln, in East Anglia Norwich and King's Lynn. The

real purpose of the progress was to raise more money for the War; commissioners travelled after Henry raising loans from the clergy, the landowners, the burgesses and even villagers and artisans. By the beginning of May these monies amounted to some £38,000, of which £22,000 had been contributed by Bishop Beaufort, the King's uncle. Parliament, meeting at Westminster that month, spoke of poverty and distress among Henry's subjects but nonetheless granted further subsidies—a fifteenth, together with a tenth from the clergy. The King needed every penny. When he died a year later the government had to face a deficit of £30,000 together with debts of £25,000: this was largely due to the expense of the War which not even the revenue from conquered territories could defray, because of constant raiding and unrest.

In April 1421 the King received news of the defeat and death of his brother Clarence, the heir to the throne. The Duke, although an experienced soldier who had been campaigning in France since 1412, was impulsive and envious of his elder brother's glory. On 22 March 1421, an Easter Saturday, while he was at dinner at Pont de l'Arche in Normandy after returning from a raid across Maine and over the Loire, Clarence was informed that there was an Armagnac army at Baugé nearby. When Sir Gilbert Umfraville—Henry's 'Marshal of France'—and the Earl of Huntingdon advised him to wait until his archers arrived, the Duke told them scornfully: 'If you are afraid, go home and keep the churchyard.' Clarence then set off with less than 1,500 men-at-arms, galloping the nine miles to Baugé. As soon as he was there, crossing the bridge over the river Couesnon, he made contact with the enemy and at once charged them up-hill, although they outnumbered his troops two to one and he had to attack over boggy ground. The Armagnacs, who included a Scots force under the Earls of Buchan and Wigtown, counter-charged down the slope on to the English who, having been beaten back, were reforming on the bank of the river. Clarence, easily identified by the coronet on his helmet, was quickly cut down and most of his men fell with him or were taken prisoner; Umfraville and Lord de Roos died with the Duke, while the Earls of Huntingdon and Somerset were captured. The Earl of Salisbury, who came up shortly afterwards, managed to retrieve Clarence's corpse—which had been put in a cart to take to the Dauphin—and extricated the survivors.

The defeat demonstrated that the English still had to rely on their traditional combination of archers and dismounted men-at-arms. As a contemporary Englishman wrote, his fellow-countrymen had been beaten 'By cause they wolde nott take with hem archers, but thought to have doo with the ffrenshmen them selff wythoute hem. And yet whan he was slayne the archers come and rescued the body of the Duke.' The victory was a marvellous encouragement to the Armagnacs; even if it gained them no lasting advantage, it showed that the invaders were not invincible. The Dauphin joked to his courtiers: 'What think ye now of the Scottish mutton eaters and wine bibbers?'—there had been some unfavourable comment about these valiant allies. He made the Earl of Buchan Constable of France.

Henry returned in June 1421, landing at Calais with 4,000 troops and marched to Paris to relieve Exeter. Paris was threatened by a chain of Armagnac forces on three sides, based on Dreux in the north, Meaux in the east and Joigny in the south. Dreux, the King quickly besieged and captured. He then marched south into the Beauce, capturing Vendôme and Beaugency and going on to camp in front of Orleans. He was too short of supplies to invest so well-fortified a town, and after three days he swung north and captured Villeneuve-le-Roy. He was in an ugly mood; when he took the Armagnac castle of Rougemont he hanged the entire garrison, demolishing the building and then drowning other of the defenders who had escaped and whom he caught later on. He marched on Meaux.

This town, on a bend of the Marne and forty miles east of Paris, was defended on three sides by the river and on the fourth by a canal, all in flood because of heavy rains. The King began the siege in October, building a camp and

bringing up cannon and provisions. Mining and bombardment soon began to break down the walls, yet the defenders
under the Bastard of Vaurus, who was a cruel and evil man
but a brave commander, held out despite famine. Outside
the walls the ground was waterlogged by rain and floods,
and then a sharp frost set in, while there was more than the
usual amount of disease ; it has been estimated that a six-
teenth of the English army died from dysentery and small-
pox. Henry himself fell ill and a physician was sent from
England. Yet despite sickness and the misery of another
harsh winter, Henry insisted on staying with his men even
during Christmas. His sole encouragement was that Queen
Catherine had given birth to a son and heir at Windsor on
6 December. (The gloomy legend that he commented :
'Henry born at Monmouth shall small time reign and get
much, and Henry born at Windsor shall long reign and all
lose, but as God wills so be it,' was invented at least a century
later.) In early March a few Armagnac troops succeeded in
getting into the city at night, but most of them were captured after their leader fell into the ditch with a splashing
which woke the English. Disheartened by the failure of this
attempt at relief, the garrison withdrew to the Market which
was a fortified suburb, taking the remainder of the food with
them. The rest of the town surrendered on 9 March 1422,
but the garrison still held out. Henry's artillery, mounted
under wooden shelters on an island in the river, battered
them relentlessly and eventually they too surrendered on
10 May, after a siege of eight months. The Bastard was
beheaded, his body being hanged from the tree where he
had gibbeted his own victims. Henry also beheaded a
trumpeter called Orace who had jeered at him ; while some
of the defenders who had mocked him by beating a donkey
on the wall until he brayed and saying that it was the King
speaking, were incarcerated in particularly nasty prisons.
The rich captives were sent back to England to await
ransom, and all plate, jewellery and valuables were collected
for Henry's use.

Such sieges caused misery which was not confined to the

defenders and the townspeople. When the English were before Meaux they pillaged far and wide throughout the local countryside, the Brie. According to the Bourgeois of Paris, many peasants there abandoned their farms and families in despair, saying: 'What can we do? Let us put everything into the hands of the Devil for it cannot matter what becomes of us ... They cannot do more to us than kill us or take us prisoner, for by the false government of traitors we have had to leave our wives and children and flee into the woods like wandering beasts.'

Henry returned to Paris. By now he was an ill man, and prayers were being offered for his recovery. His illness was probably a form of dysentery, no doubt contracted during the siege of Meaux. En route for Cosne-sur-Loire, a key point on the road to Dijon which was besieged by the Armagnacs, he suddenly found himself unable to ride and had to be taken back by litter to the castle of Vincennes which he reached on 10 August. Plainly he was dying. He made arrangements for the government of the two kingdoms with his customary thoroughness. He appointed his brother Bedford provisional Regent of France and guardian of the baby Henry VI, while Gloucester was to be Regent of England. He told Bedford that he must preserve the alliance with Burgundy at all costs, and that he should only keep the Regency if Duke Philip declined it. He also ordered that if things went badly the English should concentrate on saving Normandy. In addition he claimed he had invaded France not from any desire for glory but simply because his cause was just and would bring lasting peace. That he genuinely believed that he might have succeeded in conquering France is borne out by his claim that if God had spared him he would have gone on to Jerusalem to expel the infidels. However at one point he seems to have feared for his salvation; suddenly he shouted: 'Thou liest, thou liest, my portion is with the Lord Jesus Christ!' as though replying to an evil spirit. Henry V died peacefully at Vincennes on 31 August 1422. He was only thirty-five.

8

John, Duke of Bedford, Regent of France
1422–1429

... regent I am of France:
Give me my steeled coat, I'll fight for France.

King Henry VI

A vous entier

motto of the Duke of Bedford

For the English the seven years after Henry V's death were some of the most successful of the entire War. They continued their advance southward, down into the Loire Valley, and appeared to have a real chance of bringing the rest of the country under the rule of the infant Henry VI who was also 'Henri II' of France, King Charles having died only six weeks after his son-in-law. The dual monarchy (anticipating Sir Winston Churchill's wartime fantasy of a Franco-English state) worked surprisingly well; on occasion even Parisians fought loyally for it. All this was due to two men— the Regent Bedford and his great general the Earl of Salisbury.

John of Monmouth, Duke of Bedford, was thirty-three years old in 1422. He had been the Admiral who won the sea fight off Harfleur, and had twice been Guardian of England during his brother's campaigning abroad, besides seeing some hard fighting in France. A big, florid, fleshy man, beneath his cropped brown hair he had an eagle's beak of a nose with an oddly receding forehead and chin (to judge from the miniature in *The Bedford Book of Hours*). If hot-tempered, he was nevertheless more human and amiable than Henry V; and though no genius he was an excellent soldier, administrator and diplomatist, and possessed a rugged determination. His most agreeable quality was the loyalty proclaimed by his motto, a loyalty which he gave devotedly to his nephew Henry VI. Although he believed uncompromisingly in the Plantagenet right to the throne of France, he also genuinely loved the French and their country, where he was eventually Duke of Alençon and Anjou, Count of Maine, Mortain and Dreux, Viscount of Beaumont and Lord of many other seigneuries besides, and where he possessed delightful *hôtels* and châteaux. Dutifully, he offered his Regency to the Duke of Burgundy and was no doubt much relieved when Philip declined it.

Thomas Montagu, Earl of Salisbury and Count of Perche, was—after Henry V—the most distinguished commander produced by England during the entire Hundred Years War. Henry's favourite general, he had been made a Knight of the Garter and in 1419 Lieutenant-Governor of Normandy. A strategist as well as a tactician, he was always original and imaginative yet practical and patient at the same time. The Bourgeois of Paris calls him 'the knightly, skilful and subtle Comte de Salisbury'. Furthermore, he was an all-round soldier, as good at staff work as he was at fighting, while he was probably the first English commander (after King Henry) to be a gunnery expert. His men liked and trusted him, though fearful of his strict discipline. Above all, he worked well with Bedford. The French dreaded the Earl, who was known to drag his captives back to Paris at the end of a rope. In *King Henry VI* Shakespeare makes the Duke of Anjou say:

Salisbury is a desperate homicide;
He fighteth as one weary of his life.

This may well have been how the Dauphinists saw him, and
at this period they themselves were short of even moderately
good commanders.

There was a third Englishman of the same calibre as
Bedford and Salisbury, Richard Beauchamp, Earl of Warwick and Count of Aumale. However although undoubtedly
as capable, despite long and conscientious service in France
he achieved less. Warwick's fascination is that he is almost
the only English commander in the Hundred Years War
(other than a monarch) of whom a probable natural like-
ness has survived. His effigy at Warwick shows a fine-
boned face, fastidious yet powerful and unmistakably
patrician, with an expression which is both graceful and
arrogant. Even his hands have the same haughty elegance.
Moreover we know a good deal about his life from the
account written a generation later by the antiquarian John
Rous. Born in 1382, Warwick fought and routed Owain
Glyndŵr when he was only twenty. In 1408 he went on a
remarkable pilgrimage to Jerusalem, and en route was the
guest of Charles VI at Paris and of the Doge at Venice,
besides fighting a triumphant tournament with Pandolfo
Malatesta at Verona. On the way home he visited Poland
and the Teutonic Knights in Prussia and Germany. After
taking part at the siege of Harfleur in 1415 he received
Emperor Sigismund at Calais, when he declined to accept
the gift of a sword for King Henry, suggesting that the
Emperor should present it in person. Warwick played an
important part in the conquest of Normandy and in the
negotiations which led to the Treaty of Troyes. At various
times Captain of Calais, Rouen, Meaux and Beauvais,
'Captain and Lieutenant General of the King and the
Regent in the Field' in 1426–1427, and a member of
the Council of Regency in England, he was a pillar of the
Anglo-French state. Immensely wealthy, with an income of
nearly £5,000, and of ancient lineage—the Beauchamps

had been Earls since 1268—he had the honour of being appointed tutor to the young Henry VI. Due to lack of space there is not much about chivalry in these pages, but its ideals were real enough, and there was no better fifteenth-century English exponent of it than Warwick. It is therefore all the more interesting that this was the man who would burn Joan of Arc.

Salisbury and Warwick could rely on an unusually gifted team, most of whom worked together for twenty years or more. They were not knights-errant like the Earl of War-wick, but professional soldiers. They included Lord Willoughby d'Eresby, Lord Talbot, Lord Scales, Sir John Fastolf, Sir Matthew Gough, Sir Thomas Rempston, Sir Thomas Kyriell and Sir William Glasdale. Brave, brutal men, they throve on a life of battles, raids and skirmishes, an existence which even when not campaigning was a routine of camp, saddle and fortress. One or two lived to be killed in the Wars of the Roses, and nearly all made fortunes.

Many took French titles, for the expropriation and hand-out of these continued, each one being accompanied by large estates (although in most cases there was a rightful holder alive in Dauphinist France). They included some of the best-known dignities in French history; Lord Willoughby became Count of Vendôme, Lord Talbot Count of Clermont and Lord Scales Vidame of Chartres. Nor was such ennoblement confined to peers. Sir John Fastolf was made Baron of Sillé-le-Guillaume and of La Suze-sur-Sarthe, and Sir Matthew Gough Baron of Coulonces and Tillières. Such counties and baronies were eagerly sought after.

King 'Henri' was eventually recognized by all France north of the Loire, save for isolated Dauphinist enclaves. A good deal of this was controlled by the Duke of Burgundy —he occupied most of Champagne—while Brittany was independent under Duke John V. At its widest extent the territory directly under English rule consisted of Normandy (with the *Pays de Conquête*—the rest of the Seine valley—and Maine and Anjou), Paris and the Ile de France, some of

Caister Castle, Norfolk—in its day furnished with splendour and luxury. Built by the soldier Sir John Fastolf, originally an esquire of £46 a year, who out of the profits of war in France and their careful investment had increased his income to £1,450 a year when he died in 1459.

The man who burnt Joan of Arc: Richard Beauchamp, Earl of Warwick and Count of Aumale, Captain of Rouen and many other French cities (1382–1439). He was finally Lieutenant-General of France from 1437–1439.

Champagne and Picardy, and of course the Pas de Calais and
Guyenne. The Dauphin reigned over the rest, after a
fashion. His Council was at Poitiers but as his court was
sometimes at Bourges he was contemptuously called 'The
King of Bourges'. In practice he was seldom there, moving
from château to château.

The Anglo-French realm was kept entirely separate from
England and governed through long-standing institutions
by Frenchmen supervised by a few senior English officials.
Despite the promises made at Troyes, Normandy (with the
Pays de Conquête, and Maine and Anjou) was administered
as a state apart—the Regent being determined to turn the
duchy into a Lancastrian bastion—by a council at Rouen.
Though the *baillis* were always Englishmen, almost all other
civil officials were natives. Bedford did his best to make
English rule popular with the Normans, encouraging trade,
founding a university at Caen and issuing an excellent gold
coinage in his nephew's name—the *salut*.

The government of Paris was quite distinct. It possessed
what has been described as the beginnings of 'an Anglo-
French secretariat', for even before an English garrison had
been installed, its bureaucracy had been purged of Dauphinist symphathizers and had no qualms at co-operating with
the English. Some of these Burgundian officials worked in
Rouen and in London as well as in Paris. When at the
capital Bedford lived at the Hôtel des Tournelles, where he
gave splendid parties for the Parisians like that in June
1428 for 8,000 guests ; the Bourgeois says that the nobles
and clergy were invited 'then the doctors of every science and
the lawyers from the *Parlement*, the Provost of Paris and the
officials from the Châtelet, then the Provost of the Merchants, the Aldermen, the Bourgeois and even the commons'.
The Regent was particularly careful to keep on amiable
terms with the University, the *Parlement* and all the civic
dignitaries.

Yet however anxious he may have been to make Plantagenet rule popular, Bedford none the less tried to force
his subjects to contribute to the war effort. Paris had to

endure ferocious taxation, but the Normans suffered most—
'Normandy was indeed, in the full sense of the term, the
milch cow of Lancastrian rule,' is Perroy's comment.
Besides the subsidies granted by the Estates there was a
gabelle, a *quatrième* on wine and cider, and a sales tax on all
goods. In addition the *guet* was levied, a hearth tax to pay
the troops. During crises such as the great campaign in
1428, even more was demanded. The peasants also had to
suffer from the English garrisons—foraging, looting and
kidnapping for ransom, and the *pâtis* or protection racket.
The same sort of demands, official and unofficial, were made
in Anjou and Maine and in the Ile de France. As time
passed and the English became increasingly desperate for
money, both the taxation and the plundering grew still more
oppressive.

Life was made almost intolerable for the peasants by
English freebooters and by *écorcheurs*. One of the most
notorious of the former was Richard Venables, who came
to Normandy in 1428 with only three men-at-arms and a
dozen archers but who soon collected an army of deserters
and set himself up in the fortified Cistercian monastery of
Savigny, from where he rode out to rob and murder. His
bloodiest exploit was at Vicques near Falaise where he
massacred an entire village. Venables's band was only one
among many. The *écorcheurs*, or flayers, were gangs of high-
waymen who were the heirs of the *routiers*: they took their
name from their custom of stripping victims to the skin and
even flaying them alive. Bedford did his best to defend the
unfortunate country people. In Normandy he gave them
arms and tried to make them practise archery on Sundays.
In Maine he issued certificates of protection under his own
seal (for a household or for a parish as a whole) together with
travel permits and safe conducts, though all these had to be
paid for in hard cash.

But despite Bedford's heroic endeavours, Lancastrian
France eventually became a wilderness laid waste by its garri-
sons, by deserters, by *écorcheurs* and by Dauphinist raiders.
At the end of the 1420s the revenues from Normandy

began to fall drastically. It was painfully obvious that the conquered territories were not going to pay for the War.

From the very beginning only Burgundian support made it possible for the dual monarchy to function at all. 'Burgundian' in this context did not of course mean someone from Burgundy but was the name of a political allegiance —those Frenchmen who preferred to be governed by the Duke of Burgundy or his allies rather than by Dauphinists. Many now genuinely believed that a strong English régime would bring peace and put an end to the bloody civil war of the last dozen years; moreover they also thought that—on past form—the English were bound to win a war with the Dauphinists (in much the same way that Pétainists estimated German chances in 1940). Remembering the Armagnac terror, every Parisian dreaded the massacres which would surely follow the return of the Dauphin, a fear echoed in every town in Anglo-Burgundian France. Even before the Lancastrian occupation, the Bourgeois of Paris thought it better to be a prisoner of the English than of the Dauphin 'and those people who call themselves Armagnacs'. Later, describing Armagnac campaigns, the Bourgeois said they perpetrated crimes worse 'than any man or demon could commit'; this rational and decent observer, probably a Canon of Notre-Dame, uses such terms as 'worse than Saracens' or 'unchained devils'. Unfortunately the English position depended on more than fear of Armagnacs.

The most dangerous threat was the difficult nature of Duke Philip. Splendid in appearance, he was arrogant and violent-tempered—in his rages his face took on a bluish hue —and extremely touchy. Still more disconcerting, this pillar of chivalry was a notorious liar; little reliance could be placed on his word, for he was whimsical and changeable. Although intent on strengthening his power in his own domains and on acquiring more territory in the Low Countries, and though bored by French politics, the Duke was proud of his Valois blood and could never really accept a Plantagenet France. As the memory of his father's murder faded he was increasingly ready to flirt with the Dauphinists.

He showed his hand by declining to become a Knight of the Garter and thus refusing to swear an oath of loyalty to English brethren. Bedford strove desperately to keep on good terms with him.

In April 1423 the Dukes of Bedford, Burgundy and Brittany met at Amiens to sign a treaty in which each swore 'brotherhood and union as long as we live' and tacitly pledged himself to work for the Dauphin's final overthrow, though entering into no military commitment. Burgundy and Brittany signed with reservations, later making a secret treaty in which they promised to remain friends should either of them ally with the Dauphin. In May the Regent married Philip's sister, Anne of Burgundy, a purely political match which became a noticeably happy marriage—although she was 'as plain as an owl'. A contemporary commented : 'My Lord the Regent loves Madame Regent so well that always he brings her with him to Paris and everywhere else.' Intelligent, gay and devout, Anne tried hard to preserve the alliance between her husband and her brother.

If there was no proper strategic co-operation between the English and the Burgundians, a good working military relationship often existed in the field. This was very much in evidence throughout 1423. An allied army took Le Crotoy, while a similar force under the Duke of Norfolk and Jean de Luxembourg routed the Dauphinist Poton de Xaintrailles. Everywhere English and Burgundians joined in raids and skirmishes. In the south-west however, the English and Guyennois had to fight by themselves, raiding and counter-raiding on the borders of Guyenne, over into the Saintonge and Poitou and into the Limousin and Périgord ; they had to repel Dauphinist attacks on La Réole and in the Entre-deux-mers.

The one important action of 1423 was at Cravant. The Dauphinists had gathered a new army which included a large Scots contingent under Sir John Stewart of Darnley, the Constable of Scotland, and Italian and Spanish mercenaries. They marched on Cravant, a little town on the right bank of the river Yonne which was a key stronghold on the frontier of ducal Burgundy ; if it fell, Dijon, Philip's capital, would be exposed to attack—though the enemy's primary objective was to relieve isolated Dauphinist garrisons cut off in Champagne and Picardy. The defenders, mainly local gentry, put up a determined resistance but by July had already eaten their horses—'there was neither cat nor dog, rat nor mouse that was not eaten up', relates the chronicler Jean de Wavrin.

The Earl of Salisbury marched as quickly as he could to relieve them. At Auxerre he was joined by a Burgundian contingent and a council of war was held in the cathedral, where they drew up a joint order of the day which has survived. There was to be an English and a Burgundian Marshal, the advance guard was to be half English, half Burgundian, discipline was enforceable on pain of death, and no prisoners were to be taken until victory was certain. Archers had to bring the usual pointed stakes, and everyone had to furnish himself with two days' rations. At night everyone must pray as devoutly as possible. Salisbury pressed on, although the weather was so hot that when they halted men-at-arms lay face downward on the ground in their armour to cool off. In all he had about 4,000 troops.

When Salisbury reached Cravant on Friday 29 July the Dauphinists were waiting on the other side of the river, on the crest of a hill about a mile and a half from the town. However they then came down to the bank, and to attack them the English would have to cross the river, an operation which could easily end in disaster. Salisbury gambled on the garrison coming to his assistance and, covered by archers, waded across the river in front of the town. At the same time Lord Willoughby led an assault on the main bridge. Salisbury's detachment crossed safely and was soon engaged in savage fighting, while at the bridge Willoughby's men had an even hotter reception from the Scots. At last the Dauphinists began to falter, whereupon the garrison, although weak from lack of food, charged them from the rear as Salisbury had hoped. The enemy army disintegrated and to escape had to run the gauntlet between the town and the river bank ;

1,200 were slaughtered, including many Scots. Sir John Stewart, who had lost an eye, was taken prisoner.

By 1424 the Regent, Bedford, felt sufficiently confident to strike south and complete the conquest of Maine and Anjou, although he knew that the enemy had gathered another army and was intending to launch a full-scale offensive. He assembled 10,000 troops at Rouen and sent the Earl of Suffolk to retake Ivry which had fallen to the Dauphinists. Suffolk captured the town quickly enough but the garrison held out in the citadel, expecting to be relieved by the Dauphin's new army. Before the army could reach Ivry, Bedford came up with the main body of his troops and the citadel surrendered. The enemy commanders—the Duke of Alençon, the Count of Aumale and the Viscount of Narbonne, had too many unfortunate memories of Agincourt to want a battle, but their Scots allies insisted on fighting. They compromised, deciding to capture some towns while avoiding a pitched battle in the field. On 14 August they appeared before the English town of Verneuil on the Norman border with prisoners tied to their horses' tails; the townsmen, thinking these were English captives and that Bedford must have been defeated, promptly opened their gates, only to discover that the 'prisoners' were Scots. Meanwhile Bedford had left Ivry for Evreux, where reconnaissance troops informed him that the enemy had taken Verneuil. Next day he set out for Verneuil, so sure of himself that he ordered 3,000 Burgundians to leave him and return to the siege of Nesle.

On 17 August the Regent drew up his army on the road from Damville to Verneuil where it emerged from a forest on to the plain in front of Verneuil. He had about 9,000 men. He used the same formation employed at Poitiers and Agincourt, with his men-at-arms at the centre and archers on the wings; the men-at-arms were in two 'battles', the right commanded by himself, the left by Salisbury. He also posted a reserve of 2,000 mounted bowmen a quarter of a mile behind. As an added refinement, he fortified his baggage-train, laagering the wagons in a hollow square still further

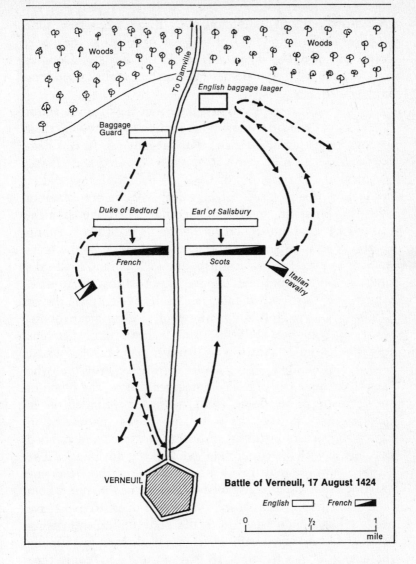

Woods

Woods

To Damville

English baggage laager

Baggage
Guard

Duke of Bedford

Earl of Salisbury

French

Scots

Italian
cavalry

VERNEUIL

Battle of Verneuil, 17 August 1424

English ☐ French ◼

0 ½ 1

mile

back ; the horses were tethered head and tail, three or four
deep, in a circle round the square to serve as an extra barrier.
The Dauphinist army was further down the road towards
Verneuil, about 17,000 troops formed into two divisions of
dismounted men-at-arms linked by archers, their wings
being protected by mounted men-at-arms who were meant

to deal with any flanking attacks by English bowmen. One division was commanded by the Count of Aumale; the other, consisting of 6,000 Scots, was under the Earls of Douglas and Buchan who sent a message to the English that they intended to give no quarter.

Neither side wanted to attack. From dawn until about 4 o'clock in the afternoon both armies sweltered in their armour beneath a blazing sun without moving. At last Bedford ordered his men to advance. After kneeling and kissing the ground and shouting 'St George! Bedford!' they did so at a slow steady pace, giving deep, deliberate roars of defiance. Simultaneously some mounted Dauphinist men-at-arms charged the archers on Bedford's right flank, riding through and past them until they were stopped by the bowmen in reserve; many English turned and ran. Bedford's division continued to march grimly towards that of Aumale, which was also advancing, shouting 'Montjoie! Saint Denis!' The two gleaming masses of faceless steel robots, war-cries booming hollowly from beneath their helmets, met with a loud crash to begin a hand-to-hand combat whose ferocity astounded even contemporaries. Wavrin, who fought in the battle himself, remembered how 'the blood of the dead spread on the field and that of the wounded ran in great streams all over the earth'. For three-quarters of an hour English and Dauphinists hacked, battered and stabbed each other without either side gaining any advantage. The Regent, swinging a two-handed pole-axe, did fearsome execution and killed many men—'He reached no one whom he did not fell.' (Such weapons smashed open an expensive armour like a modern tin can, the body underneath being crushed and mangled before even the blade sank in.) Finally the enemy began to falter, to give ground; suddenly they turned to lumber away as quickly as their armour would permit towards Verneuil, where many were driven into the moat and drowned, including Aumale himself.

On the left the gallant Salisbury had been almost overcome by the Scots. Moreover 600 Italian cavalry had swept past him to plunder the baggage laager; the archers in the

reserve were still dealing with the Dauphinist men-at-arms
who had broken through on the right, and the Italians,
despite a brave resistance by the pages, started to rifle the
wagons and drive off the horses. Luckily the reserve managed to repel the enemy men-at-arms and came up to beat
off the Italians. They then ran forward to help Salisbury,
taking the Scots in flank with a loud yell (*'un merveilleu cri'*).
Meanwhile Bedford had reassembled his weary but triumphant division. He returned to smash into the Scottish rear,
overwhelming them. The English troops nursed a particular
hatred for their northern neighbours, very few of whom
escaped alive ; among the slain were Archibald, Earl of
Douglas with his son James, Earl of Mar, and John Stewart,
Earl of Buchan. Bedford wrote later : 'The moste vengeance
fell upon the proud Scottes, for thei went to Dog-wash the
same day, mo than 1700 of cote Armoures of these proude
Scottes.' In addition, over a thousand Dauphinist French
were killed including the Viscount of Narbonne, which
brought total enemy casualties to more than 7,000. The
most important prisoners were the Duke of Alençon and
Marshal Lafayette.

Yet although the English had lost only a thousand men,
there had been a moment at the beginning when they were
nearly beaten. Many had fled from the first Dauphinist
charge, shouting that it was all over. A captain called
Young was afterwards found guilty of running away and
taking 500 men with him ; he was hanged till half dead,
then drawn and quartered.

Verneuil was seen as a second Agincourt and the Regent's
prestige soared. The Dauphinists had been completely
broken as a fighting force in the field ; the way lay open for
an advance on Bourges and perhaps the final reckoning.
However, Bedford, true to his brother's example, preferred
the less spectacular but more solid gain of completing the
conquest of Anjou and Maine, and began a methodical re-
duction of enemy strongholds. An additional advantage was
the end of the threat of Scots intervention ; the flower of their
best fighting-men had fallen. (Ironically, the Dauphinists

were not altogether sorry for this ; their chronicler, Basin, tells us that the disaster of Verneuil was offset by being rid of the Scots whose insolence was intolerable.)

At this moment of triumph the Regent's position was suddenly undermined by events outside France which threatened to ruin his relations with Burgundy. Humphrey of Gloucester, a frivolous and irresponsible intriguer, fell in love with Jacqueline of Hainault, Countess in her own right of Hainault, Holland and Zeeland, who had deserted an unsatisfactory husband and taken refuge in England. After obtaining a dubious dispensation from the deposed anti-Pope Benedict XIII (who still lived at Avignon), Gloucester married her and styled himself Count of Hainault, Holland and Zeeland, which in 1424 he invaded with an army of 5,000 men. The expedition was a farce and 'ambitious Humphrey', having made a fool of himself, had to return to England within the year, where he tried to get up a further invasion. Nothing could have been better calculated to infuriate Philip of Burgundy who wanted Jacqueline's territories for himself. When Philip visited Paris in the autumn of 1424 he shouted insults at Bedford and informed him that he had made a defensive treaty with the Dauphin. Only the influence of Philip's sister, Bedford's wife—together with a fear that a complete rupture might provoke his brother-in-law into going to Gloucester's assistance—prevented the total collapse of the Anglo-Burgundian alliance.

Philip of Burgundy was never an easy ally. During his visit to Paris he mortally offended the Earl of Salisbury. Philip, a notorious lecher with thirty mistresses, made outrageous advances to the nineteen-year-old Countess of Salisbury (Chaucer's granddaughter), who was a famous beauty. Salisbury was so angry that he swore he would never again serve in the field with Philip but would go to Hainault and fight for Gloucester.

By the end of 1425 Gloucester had stirred up more trouble, this time in England. Here although he was titular Protector the real government was the Council, which had refused to recognize him as Regent and which was dominated by the Chancellor, Henry Beaufort, Bishop of Winchester. Beaufort, a half-brother of Henry IV (being a bastard but legitimized son of John of Gaunt by Catherine Swynford), was one of the most formidable ecclesiastics in English history and regarded himself as the man best fitted to rule England. Inevitably he quarrelled with Gloucester, who hated him for taking away the Regency. Duke Humphrey tried to raise the London mob against Beaufort and there was very nearly civil war. In October 1425 Beaufort wrote desperately to Bedford, imploring him to return to England as quickly as possible—'If you tarry, we shall put this land in peril with a battle. Such a brother you have here.' He also reminded him that 'the prosperity of France stands on the welfare of England'. In consequence the Regent was out of France from December 1425 until March 1427, fifteen months when he was too busy reconciling his brother and his uncle to attend to matters across the Channel. Although the reconciliation was reasonably successful, Bedford must always have been worried that Gloucester and Beaufort would come to blows again.

During his stay in England Bedford had difficulty in obtaining money from Parliament for fresh troops. The endless expense of the War was now making it unpopular with the English, who in any case thought that the occupied territories should pay for it. As expeditionary forces grew smaller, fewer and fewer Englishmen took part.

On the other hand a greater proportion of the aristocracy was serving in France. Unlike the previous century when many commanders came from the lesser gentry and even humbler backgrounds, in the fifteenth century senior officers were predominantly noblemen—the Earls of Salisbury, Warwick, Suffolk, Lord Talbot and Lord Scales, to name only the most famous. There was an excellent economic reason why they should be greedy for the profits of war : because of the agricultural depression the income from many baronial estates was lower than it had been for decades.

Nevertheless, if there were no more Robert Salles or

Nicholas Hawkwoods, men from the higher gentry continued to rise in rank and fortune through the War. It is reasonable to suppose that, like the magnates, they were driven by dwindling revenues. A good example is Sir John Stourton of Stourton in Wiltshire. Born in 1399, the son of a Speaker of the House of Commons and the head of an ancient West Country family, he was at the siege of Rouen in 1418 and took part in many other campaigns; by 1436 he was raising over a hundred bowmen to bring to France. In 1438 he was appointed a Privy Counsellor, henceforward attending Council meetings where he played a key role in planning military operations; he recommended campaigning in Normandy rather than Guyenne because it was nearer, though his real reason may have been that he had lands in Normandy (admittedly these have not been identified). A member of several important embassies to the French, for nearly two years he was also keeper of the unfortunate Duke of Orleans—the poet, who had been a prisoner since Agincourt—whom he kept at Stourton from 1438–1439 and whom complained of his strictness. Later he was one of the Guardians of Calais. In 1448 he was created Baron Stourton and he survived the troubled political world of the 1450s, dying in his bed in 1462. Plainly this strenuous career was not without financial reward. Much of it must have come from loot and ransoms. Leland says that French prize-money paid for the splendid castle at Stourton (demolished in the eighteenth century, but built on the site of what is now Stourhead) with its two courtyards—'the front of the inner court is magnificent and high embattled, castle like'. It is more probable that Lord Stourton simply renovated and extended the house of his ancestors, but undoubtedly he could have afforded to build a new one. He bought an imposing mansion near the capital, Stourton House at Fulham—next door to the palace of the Bishops of London—and also built most of the priory church of the Augustinians at Stavordale in Somerset.

Many others rose through the War, and a successful career in France was frequently a prelude to high office in

England. The Fiennes brothers, James and Roger, did so
well that the first built Knole and the second built Hurst-
monceux; James, who had been Captain of Arques and
Captain General of the Seine towns, and was Seigneur of
Court-le-Comte, became Lord Saye and Sele in 1446 (only
to be lynched by Jack Cade a few years later). Another new
peer, who had also been Captain of Arques and who owned
lands in France, was Lord Sudeley, the builder of the magnificent castle of that name in Gloucestershire. That very
professional warrior the first (and last) Lord Wenlock, who
was granted land at Gisors in 1421 and who went on to fight
in the Wars of the Roses until he was killed at Barnet,
erected the Sommaries outside Luton. The fortress of
Raglan was the creation of Sir William ap Thomas, and
Heron Hall that of Sir John Tyrrel, both of whom had
fought in France. Sir John Montgomery (who took part in
the capture of Joan of Arc) built Faulkbourne Hall, and his
son Middleton Towers. Most of these great houses were of
red brick, for which their creators must undoubtedly have
acquired a taste in France. In addition these lordly soldiers
built beautiful Perpendicular churches, if not so many as the
bourgeois wool men; McFarlane calls them 'the war
churches' as opposed to the wool churches. Of these the best
known is the chapel at Warwick, with its armoured effigy
in gilded metal of a Beauchamp Earl who died in 1439.

Ransoms still formed a large part of such money. The
Count of Vendôme was bought at a high price by Henry V
from Sir John Cornwall, later Lord Fanhope and the builder
of Ampthill. Sir John has been described by E. F. Jacob as
'an example of a highly well-placed speculator in ransoms';
his purchases included the Lords of Gaucourt and Estouteville in 1423 (taken prisoner at Harfleur eight years before)
and the Duke of Bourbon. Sir Rowland Lenthall built
Hampton Court in Herefordshire with prize money from
prisoners captured in Henry V's campaigns.* Sir Walter

* 'This Lenthall was victorious at the battaile of Agin-Court and tooke
many prisoners there, by the which prey he beganne the new building and
mannour place at Hampton.' John Leland, *Itinerary*.

Hungerford, later Lord Hungerford, rebuilt the castle and also the church at Farleigh Hungerford in Somerset; Leland was told that he paid for this out of loot from Agincourt, but it is known that Sir Walter brought no less than eight valuable prisoners back to England.

Besides ransom there was plunder. Apparently the French nobility had the obliging habit of campaigning with their jewels and family plate; and everyone took a cut from the *pâtis* money. There was also paid office. Understandably the dual monarchy had a very large number of captaincies to fill. McFarlane claims: 'There was hardly a knight, or indeed an esquire of Henry V's army that was not given one or more of these offices of responsibility *and* profit under his son.' He adds that some of them were entrusted with the administration of entire French provinces, not just of a town or castle. Such men bled white the territories under their rule.

Of course Englishmen were captured and had to pay ransom themselves, but because their armies won more battles—including all the larger ones—the ratio of Frenchmen to Englishmen taken prisoner was overwhelmingly in favour of the latter. It is also true that there were other and sometimes more important factors at home in England in the creation of patrician fortunes and of new noble houses—advantageous marriages, grants for services to the crown and the exploitation of English offices. Nevertheless at this time French money played a major and often a key role, and a very large proportion of the great success stories of fifteenth-century England began in France.

The Regent returned to France in March 1427, accompanied by a man from the Welsh Marches who was to become one of the most redoubtable soldiers of the War—Lord Talbot. They took with them a pitifully small new army, 300 men-at-arms and 900 archers, though they also brought a new artillery train. The English were lucky that during Bedford's absence the Dauphinists had not taken advantage of the defection of the Duke of Brittany, a shifty intriguer. In 1426 Duke John of Brittany had signed a

treaty with the Dauphin at Saumur while his brother with a
mixed force of Bretons and Scots had seized the important
English fortress of Pontorson and massacred its garrison.
Furthermore, because of Gloucester's meddling in Hainault,
Anglo-Burgundian co-operation was almost non-existent.
Bedford acted swiftly. In May Lord Warwick captured
Pontorson, after which Duke John veered back to the
English and in September 1427 formally reaffirmed his
allegiance to the Treaty of Troyes. In June the Regent and
his wife visited Duke Philip of Burgundy at Arras and began
to restore good relations ; Bedford stopped a new English
expedition to Hainault and then arranged a truce between
Gloucester and Burgundy. Humphrey abandoned Jacqueline of Hainault and her claims, obtaining a Papal Bull which
declared their marriage invalid (his chief reason being that
he now wanted to marry her lady-in-waiting Eleanor
Cobham). By the end of 1427 Bedford had entirely restored
the Triple Alliance.

A further 1,900 troops had arrived from England in the
spring but before launching a major new offensive it had
been necessary to capture a number of enemy strongholds.
Among them was the town of Montargis, sixty miles south-
east of Paris, which dominated the Yonne valley. It occupied
an extremely strong position on a headland completely sur-
rounded by the rivers Loing and Vernisson, while the
approach was criss-crossed by canals which hindered the
besiegers. It had a resolute garrison under the Sieur de La
Faille who was well liked by the townsmen. Lord Warwick
pitched his camp on the road from Paris, on both sides of
the river, and possessed a good supply line. He had brought
only 5,000 men but he had an adequate artillery train and on
15 July began a methodical bombardment of the town.
Nevertheless, after six weeks he had made little progress.
He could hardly have expected that the Dauphinists could
produce a commander capable of taking him by surprise.

John, Bastard of Orleans (popularly known later as the
'*bon et brave Dunois*' from his county of that name) was the
left-handed son of the Duke of Orleans who had been

murdered in 1407. A penniless adventurer, the Bastard became a professional soldier and fought at Baugé and Verneuil. He was now twenty-four years old. In September 1427 he and another good soldier, La Hire, were sent to reinforce Montargis with 1,600 troops. The Bastard had obviously studied the battle at Cravant, and a messenger from him reached the town with a plan of concerted action. Suddenly the Bastard and his men appeared in full view of the English on the road south of the town. Warwick's troops rushed to attack them, whereupon the townsmen opened the sluice-gates and the ensuing flood carried away the wooden bridge over the river, cutting the English forces in two and drowning many. At the same time the defenders sallied out to attack them from the rear. Warwick lost a thousand men, the rest fleeing in panic and abandoning their artillery.

On the same day as the débâcle at Montargis, Sir John Fastolf and a small force were defeated at Ambrières in Maine, and all Maine rose in revolt. The Regent, coldly determined, at once recommenced the siege of Montargis and began to put down the rising in Maine. He showed himself no less merciless than his brother: the town of La Gravelle did not honour its promise to surrender by a given date, so he beheaded the hostages which it had given as a surety. Lord Talbot was also beginning to show his quality. When La Hire seized Le Mans, Talbot retook it and rescued the garrison with only 300 men, going on to capture Laval which was one of the keys to Maine. By the spring of 1428 the situation had been restored and the way was now open for the long-hoped-for offensive.

But the English were still bedevilled by lack of money. Although taxed to the hilt the conquered territories could not provide enough, while in England Parliament had shown itself unco-operative despite Bedford's pleas. In July 1427 he had sent Salisbury home to beg the Council for help, and eventually the Earl obtained £24,000, though he had to lend part of it from his own resources. He sailed from Sandwich in June 1428 with 450 men-at-arms, 2,250 archers,

ten miners, over seventy masons, carpenters and bowmakers
and a new artillery train. Meanwhile the Regent had been
assembling troops and supplies. Salisbury marched into
Paris in July. He and the Regent differed over the objectives
of the forthcoming campaign—the former wished to capture Orleans, the key to the Loire and from whence he could
strike over the river into the Dauphinist heartland ; Bedford,
on the other hand, wanted Angers which would give the
English complete control of Anjou and enable them to link
up their northern territories with Guyenne. Moreover the
Regent had scruples about attacking Orleans ; to do so was
to breach a treaty, and as its feudal lord the Duke of Orleans
was a prisoner in England, the assault would be against all
the rules of chivalry. Salisbury prevailed, but Bedford seems
to have kept his misgivings ; some years afterwards he
wrote to his nephew Henry VI how the Plantagenet cause
had prospered everywhere in France until the siege of
Orleans, 'takyn in hand God knoweth by what avys'.

The Earl began his offensive in mid-August, capturing
more than forty towns and fortresses, 'somme wonne be
assault and somme otherwyse' as he put it. They included
the towns on the Loire nearest to Orleans—Beaugency and
Meung downstream and Jargeau upstream. On 12 October
he invested Orleans. On the northern bank of the Loire, the
city must have presented a daunting spectacle. Its thirty-
foot-high walls were so long that the English were unable
to surround them with siege works and had to rely on
patrols. Inside there were more defenders than the besiegers
outside—2,400 troops and 3,000 militia, commanded by
the same Sieur de Gaucourt who had been at Harfleur ; they
had 71 guns mounted on the walls, some firing stone shot
weighing nearly 200 lbs and far outnumbering the English
artillery. Nor were the English troops, who had dwindled
to 4,000, of the best quality ; they had been looting and
deserting ever since they landed and had sacked an especially
holy shrine at Cléry. As for Burgundians, Salisbury had a
mere 150, hired from the Duke. The Earl had no hope of
blockading the city with so few men, and the defenders

could obtain supplies and reinforcements without difficulty. Not in the least deterred, 'mad-brain'd Salisbury' decided to batter his way over the main bridge across the river, a structure 350 metres wide which stretched from the south bank to the centre of the city. It was defended on the bank by an earthwork and then by two massive towers over the first arch, known as the Tourelles. A bombardment followed by an assault was unsuccessful, but when the towers' garrison realized that miners had tunnelled beneath the foundations they fled in panic, demolishing two arches of the bridge behind them.

Salisbury climbed up on to the third floor of the Tourelles to have a closer view of Orleans and decide where to attack next, 'looking very attentively on all sides to see and devise in what way he might surround and subdue it'. An apocryphal story says that an English captain, Sir William Glasdale, said to the Earl : 'My Lord, you see your city.' Suddenly a schoolboy set off a small bombard on the walls whose gunners had left it during dinner. Salisbury heard the report and ducked. The gunstone came through the window, killing a gentleman next to him, and an iron bar flew off, hitting Salisbury's visor and slicing away half his face. To the genuine sorrow of his men 'who both feared and loved him', after a week's agony he died at Meung on 27 October, his last words being to beg his officers to continue the siege. Wavrin believed that had Salisbury lived another three months he would have taken Orleans. His death was a calamity for the English.

The Earl of Suffolk took over the command. This great-grandson of Edward III's moneylender was a very different man from Salisbury. Although a veteran of Harfleur who had seen many campaigns, he was an unimaginative and unenterprising soldier, averse to taking risks, and above all unlucky. He continued the siege, after a fashion ; a garrison was left in the Tourelles under Glasdale while Suffolk and the rest of the troops went into winter quarters in nearby towns. However, Lord Talbot and Lord Scales brought them back on 1 December, surrounding the city with a line of sixty stockaded earthworks, known as *bastilles*, linked by communication trenches. As a blockade it was hardly adequate, for there was a wide gap to the north-east. In any case the defenders inside the city had plenty of food, and were reinforced by the Bastard of Orleans, La Hire, Poton de Xaintrailles and 500 fresh troops. But the English hung on grimly during the winter. The courtesies of chivalry were scrupulously observed. On Christmas Day Suffolk sent some figs to the Bastard and received a fur coat in exchange while the city lent the besiegers an orchestra.

We know the names of Sir William Glasdale's garrison in the Tourelles, and they sound astonishingly modern and ordinary—they would not have been out of place at Torres Vedras or Tobruk. Among them were Thomas Jolly, Bill Martin, Davy Johnson, Walter Parker, Matthew Thornton, George Ludlow, Patrick Hall, William Vaughan, Thomas Sand, Dick Hawke, John Langham, William Arnold, George Blackwell, and John Reid from Redesdale.

On 12 February 1429 Sir John Fastolf, who was taking a convoy of Lenten food—herrings and lentils—from Paris to the English at Orleans, learnt at Rouvray near Janville that he was about to be attacked by a Dauphinist force of 4,000 men under the Count of Clermont. Fastolf, who only had 500 English archers and 1,000 Parisian militia (probably crossbowmen) immediately halted and laagered his wagons, leaving two narrow entrances fortified by the pointed stakes of his archers. Clermont had some small cannon and began to use them on the laager with considerable effect. But then a Scots detachment under Sir John Stewart of Darnley insisted on attacking on foot, and the French men-at-arms joined them, though remaining on horseback. They were bloodily repulsed by arrow-fire, whereupon Fastolf mounted his archers (who almost certainly carried lances) and charged out to complete the enemy's rout, killing about 500—mainly Scots. Fastolf lost only four men, apart from some wagoners who had tried to run away. It was heartening that the Parisians should have shown themselves so loyal. The Regent had a service of thanksgiving held in Paris and paid special honour to the militia men.

By the spring of 1429, the English were still no nearer capturing Orleans. In April Bedford begged the Council for more men and was sent only 100 men-at-arms. The Dauphinists then made a shrewd diplomatic move by ceding Orleans to the Duke of Burgundy, on the pretext that its lord the Duke of Orleans was a prisoner in England. Philip was eager to accept but Bedford, although concerned at putting the alliance with him at risk, refused to agree. Angrily Philip ordered Burgundian troops to leave the siege. By 15 April the Regent was again writing to the Council, deploring the low morale of his army, pleading for reinforcements and warning that without military or financial assistance he would be force to raise the siege.

The walls were still unbreached. Suffolk held on, without much hope. He had forgotten to put chain-booms across the Loire, so the enemy were able to use the river for moving troops and supplies. On 29 April barges laden with food sailed from Chézy only five miles upstream and, while the English were distracted by a mock assault on one of their earthworks, got through to the city. Next day, accompanied by a small escort, the leader of an army of relief rode into Orleans on a black charger, carrying a small battle-axe. She was Joan of Arc.

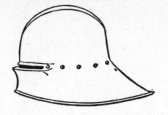

9

'The Witch of Orleans'
1429–1435

Foul fiend of France and hag of all despite.

King Henry VI

'ffalse witche'.

a London chronicler

In 1428 an illiterate shepherdess of seventeen decided she had been called by God to save France and expel the English. In fact, far from driving out the English, Joan of Arc merely checked the English advance by reviving Dauphinist morale, and the Regent managed to halt the counter-offensive. It was not the Maid who ended English rule in France.

Playwrights tend to concentrate on Joan's trial and martyrdom, and seldom give Bedford and his troops any credit for sincerity. Yet the English army can be forgiven from mistaking her for a witch sent by the Devil to be their ruin. For a decade God had apparently blessed the cause of the Lancastrians and looking back, in a report of 1434 to the English Council, the Regent spoke of 'a greet strook upon your peuple'; he attributed it to sudden misgivings among the English about the justice of their cause, induced by 'a disciple and lyme [limb] of the Feende, called the Pucelle, that used false enchauntments and sorcerie'. Shakespeare in *King Henry VI, Part I* echoes this attitude, referring to the Maid in such terms as 'fell, banning hag, enchantress', and shows her bargaining with fiends.

In 1428 the Dauphin's cause seemed lost. The English appeared invincible, their continuing victories proof that God was with them, while it was unthinkable that Burgundians could ever be reconciled with Armagnacs. The Dauphinists' worst handicap was the character of their leader, Charles VII as he styled himself without conviction, who even at thirty showed no signs of being a late developer. As usual Perroy has a particularly convincing portrait. 'Physically and mentally, Charles was a weakling, a graceless degenerate. He was stunted and puny, with a blank face in which scared, shifty, sleepy eyes, peering out on either side of a big, long nose, failed to animate his harsh, unpleasant features.' Charles was afflicted by strange fears; he disliked entering houses, frightened they might fall on him (after one did so at La Rochelle) and he would never cross a wooden bridge. So shaken was he by his mother's smear that he was a bastard, that he seriously considered abdication. He left government to a series of greedy favourites who were too busy quarrelling with each other to have any time for fighting the English.

Moreover, there was something sinister about his fugitive court. The first of Charles's favourites, a poisoner and wife-murderer (and also a former lover of Queen Isabeau), was dragged naked from a new spouse's bed and drowned in a river; before dying he frantically begged his assassins to cut off his right hand which he had pledged to the Devil. A second favourite, Le Camus, was clubbed to death and his hand was similarly chopped off to stop it raising the Fiend. (As had been done with Duke John of Burgundy on the bridge at Montereau.) This would have been no surprise to a court which included Marshal Gilles de Rais, the Satanist and child-murderer. The King himself was obsessed with forbidden astrology and prophesy, a taste which seriously worried his confessors and attracted charges of heresy. (Such a man as Charles could only too easily have suspected that Joan of Arc, with her gift of foretelling the future, was a sorceress.) Perhaps the most sinister figure of all was the chief favourite, the gross and murderous La Trémoille, who ruled Charles and whose sole concern was to acquire as much money as possible.

Yet there were healthier elements in Charles's entourage. His mother-in-law Yolanda of Sicily was a sensible and steadying influence, as later was his mistress Agnes Sorel. There were some useful soldiers, such as Poton de Xaintrailles, Etienne de Vignolles (better known as La Hire) and the Bastard of Orleans. The foremost was the Constable de Richemont (the future Duke Arthur III of Brittany) so hideously disfigured by facial wounds received at Agincourt that he looked like a frog. He entered the King's service in 1425 and eventually overthrew La Trémoille. Richemont developed into a formidable commander and was supported by a small band of faithful Bretons which included the Marshal André de Laval and the Admiral Prégent de Coëtivy.

It was also true that Dauphinist France was much richer than Lancastrian France. Where the Regent's revenue averaged from 100,000 to 200,000 *livres* a year, Charles's potential revenue was three and sometimes five times as much, partly because the area under his control was larger and less devastated. However, in the early years of the King of Bourges his taxes were not properly collected or else went into other pockets, and he was so poor that his clothes had to be patched. Charles VII had both the men and the money to fight the English, but it would take a miracle to make him do so.

Joan of Arc was born about 1412 in a village called Domrémy on the Meuse in eastern Champagne. As a girl she worked as a cowherd and differed from her companions only in her piety, spending long hours in the parish church.

She saw visions, and from the age of thirteen heard voices which eventually told her to go and rescue Orleans. In May 1428 her uncle took her to a Dauphinist stronghold, where the captain was unimpressed. However, she returned the following January; the captain then sent her to the Dauphin and in February she met Charles at Chinon. Although he hid among his courtiers she at once recognized him and told him that God had ordered her to fight the English and to see that he was crowned at Rheims. The Dauphin was doubtful about the peasant girl dressed like a man—in the fifteenth century this was probably even more shocking than male transvestism in the early twentieth—but the theologians who then examined her detected no signs of heresy or insanity, and advised Charles to let her try at Orleans.

Joan had already dictated an extraordinary letter to the Regent and his officers. 'Jhesus Maria', it began, 'King of England and you Duke of Bedford [Bethforth] calling yourself Regent of France; William de la Pole, Earl of Suffolk, John, Lord Talbot and you Thomas, Lord Scales, calling yourselves Lieutenants of the said Bedford . . . deliver up to the Maid sent by God, the King of Heaven, the keys of all the good towns which you have taken and violated in France.' She explained: 'I have been sent by the King of Heaven to throw you out of all France,' and ended: 'Take yourself off to your own land, for God's sake, or else await tidings from the Maid whom you will soon see to your hurt.' No chronicler has recorded Bedford's reaction to the letter.

The Maid set out for Orleans at once, wearing armour, with an army of 4,000 men under the young Duke of Alençon who believed fervently in her mission. As has been seen, she entered Orleans at the end of April. On 3 May the main body of her relief force reached the city. Joan rode in at their head, accompanied by priests chanting psalms; she was claiming the divine support which the English regarded as their special prerogative. Within a few days her troops had overrun the main English earthworks and recaptured the Tourelles, killing the garrison including Glasdale. On 8 May 1429, after an investment which had lasted ninety

days, the Earl of Suffolk raised the siege. The outnumbered
English made a last defiant gesture to show that God was on
their side ; they paraded in battle formation on open ground
opposite the walls, challenging the defenders to come out
and fight, but even now the enemy dared not face them.
Suffolk then marched off in excellent order, taking a detachment to Jargeau and sending the remainder to Meung and
Beaugency under Lord Talbot and Lord Scales.

Dauphinist morale rose wonderfully and Alençon's army
immediately set about the English strongholds on the Loire.
On 12 June Jargeau was stormed, Suffolk being caught as he
tried to flee, while—apart from those worth good ransoms—
his garrison were put to the sword. The bridge over the river
at Meung was captured three days later ; at Beaugency the
English had to take refuge in the citadel.

Lord Talbot was determined to relieve the Beaugency
garrison. He joined Sir John Fastolf at Janville, their combined forces amounting to little more than 3,000 men ; the
Dauphinists had 8,000 but on past form these were far from
impossible odds. Fastolf, however, was uneasy and did not
trust his Parisian militia (or *Faux Français* as the Dauphinists termed them) ; he wanted to fall back and wait for fresh
troops who were expected daily. But the aggressive Talbot
insisted on advancing. Then on Saturday 18 June news
came that the citadel at Beaugency had surrendered and
the English began to retreat through the woods towards
the village of Patay. Joan told the Dauphinist commanders
to attack—'You have spurs, so use them !'—and promised
that they would win a victory greater than Charles had ever
known. Nevertheless, their scouts could not find the English
until they heard them cheering when a stag broke cover.
Talbot, realizing that the enemy was near, began to form up
his archers south of Patay in a dip while Fastolf tried to
position his militia on rising ground behind him. Without
warning Dauphinist men-at-arms suddenly appeared at the
top of the dip and charged down the slope into the flank of
Talbot's archers as they were still fixing their stakes, and
overwhelmed them. Fastolf's levies thereupon bolted. Talbot

and Lord Scales were captured though Fastolf and a band of archers managed to escape, beating off their pursuers. After a gruelling march Sir John reached Corbeil on the following day, where he had to report the defeat to the Regent in person. Monstrelet says Bedford was so angry that he took away Fastolf's Garter, and a legend grew up which branded the unfortunate knight as a coward—later Shakespeare transformed him into Sir John Falstaff. Yet Fastolf had advised against confronting the Dauphinists, had done his best to rally the troops and had at least saved some of them. In the event, Bedford soon restored his Garter and made him Lieutenant of Caen.

Joan was now at the height of her fame. Monstrelet tells us how after Patay all Dauphinists believed that the English and Burgundians were powerless against her. Instead of marching on Paris she persuaded the Dauphin to accompany her to Rheims to be crowned. Somehow an army of 12,000 men was assembled and then marched through English territory to Rheims where Charles was consecrated King of France; Joan stood near him throughout the ceremony, holding her white banner, and afterwards she addressed him as King for the first time. (Yet it is arguable that both Charles and the Archbishop who anointed him believed she was a witch.) The coronation of Charles VII, as we must now call him, did wonders for Dauphinist morale; according to Monstrelet, a Burgundian: 'The French believed that God was against the English.'

It is impossible to know whether Joan's inspiration was restricted to a small circle of court soldiers or if—as today's social romantics would like to think—she spoke to the rank and file as one peasant to another. What is undeniable is that for a few months many Frenchmen thought they were fighting a holy war, and the English went in terror of the Maid and her sorceries.

The Dauphinist expedition to Rheims gave Bedford a breathing-space. When Charles's army marched on Paris the Regent was ready, and after some slight skirmishes made it fall back in August; he did his best to provoke Charles into fighting, sending a letter addressed to 'You who call yourself King' which accused him of consorting with 'a disorderly and disgraced woman wearing the dress of a man'. But the Dauphinists refused battle. The Parisians stayed loyal to the Regent; no doubt they still feared reprisals if the Armagnacs entered their city. On the afternoon of 8 September Joan led an assault on the walls between the Porte Saint-Honoré and the Porte Saint-Denis; it was not properly supported by Charles's commanders and, though the outer ditch was crossed, the attackers failed to get over the inner moat and retreated in disorder. The Maid, wounded in the thigh by a crossbow quarrel, was left lying in the open until nightfall; the commanders made no attempt to rescue her, perhaps hoping she would perish. The legend of her invincibility had been broken. Charles retired to Gien, dismissing his army. Nevertheless Bedford was so alarmed by Joan's offensive that he temporarily gave up the Regency of France (save Normandy) to Philip of Burgundy, together with the governorship of Paris.

The Maid began to campaign again in October. She took Saint-Pierre-le-Moutier on the upper Loire, but failed to capture the nearby town of La Charité. She was not always merciful; on at least one occasion she ordered the beheading of an enemy commander who had been taken prisoner. In May 1430 she moved to Compiègne. During a skirmish outside the town on 24 May she was plucked from her charger by a Burgundian soldier. Monstrelet noted that the English and the Burgundians 'were much more excited than if they had captured 500 fighting men, for they had never been so afraid of any captain or commander in war as they had been of the Maid'. In November Joan was handed over to the English. At Rouen she received rough treatment from Warwick's soldiers—they tried to rape her, and Lord Stafford actually drew a dagger on the girl.

Joan's trial began on 21 February the following year after a lengthy and unscrupulous investigation by canon lawyers. The prosecution's case (no doubt with rumours about Charles VII in mind) was that this 'false soothsayer' had rejected the authority of the Church in claiming a personal revelation from God, in prophesying, in signing her letters with the names of Christ and the Virgin, and in asserting that she was assured of salvation. These not unreasonable accusations were accompanied by lesser charges, such as her sexual perversity in wearing male dress—'a thing displeasing and abominable to God'—and her insistence that the saints spoke French and not English. The entire justification of the Lancastrian right to the French throne was at stake : she had to be found guilty. After much bullying, trickery and misrepresentation the lawyers trapped her, and on 30 May 1431 she was burnt by Warwick's soldiers in the market-place at Rouen as a relapsed heretic. She died quickly and the executioner pulled the charred corpse out of the fire so that people could see that it was that of a woman. She was only nineteen.

King Charles had made no attempt to save her. However, twenty years later he ordered an enquiry, and eventually the Papacy annulled the sentence. She was not canonized until 1920. For at least two centuries the English remained convinced that she was a witch; as Bedford wrote, in a letter to the Duke of Burgundy, she had 'turned away the hearts of many men and women from the truth, and turned them towards fables and lies'.

Joan's execution made little stir. However, since then the sorceress maid from Domrémy has aroused far greater interest than in her own short day. In the 1460s François Villon referred to Joan among other of the world's famous women :

> *Et Jehanne la bonne Lorraine*
> *Qu'Englois brulèrent à Rouen*

and from Voltaire to Shaw to our own day, a surprising range of gifted writers have been fascinated by this Catholic saint. In France some traditionalist Frenchmen still consider veneration of their *petite pucelle* to be one of the hallmarks of a true patriot. In a different way she inspires no less devotion in England and America. Nevertheless she failed in her mission.

The Regent saved the dual monarchy through sheer determination. It was a very near thing, for although Charles was incapable of exploiting the situation, towns all over northern France had opened their gates to his supporters; English Champagne was lost and Maine looked like going the same way. There were even risings in Normandy, where between 1429 and 1431 Bedford had his headquarters, in Rouen at a modest *hôtel* ironically named *Joyeux Repos*. English troops deserted in large numbers, some making for the Channel ports, in the hope of finding a passage to England, while others became bandits. Luckily, Philip of Burgundy was impressed by the fact that the English had held Paris, and until he had complete control of Hainault and Holland—which he did not achieve until 1433 —he was nervous of losing the Regent's friendship.

The English had to pay heavily for such support. Between 1429 and 1431 Philip obtained £150,000 from them for his services and was owed a further £100,000. After 1431 he was paid a monthly pension of 3,000 francs (about £330). In addition in March 1430 the English ceded Champagne to him—though this was already occupied by Dauphinists— together with 50,000 gold *saluts* (Anglo-French gold crowns minted at Rouen), in return for military assistance against the Dauphinists for two months.

Slowly the Regent restored the situation. Château Gaillard was recovered in June 1430, and the English continued to regain ground everywhere throughout 1431. In March Bedford himself retook Colummiers, Gourlay-sur-Marne and Montjoy; at the same time the Earl of Warwick annihilated a raiding force which had tried to ambush the Regent, capturing its commander Poton de Xaintrailles, together with a shepherd boy who was supposed to be Joan's successor (he deliberately bloodied his hands and feet in imitation of St Francis's stigmata). In October Louviers fell to Bedford, after a siege of nine months. The Duke of Burgundy was not so successful, losing territory to the Dauphinists.

The impetus generated by Joan's revivalism had ground to a halt. The apathy of the Dauphinists is understandable enough. It was not simply because of the supine nature of the man who was the leader and the symbol of Valois France, but because more fighting meant more devastation. Basin wrote how 'from the Loire to the Seine the peasants had been slain or put to flight'. The bishop continued : 'We ourselves have seen the vast plains of Champagne, of the Beauce, of the Brie, of the Gâtinais, Chartres, Dreux, Maine and Perche, of the Vexin (French as well as Norman), the Beauvaisis, the Pays de Caux, from the Seine as far as Amiens and Abbeville, the countryside round Senlis, Soissons and Valois right to Laon and beyond towards Hainault absolutely deserted, uncultivated, abandoned, empty of inhabitants, covered with scrub and brambles ; indeed in most of the more thickly wooded districts dense forests were growing up.'

The capital itself was in a frightful state. As a result of interrupted communications and exposed supply routes, together with harassment by brigands and peasants, many Parisians were starving, while travellers were ambushed by raiding parties lurking outside the city. At night wolves continued to prowl the streets, looking for dead bodies or children. Thousands left in despair. Now that Burgundy had relinquished his governorship Bedford could act, and on the last day of January 1431 he returned to Paris '*en très belle compagnie*', bringing up with him seventy barges laden with food. The Bourgeois records how Parisians said that 'for 400 years people had never seen so much to eat'. But it was only a drop in an ocean, and the famine became even worse, the price of wheat doubling. The Parisians 'often cursed the Duke, not only in private but in public as well, giving way to despair and ceasing to believe in his fine promises'.

Bedford decided to play his trump card. At the end of November the nine-year-old 'Henri II' arrived at Saint-Denis and on 2 December made his *joyeuse entrée* into the capital of his Kingdom of France. Yellow-haired and in cloth of gold, he rode on a white charger through the icy streets to be greeted by the Provost and the Councillors of the

Parlement in their red satin. Although starving, the Parisians gave the King a tumultuous welcome, crying 'Nowell'; obviously they hoped for a rich bounty from the royal largesse. On Sunday 16 December he went on foot to Notre-Dame, accompanied by citizens who sang melodiously. A huge dais had been erected in front of the choir, its steps painted sky-blue and studded with golden fleur-de-lys, and here Henry was anointed King of France by Cardinal Beaufort. Alas, Beaufort, who was in charge of the proceedings, ruined everything by tactlessness, ill-management and parsimony. The Bishop of Paris, whose cathedral it was, had to take a back seat, while the service was conducted according to the English Sarum rite and not the Gallican usage of France, and a silver-gilt chalice was stolen by English officers. The coronation banquet was little better than a riot. The Paris mob forced its way into the Hôtel des Tournelles 'some to see, others to devour and others still to steal', and in the end the representatives of the University and the *Parlement* and the aldermen gave up trying to throw them out; those who managed to find something to eat learnt with horror that the food had been cooked the preceding Thursday, 'which appeared very strange to Frenchmen'. Later the sick at the Hôtel-Dieu complained they had never known such a poor and meagre bounty. In the Bourgeois's view, Paris had seen merchants' marriages which had been 'of more profit to the jewellers, goldsmiths and other purveyors of luxury than this coronation of a King, with all its jousts and Englishmen'. Henry left Paris the day after Christmas, without having pardoned any prisoners or abolished any taxes as was customary. 'One heard nobody, in private or in public, commend his stay and yet no King was ever more honoured than he had been at his *joyeuse entrée* or at his consecration, especially when one considers the depopulation of Paris, the evil times and that it was full winter and how dear was food.' Instead of making the régime popular, the coronation had merely infuriated the Parisians.

Beaufort had now upset even Bedford. The Cardinal

insisted that he must resign his Regency while the King was present. Not only was it an insult but it prevented Bedford from correcting Beaufort's mistakes and from curbing his arrogance.

Undoubtedly Bedford was unusual among contemporary Englishmen in his genuine affection for the French. 'For though the English ruled Paris for a very long time, I do honestly believe that there was not one of them who had any corn or oats sown or so much as a fireplace built in a house, save for the Regent, the Duke of Bedford,' the Bourgeois informs us. 'He was always building wherever he went ; his nature was quite un-English, for he never wanted to make war on anyone, whereas in truth the English are always wanting to wage war on their neighbours without cause. Which is why they all die an evil death.' The Bourgeois was not the only Frenchman to respect the Regent. Basin admits that Normandy was better cultivated and more highly populated than the rest of northern France because of Bedford, who was 'courageous, humane and just'. He adds that the Regent 'was very fond of those French lords who obeyed him and took care to reward them according to their deserts. As long as he lived the Normans and the Frenchmen in this part of the realm had a great liking for him.'

In 1432 the English position began to deteriorate noticeably. On the night of 3 February a force of 120 Dauphinists scaled the walls of the *Grosse Tour* of the citadel at Rouen with ladders let down by a traitor and seized the great fortress. Though the Rouennais stayed loyal and within a fortnight the enemy surrendered (to be beheaded), it was nonetheless a serious blow to English prestige. In March, on the eve of Palm Sunday, some Dauphinists entered Chartres hidden in provision wagons and took the city after a fierce battle in the streets ; the English lost an important source of supplies for Paris.

In May, anxious to regain the initiative, the Regent laid siege to Lagny, a fortress which commanded the Marne and whose garrison was continually ambushing convoys on their way to Paris. The town was strongly fortified, guarded

The Beauchamp chapel at Warwick, built by Earl Richard from a fortune
which owed much to the French wars.

Royal plunder. The Cup of the Kings of France and England, made for
Charles V c. 1380, was in Bedford's hands by the 1430s and was later taken
to England.

on two sides by the Marne, so Bedford blockaded it. A relief army under the Bastard of Orleans and the Castilian mercenary Rodrigo de Villandrando arrived on 9 August; no doubt the Bastard hoped to use the tactics he had employed at Montargis five years earlier.

On 10 August, a day of blazing heat, the Dauphinists tried to fight their way into Lagny and the besiegers tried to stop them. The struggle centred round a redoubt which defended the west gate; the English left wing captured it, but when their right wing was routed the Bastard attacked them and the townsmen joined in, the redoubt being retaken by the enemy. The Regent led another ferocious assault on the redoubt to stop Dauphinist wagons entering the city, and the fight surged backwards and forwards. At 4 o'clock Bedford reluctantly gave the order to disengage; the confused, untidy battle had lasted eight hours, several of his troops had died from heat-stroke and every man-at-arms, including himself, was exhausted—dehydrated, choked by dust, blinded by sweat, stunned and deafened by blows. (It is probable that Bedford's exertions damaged his health permanently.) He had lost only 300 men but had suffered a moral defeat. He was further discouraged by a sudden change in the weather which brought heavy rain and caused the Marne to flood. When the Bastard made a feint as if to march on Paris, Bedford decided he had had enough and on 13 August raised the siege, abandoning his artillery.

At the end of 1432 the Regent's wife, Anne of Burgundy, fell ill. She died in Paris on 14 November. According to the Bourgeois she had been the most agreeable of all ladies in France—'bonne, belle et jeune'—and Monstrelet says that Bedford 'had at heart very great sorrow'. Moreover, in the current situation it was political disaster. Wavrin explains that the English and all those Frenchmen who supported the dual monarchy 'feared that because of this unhappy event the love and alliance which had existed for a long time between her husband and Duke Philip of Burgundy, who had loved her very dearly, would grow somewhat cold'. No doubt wishing to ally himself with another powerful

Burgundian family, Bedford remarried in April the following year, despite his sorrow. His new wife was Jacquetta of Luxembourg. Duke Philip was angered by this marriage to the daughter of one of his richest nobles and best generals, which had taken place without his consent.

The only thing that saved Bedford now was the poverty of the Dauphin, who was unable to exploit his superior revenues and mount a really formidable offensive. But Burgundy, in complete control of Hainault and Holland, feared a possible alliance between Charles and the Emperor and was also nervous of a compromise agreement between Charles and the English. He himself began to make tentative diplomatic approaches to the Dauphinists. In June 1433 he sent envoys to England to explore the possibilities of a general settlement; they received a very cold reception. Philip was not deterred, and he was helped by the activities of the Papal Legate, Cardinal Niccolò Albergati, who had been working for peace since 1430.

In June 1433 the Regent returned to England, to deny before Parliament rumours that he was incompetent and neglectful. He did so to such effect that in November the Commons complimented him on his management of affairs in France where, they claimed, he enjoyed obedience 'right tender, young and green', and they noted how he had 'exposed his person to the labour and adventure of war, as the poorest knight or gentleman there in the King's service, and achieved many great and fair things, worthy to be had in perpetual remembrance; and especially the battle of Verneuil, which was the greatest deed done by Englishmen in our days, save the battle of Agincourt'. Both Houses begged Bedford to stay in England as the King's chief counsellor. He accepted. Yet, despite his popularity, he was unable to extract fresh money for the War which had now come to be regarded as a burden.

Bedford ordered a careful investigation into the royal finances. This revealed that the deficit for 1433 was nearly £22,000, and that £57,000 had been spent on war; total debts amounted to £64,000—almost three times the annual revenue. He at once cut down the pay of officials, including his own, and begged Parliament—unsuccessfully —to vote a yearly sum which would remove the threat of state bankruptcy. The agricultural depression and a decline in overseas trade had lessened the yield from taxation, and diminished revenues were a far greater threat to the Lancastrian dual monarchy than any Joan of Arc.

The War was much more expensive than it had been in Edward III's time. Armour and weapons were increasingly elaborate, while large numbers of the new big guns had become indispensable for siege warfare both in attack and defence. Moreover the maintenance of garrisons was a constant drain: Calais alone cost nearly £17,000, half the government's total revenue. It required a peace-time strength of 780 men, raised to 1,150 in war-time. Again and again Captains of Calais had to pay starving troops out of their own pockets; there was a mutiny in 1431 and another in 1441. There must have been similar mutinies in many garrisons. A significant number of men deserted and became brigands.

Yet there was no difficulty in finding soldiers if one had the money to pay them. Every English magnate possessed his own private army, recruited from what has been described as 'a new and potentially dangerous type of semi-noble' who had acquired a little wealth and status during the War and who was paid wages. Such armies were often surprisingly large; in 1453 the Earl of Devon, waging a personal war in the West country against Lord Bonville (a former Seneschal of Guyenne), is said to have mustered 800 horse and 4,000 foot. Troops like this were far from untried; violence was part of everyday life under the weak régime of Henry VI, and readers of *The Paston Letters* will know how often great men had recourse to armed robbery and intimidation. Even so, the best pickings were still to be had in France.

A partnership document between two of the new semi-nobles, the esquires John Winter and Nicholas Molyneux, has survived from 1421. They swore in a church at Harfleur to be 'brothers in arms'. Should one be taken prisoner the other must ransom him, providing the money needed did not exceed 6,000 gold *saluts* (£1,000). If it were more, the one who remained free was to surrender himself as a hostage for the other to go home and raise the additional money. More optimistically they promised to share 'all the profits [from war] which by God's grace they shall gain', and to send them back to London for safe-keeping in a coffer at a church in Cheapside of which each had a key; 'in which coffer shall be kept such gold, silver and plate as each or both of them may wish to keep to purchase lands in the realm of England'. When they retired everything was to be divided between them. If one were killed, the survivor was to inherit the whole, but must allow a sixth to his brother's widow and pay for his children's schooling, allowing them £20 a year for life. The partnership prospered. As late as 1436 they were still sending money home to buy manors and even bought a pub—the Boar's Head in Southwark (something of a medieval Claridges), which Winter seems to have managed. Molyneux obtained a lucrative post at Rouen—Master of the *Chambre des Comptes*—and when Normandy fell was able to salvage something from the wreck.

The year 1434 began well for the English, the Earl of Arundel operating with considerable success in Anjou and Maine as far as the Loire. Lord Talbot—who had been exchanged for Poton de Xaintrailles—was even more successful, taking Gisors, Joigny, Beaumont, Creil, Clermont and Saint-Valery. But Lord Scales and Lord Willoughby failed to overcome the indomitable garrison of Mont-Saint-Michel.

Then Bedford received a letter from the Provost of Paris, saying that unless he came back soon the capital was lost. When he returned in July he was greeted with news of a general rising by the Norman peasants against English garrisons; even Caen and Bayeux were threatened. It had been provoked by Richard Venables (see p. 194), who had massacred the entire village of Vicques near Falaise. Raising a special subsidy from the Estates, the Regent organized a full-scale military operation against Venables who, with his second-in-command Waterhouse, was captured, brought to Rouen and hanged. Bedford hoped that this would reassure the peasants, but in August another English band perpetrated a similar massacre at the village of Saint-Pierre-sur-Dives. The peasants fought on, using against the English the weapons supplied to them by the Regent for their protection. Eventually he managed to crush them, but it must have been a sad blow to find such enmity in a province which was the heart of the dual monarchy.

More money was needed desperately. The Regent summoned the Estates of Normandy, beseeching their help, and they voted 344,000 *livres tournois*, more than ever before, but even this was not enough. The garrisons alone were costing 250,000 *livres* a year, while there were expenses arising from the peasants' revolt—Arundel and the troops putting them down had to be paid. Even before he had left England, Bedford had submitted a thoroughly gloomy report to the Council, pointing out that 'the press of war' had driven the peasants 'to an extreme poverty such as they may not long endure' because they dared not plough their lands, tend their vines or feed their livestock. But even so he was not without hope, stressing that the French of the dual monarchy were by and large loyal to King Henry. 'Throughout the years of my service there I have found the multitude of your subjects there as well disposed and as desirous to keep their faith and truth to your Highness as any people ever was.' He suggested three positive measures. First, that the Duchy of Lancaster's revenues (separate from those of the Crown) should be diverted to the French war, and in particular to maintaining 200 men-at-arms and 600 archers. Second, that the garrisons of Calais and the Calais March, who were not in the front line, should be combined and employed as a mobile reserve. Third, that provided that these two proposals were adopted, he would maintain another 200 men-at-arms and another 600 archers from his personal resources.

In December Bedford returned to Paris where the misery was greater than ever and a further terrible winter had set in —'day and night the snow never stopped falling . . . never were frost and snow so bitter'. The vines and the fruit trees perished. Wine, flour and all food were impossibly dear. The city was now so depopulated that empty houses were being pulled down for firewood. In February 1435 the Regent left Paris for the last time.

The Duke of Burgundy was now preparing to withdraw his support from the English. He was anxious not to appear treacherous, so his lawyers found a legal quibble in the Treaty of Troyes : Henry V, they said, could have handed down the French Crown had he inherited it himself, but his son could not inherit it directly from Charles VI. In February 1435 Philip of Burgundy met the Duke of Bourbon and other Dauphinists at Nevers, where with noticeable friendliness it was agreed that a conference between Burgundians, Dauphinists and English should be held at Arras in the summer to arrange a general settlement.

Philippe Contamine makes the point that the Hundred Years War saw quite as many conferences as it did battles, sieges and *chevauchées*. These usually took place at a border town, such as Leulinghen or Gravelines, or at somewhere neutral like Avignon, though occasionally they were held in one of the protagonist's territories and even in London or Paris. Often the delegations of both sides were led by a Prince of the Blood, who brought a large staff of officials and a vast retinue of servants, together with wagon-loads of furniture, plate and provisions. There were formal orations in Latin, public banquets and private interviews in addition to round-table negotiations.

When the congress at Arras began in August, Bedford who was seriously ill at Rouen, was ready to make territorial concessions but would not compromise on his nephew's claim to the throne of France ; the English envoys were instructed to state that this was a matter too sacred for discussion— Henry derived his right from God. The Regent also insisted that Normandy belonged to King Henry and could not be held as a fief from Charles. On 5 September, after six weeks of debate during which Philip argued so energetically that the sweat ran down his face, Cardinal Beaufort led the entire English delegation out of Arras without having reached any agreement. They suspected, with justice, that 'King Charles and the Duke of Burgundy were growing cordial towards each other'.

Just over a week later, on 14 September 1435, John, Duke of Bedford died at Rouen. 'Noble in birth and worth ; wise, liberal, feared and loved', was the epitaph bestowed on him by the Bourgeois of Paris. The Regent is generally pitied by historians as a gifted statesman and soldier who wasted his life in a futile endeavour. Yet he might well have succeeded. The Dauphin very nearly abdicated, and had he done so the next Valois claimant, Charles of Orleans, was a prisoner in England. Moreover if Duke Philip had been clear-sighted he would surely have realized that his best hope lay with the English, for a strong Valois monarchy must inevitably destroy Burgundy. The structure which Bedford built with such limited resources was strong enough to survive his death by fifteen years. Beyond question he was a very remarkable, indeed a very great, Anglo-Frenchman.

The Regent was buried under a fine tomb in the chancel of the Cathedral of Notre-Dame in his beloved city of Rouen. Many years later someone suggested to Charles VII's son that the monument should be demolished. Louis XI replied : 'In his lifetime neither my father nor yours, for all their might, could make him budge one foot . . . Let his body rest.' The King added : 'I account it an honour to have him remain in my domains.' The tomb has long since vanished, but Bedford still lies in Rouen Cathedral.

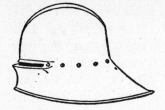

10

'Sad Tidings' 1435–1450

Sad tidings bring I to you out of France,
Of loss, of slaughter and discomfiture.

King Henry VI

And this same Wednesday was it told
that Shirburgh is goon and we have not
now a foote of londe in Normandie.

The Paston Letters

On 20 September 1435, less than a week after Bedford's death, Charles VII and Philip of Burgundy signed the Treaty of Arras. In return for recognizing Charles as King of France, Philip received Macon, Auxerre and Ponthieu, together with the Somme towns and the royal lands north of that river (all territories which he already occupied). Charles ended his alliance with the Emperor and formally denied any part in the murder of Philip's father, promising to punish the surviving assassins. He also agreed to erect a monument to the late Duke and have Masses said for his soul. In effect he abandoned what was left of the Armagnac party; France was to be made whole, and later an edict ordered that anyone found guilty of using the names 'Burgundian' or 'Armagnac' should have his tongue pierced with a red-hot iron.

The Treaty was to prove a terrible mistake for the Burgundians—it meant not only the ruin of the dual monarchy but ultimately that of Burgundy too. Perhaps Philip thought Charles VII would be more dependent on him than Henry VI; if so, he miscalculated, for Charles hated him. The two advisers who persuaded the Duke to abandon the English, Nicholas Rolin and Anthoine de Croy, were undoubtedly in Charles's pay. One day Philip was to realize his blunder and marry his only (legitimate) son to an English princess.

England was shattered by Duke Philip's betrayal. When Henry VI received a letter from him in which he was not addressed as Philip's sovereign, the tears rolled down his cheeks. In London, mobs lynched Philip's merchants and sang rude songs about the 'false, forsworn Duke'. Counsellors like Cardinal Beaufort knew very well that the country could not continue the War against such odds, but did not see how to end it without enraging all England—the claim to the French throne might have been abandoned in exchange for Normandy and Guyenne in full sovereignty, if only Henry V had not made such a compromise morally impossible. The realism of Beaufort—the 'luxury-loving prelate who was the favourite of the aristocracy' as Perroy terms him—may have been preferred by certain magnates, but the House of Commons supported the Duke of Gloucester who led a War party. The 'Good Duke Humphrey', affable and charming, was also the darling of the London mob. Although frivolous and unstable, he had none the less fought at Agincourt and played an important role in the conquest of Normandy, and the 'son, brother and uncle of Kings' (as he signed himself) was both senior Prince of the Blood and heir presumptive. His position was made even stronger by Bedford's death. But in 1435 Henry VI came of age at sixteen. He was completely under the thumb of the Beauforts and henceforward, despite loud protests, Gloucester had little influence on government policy.

The successor of Henry V and Bedford was a lanky, gangling, awkward youth with a pointed chin and mournful, worried eyes, weak in body and mind. Infinitely well-intentioned, gentle, pious and even saintly, he would have been far happier as an obscure monk. Detesting violence and cruelty, averse to any form of bloodshed, no man could have been less suited to late-medieval kingship. But he was as incapable of leading his country in peace as he was in war, for he had no understanding at all of politics or state-craft, and was a liability to the men who tried to govern for him.

The years from 1435 to 1450 constitute a protracted rearguard action by the English in France, and it is astonishing that they managed to hold on for so long after being deserted by the Burgundians. It took a reunited France to drive them out of the Ile de France completely, and when Charles VII at last rode into Rouen, Normandy had been English for thirty years—as though the German occupation of France had lasted until 1970. The English people now regarded Normandy and Calais almost as integral parts of their own country. When the end came it shocked all England and brought down the government of the day. The dynastic dispute had turned into a national struggle.

Soon after the Treaty of Arras there were risings all over Anglo-French territory. Dieppe, Fécamp and Harfleur fell to the enemy, Arques went up in flames. In February 1436 the Constable de Richemont with the Bastard of Orleans, Marshal de L'Isle Adam and 5,000 men blockaded Paris, still held by the English, and contacted Burgundian supporters inside the city, which was once again threatened with famine. The English garrison under Lord Willoughby —the Bourgeois calls him the 'Sire de Huillebit'—was weakened at Easter by 300 desertions, and the militia refused to man the walls. The starving Parisians began to riot, and on 13 April let down ladders to admit the Bastard with some picked troops who opened the gates. English archers were too late to stop them; they had run through the empty streets, trying to cow the city by shooting at ominously shuttered windows, but when they found their way barred by chains and were fired on by cannon, they took refuge with the rest of the garrison in the Bastille. The houses of the English community were broken into and their contents plundered. The Constable replaced the city's senior officials, though otherwise there was a general amnesty. Shortly afterwards Willoughby—a veteran of Harfleur and Agincourt—was allowed to withdraw with his men 'by land and water' to Rouen, departing amid hoots and catcalls.

The French, who began to refer to their foes as 'English and Normans', attacked up to the gates of Rouen. Yet Maine held, with a string of fortresses which shielded Normandy. King Charles, still poverty-stricken and as timid as ever, proved incapable of mounting an adequate offensive.

In July 1436 Burgundian troops began a siege of Calais. However, they failed to blockade it and the garrison's sorties first demoralized the besiegers, then panicked them into flight by the end of the month. On 2 August Humphrey of Gloucester landed with a relief force and led a most effective *chevauchée* against Burgundy, deep into Flanders, before returning in triumph to Calais. Many Flemish towns were encouraged to revolt against Philip, involving him in a struggle which continued until 1438. By then he was only too anxious to make peace with England, and in 1439 he concluded a truce—with commercial clauses—which lasted for many years.

If the English were unable to produce another Bedford or another Salisbury, they still possessed a formidable commander in the dashing Lord Talbot.

John, sixth Lord Talbot, Earl of Shrewsbury and Waterford, Knight of the Garter and Count of Clermont, had been born about 1388. A scion of a long line of marcher lords on the Welsh border, he inherited a savage tradition and his first years as a soldier were spent fighting Owain Glyndŵr. In 1414 Henry V made him Lord Lieutenant in Ireland where he harried the wild kern amid their bogs and forests. Talbot's French campaigns began in 1419; he was present at the siege of Melun in 1420 and at that of Meaux the following year, and later he fought at Verneuil. After a

second term in Ireland he returned to France but, as has
been seen, he was taken prisoner at Patay and spent four
years in captivity. Since then 'Old Talbot' had caught the
popular imagination with his string of victories. A portrait
at Compton Wynyates shows an oddly modern face with
strongly marked features beneath thick black hair. Impressive in manner, he was obviously afraid of nothing and his
men worshipped him. While possessing an enviable grasp
of strategy he had a curiously erratic sense of tactics. A
master of the surprise attack, the raid and the skirmish, who
knew just one order—'Forward!'—Talbot was really a
dashing English version of du Guesclin, though without
the Breton's caution. Indeed he was defeated at the only
two full-scale battles where he was in command. Nevertheless his opponents were terrified of him. The Irish lamented
'there came not from the time of King Herod anyone so
wicked in evil deeds'—and his name alone could make the
French retreat.

In February 1436 Talbot was joined by the new
Lieutenant-General of France—the enormously rich Duke
of York, a young man of twenty-four whose small size and
ugly features hardly matched his soaring ambition. If inde-
cisive and a poor soldier, York was none the less an ally of
Gloucester and a vigorous proponent of the War, and he
co-operated with Talbot to such effect that the latter soon
restored order in both Normandy and Maine. York himself
managed to recover Dieppe and a number of towns in the
Caux.

At the end of 1436 Poton de Xaintrailles and La Hire
appeared in front of Rouen with 1,000 troops, but the
citizens remained loyal and would not admit them. So they
established themselves in the little town of Ris, ten miles
away. Talbot, Sir Thomas Kyriell and 400 mounted men
galloped from Rouen to Ris as soon as they learnt where the
enemy was. They at once overran the French outposts on a
small hill above the town and the fleeing survivors spread
panic among their comrades; when Talbot charged into the
town there was no one to stop him, and he captured all the

enemy baggage and some valuable prisoners. In January 1437 he and the young Earl of Salisbury took Ivry. The following month, despite bitter winter weather and deep snow and with only 400 men, Talbot recaptured Pontoise twelve miles from Paris, sending in troops disguised as peasants to open a gate to a storming-party camouflaged in white. The French garrison fled, led by Talbot's former brother-in-arms, Marshal de L'Isle Adam. Talbot then appeared before Paris, where his men crossed the frozen moat and threatened to scale the city walls.

In the spring of 1437 the Earl of Warwick replaced the Duke of York as Lieutenant-General. Warwick was nearly sixty, at that time a ripe old age, but he still knew how to use Talbot. He sent him with 5,000 troops to relieve Le Crotoy on the north bank of the Somme estuary, which was besieged by twice that number of Burgundians. Talbot and his men waded across the famous ford of Blanche Taque a mile wide, although the water was chest-deep and the enemy had mounted cannon on the far bank. The Burgundians fled, abandoning their guns and baggage. Talbot also recovered Tancarville. Though Montereau, the last English fortress on the upper Seine, fell to the French in October, Paris was still so unsafe that when Charles made his *joyeuse entrée* he only dared stay there for three weeks.

In 1438 the French attacked Guyenne, the first serious invasion for nearly twenty years. At the same time the Castilian Rodrigo de Villandrando and his *écorcheurs* inflicted hideous devastation throughout the Guyennois countryside. Bordeaux was besieged but the enemy was short of cannon and soon retreated. Next year the Earl of Huntingdon recaptured all their gains.

Both sides again attempted to make peace. Significantly the King's ships were laid up by the English and left to rot; between 1437 and 1439 the derisory sum of £8 9s 7d was spent on them. Charles VII, for his part, was also discouraged; he had only recovered the Ile de France and even then, to the east of Paris, Meaux held out in Champagne. In July 1439 a conference met between Calais and

Gravelines, but the English still would not compromise over Henry's title of King of France, and the War continued.

The great business of 1440 was the release of the Duke of Orleans who had been a prisoner in England since Agincourt. Henry V had told Bedford never to release him, so that his services would be lost to France; and Gloucester was still fiercely opposed to letting him go, writing a long and angry 'declaration' to the King. Though most of the letter consisted of abuse of the Cardinal, his chief argument was that Orleans would become Regent and a most able one, as it was rumoured that Charles VII was ill. But Beaufort hoped Orleans might work for a general peace, and he may also have thought that the return of such a magnate would make France harder to govern. Moreover Orleans would fetch a valuable ransom—£40,000, one-third to be paid in advance. The money was collected by the Duchess of Burgundy who set up a fund and approached the entire French nobility; significantly King Charles did not contribute. Orleans was released in November 1440, promising to do his best to secure peace. The occasion was celebrated by a pontifical Mass on All Saints' Day, from which Gloucester stormed out angrily. In the event Orleans' political influence proved negligible and he retired to his châteaux to devote himself to his exquisite poetry and to good living. The English gained nothing apart from the ransom.

The War dragged on. The English had neglected to exploit Charles's weakness when the magnates rebelled against him in the *Praguerie* earlier in 1440. Warwick had died in April 1439, worn out by anxiety. He was buried in the splendid chapel he had built at Warwick, no doubt paid for by monies won in France, where his superb effigy in its Italian armour may still be seen. After a brief tenure by the Earl of Somerset, the Duke of York began a second term as Lieutenant-General in July 1440. Talbot, who in a brilliant night-attack had repulsed a French attempt to take Avranches the previous December, besieged Harfleur in August 1440 with only 1,000 men and captured it in October.

In 1441 King Charles took Creil and Conflans, and in June laid siege to Pontoise which still threatened Paris. York and Talbot at once marched to relieve Pontoise with 3,000 men. Talbot, the real commander, manœuvred brilliantly, unexpectedly crossing the Oise on a pontoon bridge of portable leather boats and frightening Charles into abandoning first his headquarters at Maubuisson and then Pontoise. After marching and counter-marching, crossing and recrossing the Seine and the Oise, and only just failing to trap the French, Talbot relieved and revictualled Pontoise which he is said to have 'refreshed' five times. But as soon as Talbot returned to Normandy, Charles and his gunner, Maître Bureau, recommenced the siege in September, quickly breaching the wall with their cannon. Pontoise finally fell on 25 October; Lord Clinton, the garrison commander, survived to be ransomed but 500 of his men were put to the sword. The last English stronghold in the Ile de France had gone.

In the summer of 1442 King Charles invaded Guyenne. He captured the castle of Tartas and the towns of Saint-Sever and Dax, and took prisoner Sir Thomas Rempston, the Seneschal of Gascony. La Réole also fell, but its garrison held out in the citadel. However, the French failed to take Bayonne, let alone Bordeaux as they had hoped, although they menaced the capital until the end of the year. The English Council could not make up its mind whether to send reinforcements to Guyenne or to Normandy. Eventually Talbot was sent to the northern duchy with a new army of 2,500 troops, but Bordeaux was left to fend for itself.

Talbot had been in England where he had received an enthusiastic reception and was made an Earl. He had been a national hero for many years; when he was captured at Patay in 1429 the fund for his ransom was widely subscribed. His triumphs in France were known throughout the land. Ordinary English people seem to have been surprisingly well informed about the progress of the War. Bishops were usually asked to pray for the success of major campaigns and then to hold services of thanksgiving or intercession (depending on the outcome); these were repeated at parish level and no doubt brought a certain amount of news. Great victories were celebrated by processions at St Paul's and other cathedrals. There were proclamations read out in market-squares and at county courts. Then there were the ballads, such as that composed on the discomfiture of the Burgundians at Calais in 1436. Nor must 'ale-house gossip' be despised; and a good deal of information must also have come via the retinues of the magnates, who kept open house. From the chroniclers it is clear that rumours were circulated by returned soldiers and were absorbed with avid interest.

The contemporary chroniclers' pride in English victories is (by way of Holinshed) echoed by Shakespeare. He makes a French nobleman ask:

Dieu de batailles! whence have they this mettle?
Is not their climate foggy, raw and dull?

He boasts of his nation's military superiority:

O noble English, that could entertain
With half their forces the full pride of France,
And let another half stand laughing by,
All out of work, and cold for action.

Indeed, *King Henry V*, despite anachronisms, accurately reflects how fifteenth-century Englishmen felt about the Hundred Years War.

In April 1443 Beaufort's nephew, John Earl of Somerset, was made Captain General of France and Guyenne. It was a political appointment, as the Cardinal wanted to overshadow York. To add insult to injury the Council coolly asked York to 'take patiens and forbere him for a tyme' about the £20,000 he had spent on the War from his own pocket. Somerset, one of the most incompetent commanders of the entire War, landed at Cherbourg with 7,000 troops and led a seemingly aimless *chevauchée* through Maine and into Brittany. He refused to tell his plans to his captains, saying fatuously : 'I will reveal my secret to no one. If my shirt knew my secret I would burn it.' (Basin comments that even his shirt was incapable of divining something which did not exist.) His one positive action was to seize the Breton town of La Guerche, which he only returned to its Duke for a cash payment ; it was not the best way of ensuring Brittany's neutrality. After a few weeks he returned to England where he found himself a laughing-stock and was banished from court. He died shortly afterwards, some said by his own hand.

Yet the idea of a *chevauchée* was not altogether foolish. In 1435 that old vulture Sir John Fastolf, realizing that England could no longer afford the expense of long sieges, had proposed that two small armies of 750 men each under good generals should be sent on *chevauchées* every year from June to November, 'burning and destroying all the lands as they pass, both house, corn, vines, and all trees that bearen fruit for man's sustenance', together with all livestock that could not be driven off. The object was to bring the enemy 'thereby to an extreme famine'. However, his advice was not taken and English strategy generally continued to centre round holding and retaking strongpoints.

Fastolf's career was one of the success stories of the Hundred Years War and is one of the best documented. He was born in 1380, the son of an esquire to Edward III. As a boy he was a page to the Duke of Norfolk. When he came of age in 1401 he inherited only a few farms near Caister and some tenements in Yarmouth, which gave him a total income of £46 a year. In 1409 he improved his finances by marrying Millicent Scrope, the elderly widow of a brother officer, but he gained more from the War, from offices, ransoms and loot. In 1413 he was made deputy constable of the castle and town of Bordeaux, in 1422 one of the King's Counsellors in France, at a salary of £110, a post which he held until he left France in 1440. He was later Grand Master of the Duke of Bedford's household. He held over

twenty offices at various towns, including the Captaincy of
Le Mans, the governorship of Maine and Anjou and finally
the governorship of the Channel Islands. After his retirement from active service at the age of sixty, the Council continued to consult him on military matters (though like many
other military advisers his advice does not seem to have been
taken). His most spectacular coup, the capture of the Duke
of Alençon at Verneuil in 1424, brought him prize-money
worth £13,000 and with some of this he built his castle at
Caister; its tower had five stories of fine, large rooms with
arcaded fireplaces and a summer and a winter hall with rich
tapestry hangings. In 1445 his properties in Normandy
were still worth £401 a year, though their value had been
reduced by enemy raids; they included ten castles, fifteen
manoirs and an inn at Rouen. He foresaw the loss of Normandy and sold some of them. Even after losing the
remainder, when he died in 1459 he was worth £1,450 a year
from his English estates, nearly all of which had been purchased with his profits of war. The little Norfolk squire, who
even at thirty-five had been only an esquire and household
man to the Duke of Clarence, had become a Knight of the
Garter, a French baron, and had he lived longer would
almost certainly have become an English baron as well. In
character he was typical of all too many English soldiers of
the period. 'Cruel and vengeable he hath been ever,' wrote a
contemporary who had crossed him, 'and for the most part
without pity or mercy.'

Both Fastolf and the humblest archer profited from the
systematic sharing of loot, which was strictly enforced.
Henry V's ordinance of 1419 had confirmed the existing
practice which continued until the very end of the War.
'All maner of captaynes, knyghtes, squyres, men of armes,
archers, what so euer they shall be bounde to paye the iijde
parte of all theyre gaynes in warre faithfully, and wythout
fraude, to theyre imediate captayne or maister, in payne of
lesing the hooll.' This applied to anyone accompanying the
troops, 'physiciens, surgens, barbors, marchauntes, and
suche lyke', who must hand in any plunder to a senior officer.

A document survives which lists down to the smallest sum the profits of war made in the year 1443–1444 by the garrison of the fortified islet of Tombelaine, in the sea opposite Mont-Saint-Michel, 'in the retinue of the high and powerful lord, my lord the . . . Earl of Somerset, Captain of the said place'. The archer John Flourison (a Frenchman by his name) 'took a horse; sold for 6 gold *saluts* . . . took a prisoner ransomed for 12 gold *saluts*', while the archer Roger Mill 'won a sword sold for 37 shillings and 6 pence *tournois*'. The total of the archers' profits was £28 17s 6d *tournois* (£3 4s 2d sterling), a third going to the men-at-arms; of which third a third went to the captain, and of this captain's third a further third went to the King. All was carefully registered by the garrison controller's clerk and deputy, and then certified again by the controller himself under his seal.

By 1444 Cardinal Beaufort, grown very old, had withdrawn from politics. But his faction retained control, its leader being the Earl of Suffolk, whom Warwick had despised and whose régime was as harsh as it was incapable and corrupt, he and his greedy colleagues ruthlessly using their position to extort money, estates and commercial privilege, even employing their retinues to overawe law courts and seize desirable properties. Yet there was a better side to Suffolk; he was a poet and even something of a mystic, loyal to his friends, and in his own incompetent way he tried to serve his King. After fighting in France for many years— with notable lack of distinction—he now agreed with the majority of the Council that England must make peace at all costs and would be lucky to retain Normandy and Guyenne.

Early in 1444, having first asked the Council for a formal indemnity from any blame, Suffolk led an embassy to a conference at Tours. The French were not prepared to make any concessions. In desperation Suffolk offered to surrender Maine in return for a two-year truce, presumably hoping to reach a lasting peace within that time; he dared not make this clause public and so it was kept secret. He also betrothed King Henry to King Charles's niece, the sixteen-year-old daughter of René of Anjou, titular King of Sicily.

News of the Truce of Tours was greeted with xenophobic fury throughout England. However, it was received very differently by the English in France—with 'immense and indescribable joy' according to Basin. This was the first break in hostilities since 1419, and after being 'shut up for years behind town walls or in castles as though condemned to life imprisonment, living in fear and danger, they were marvellously happy at escaping from their long incarceration', and 'gave themselves up to dancing and feasting with yesterday's enemies'. Basin's description suggests what uncertain, claustrophobic and altogether terrifying lives the English must have led in Lancastrian France.

Henry VI and Margaret of Anjou were married in 1445. The beautiful foreign Queen, dark-haired and strong-willed, was hated from the very beginning, partly because she was a Frenchwoman and partly because of her support for Suffolk and her enmity towards the Duke of Gloucester. It was said that England had bought a Queen 'not worth ten marks a year', while in a contemporary English chronicler's opinion: 'Fro this tyme forward King Henry never profited ne went forward, but fortune began to turn fro him on al sides.' Margaret speedily dominated her feeble, gullible husband, ensuring that he supported Suffolk, who was created a Duke in 1448. She also pressed Suffolk to honour his pledge to surrender Maine. News of the new Duke's secret promise had, after all, leaked out, infuriating the English still further. They had reason to be angry; most of Maine was peaceful and apparently even loyal, while between its capital, Le Mans, and Alençon, the frontier made by the river Sarthe was held by a line of strong castles. But at the end of 1445 King Henry promised the French that he would give up Maine by the following April, the truce being extended until April 1447.

Before Maine could be surrendered, Gloucester and York would have to be muzzled. The former had already lost considerable prestige after the condemnation of his Duchess, Eleanor Cobham, in 1441 on a charge of trying to kill the King by witchcraft so that her husband could succeed to the throne. Moreover old Cardinal Beaufort had turned King Henry against his uncle. But Suffolk had to make sure. After circulating a rumour that Gloucester was about to rise in revolt, he arrested him without warning at Bury St Edmunds on 18 February 1447 : probably he died of a stroke brought on by rage, but public opinion believed that Suffolk had murdered the 'Good Duke Humphrey'. The Duke of York, now heir presumptive to the throne, was recalled from France and sent to Ireland to keep him out of the way.

York was succeeded as Lieutenant-General at Rouen by the Duke of Somerset. On 16 March 1448, despite the unwillingness of their captains, Le Mans and the Maine fortresses were surrendered by specially appointed English commissioners. The truce between England and France was extended until April 1450.

Even in these last years the English behaved as though Normandy would stay in their hands permanently. Henry VI went on granting titles ; as late as 1446 Sir William Bourchier, the Captain of Calais, was made Count of Eu. Perhaps there were fewer Englishmen in the duchy than might have been expected ; many settlers had intermarried and some had returned to England—at Harfleur in 1449 there were only 500 English compared with 10,000 put there by Henry V in 1416. But a generation of Normans had known no other government and were genuinely loyal to their English Duke ; there were Anglo-Normans now, just as for three centuries there had been Anglo-Gascons and Anglo-Irish. Indeed, Rouen may well have seemed more English than Dublin. The most solid symbol of Lancastrian rule was the beautiful gold *salut*, or Anglo-French crown, which continued to be struck until 1449.

England kept fewer troops than ever in the Norman garrisons. Moreover, arrears of pay caused mutinies and a stream of desertions which reduced the number still further : Henry VI's annual revenue amounted to barely £30,000, when his household cost £24,000 a year and the Crown's debts had grown to nearly £400,000.

By contrast, France's finances were in good order. Charles VII's officials had reintroduced the special taxes levied at the end of John II's reign and were collecting them with a fair degree of success. Further, the rich merchant and tax-farmer, Jacques Coeur, was the King's *argentier*—paymaster of the household—and could supply unlimited liquid cash. Indeed Coeur had amassed sufficient capital to finance campaigns on a truly vast scale.

Charles was already spending large sums on military reform, raising a standing army. In 1445 an edict established fifteen companies of 100 'lances', each lance a unit of six men—a man-at-arms, two archers and three armed supernumeraries. By 1446 Charles had twenty such companies. Someone who saw them marvelled how 'the men-at-arms were all armed with good cuirasses, armour for their limbs, swords and sallets [light helmets] and most of the sallets were adorned with silver'. The most radical innovation was that the troops were kept on in peace-time and not, as hitherto, dismissed at the end of every short period of hostilities. A real attempt was made to enforce some sort of discipline and to stop the men from living off the country and from levying the *pâtis*, and they were paid regularly every month. In 1448 another edict ordered the raising of 8,000 'franc-archers'; every parish had to contribute and equip a crossbowman or archer. Such troops were only paid in wartime but were exempt from taxes in time of peace. Charles also spent much money on artillery and acquired a remarkable master gunner, a Maître Jean Bureau, whom he commissioned to modernize his cannon. Previously the English system of indentured soldiers under contract had produced a professional fighting force infinitely superior to the undisciplined levies of France. But now the odds were in favour of the French with this new, full-time, properly paid army.

Above all the French King himself had at last matured. His natural astuteness and flexibility had been reinforced by an implacable determination. He became a good organizer and a subtle politician, ruthless and unscrupulous, with a nice talent for espionage and bribery—from the early 1440s he had in his pay carefully selected *seigneurs* in Normandy and Guyenne.

Despite the truce Somerset used the troops evacuated from Maine to seize two Breton fortresses. When King Charles remonstrated, he was told that Brittany was an English fief. Somerset, or perhaps Suffolk behind his back, then commissioned an Aragonese mercenary, François de Surienne (who rather surprisingly was a Knight of the Garter) to take his *écorcheurs* to seize and sack the prosperous Breton town of Fougères in March 1449. The truce had been broken, but what made the French particularly angry was the constant English pressure on the Duke of Brittany to abandon his alliance with France.

On 31 July 1449 Charles VII sent 30,000 troops into Normandy. They attacked from three directions—north, south and east. Instead of at least trying to concentrate his scattered handfuls of ill-paid, mutinous soldiers, Somerset left them in a score of garrisons and told them to hold on for as long as possible. Yet as he himself had reported that because of inadequate maintenance most English strongpoints 'though they were stuffed with men and ordnance, they be so ruinous that they be unable to be defended'. In the north Pont-Audemer, Pont-l'Evêque and Lisieux had fallen by mid-August; in the centre Verneuil, Mantes, Vernon and Argentan by early October; and in the south Coutances, Carentan, Saint-Lô and Valognes. Some commanders, especially the native Normans, opened their gates to the French without any attempt at resistance.

On 9 October Charles and the Bastard of Orleans (now Count of Dunois) encamped on the Seine only a few miles above Rouen. On 16 October the Bastard nearly rushed the walls, but Talbot managed to beat off the assault. However, the Rouennais had no intention of undergoing another siege like 1418 and rioted in the streets. Three days later a mob opened the gates and the entire English garrison took refuge in the citadel. Somerset had only 1,200 men, while 'no corn, wood, meat or wine had been brought into the city for more than six weeks' and he had no proper provisions. On 22 October Charles invested the citadel, digging trenches and erecting batteries. 'Not a little alarmed', the Duke went out under a flag of truce to parley with the King, accompanied by forty knights and esquires and wearing 'a long robe of blue figured velvet lined with sable fur and a hat of crimson velvet trimmed with sable'. Charles was unimpressed and sent him back. The French refused any terms which would not give them Talbot as a hostage. After twelve days of haggling, a surrender was agreed; Somerset was allowed to retreat to Caen after handing over Talbot and promising to pay a large indemnity. Talbot had to watch glumly from a window as the French King made his ceremonial entry into Rouen, attended by his *Garde Ecossaise*. Shrewdly Charles issued an amnesty, pardoning the city's clergy, nobles and burgesses. But all English houses, estates and movable goods were confiscated, the new French Seneschal receiving Somerset's *hôtel*.

During the winter the French captured Harfleur, Honfleur and Fresnoy, Bureau's excellent artillery battering down the walls. Bribery was another powerful weapon. Richard des Epaules, Captain of Longuy in Perche, received £450 *tournois* for surrendering his fortress, together with a confirmation of his captaincy—in Charles's name. John Merbury, Captain of Gisors obtained £58 *tournois* for yielding Gisors. The Welshman John Edwards extracted no less than £4,500 *tournois* (£500 sterling) for La Roche Guyon. By the following spring the English retained little more than the Cherbourg peninsula.

The invasion of Normandy had taken all England by surprise. There was an outcry at the loss of Rouen. £10,000 was sent to Somerset, but no immediate reinforcements. In October 1449 Sir Thomas Kyriell KG, a former Captain of Gisors, began to assemble a force at Portsmouth. Billeted in the hospice called 'God's House', the troops got completely out of control, drinking and robbing, so that because of mutinies and adverse winds Sir Thomas was unable to sail for several months.

Eventually Kyriell landed at Cherbourg on 15 March 1450, with a mere 2,500 men. Instead of marching to relieve Bayeux as ordered, he delayed in the Cotentin to besiege Valognes. (Later Sir John Fastolf was highly critical of this 'negligently tarrying', which allowed the French to bring up troops.) Sir Thomas then begged Somerset for more men. The Duke sent what he could—500 from Caen under Sir Robert Vere, 600 from Vire under Sir Henry Norbury and 800 from Bayeux under Sir Matthew Gough. The combined army, just over 4,000 strong and with Gough as second-in-command, finally began to march inland towards Bayeux on 12 April.

The Constable de Richemont and the Count of Clermont planned to intercept them. After Kyriell had crossed the river Vire, by a dangerous causeway four miles long over the estuary, on 14 April he camped in a valley near the little village of Formigny some ten miles from Bayeux. Inexplicably he stayed at his camp throughout the following morning. Early in the afternoon the English outposts suddenly sighted Clermont's troops advancing down the road from Carentan to the north-west. Sir Thomas hastily formed up his troops—he had about 800 men-at-arms, the rest being archers—in a long line on top of a ridge above the valley, with three wedges of bowmen in the centre and on the wings who planted their stakes in front of them and dug small trenches with their daggers. (Ironically, it was the formation of Crécy and Agincourt.) Their rear was protected by a brook lined with trees and gardens.

Clermont, who himself had only 3,000 men, dismounted them and tried a probing frontal assault. It was easily repulsed, as were mounted charges on the wings. After a frustrating three hours the French brought up two culverins (small cannon) to make the English archers leave their positions. The bowmen did so with a vengeance, running forward and capturing both guns. If Kyriell had followed up now with his men-at-arms, he would have probably won the battle. But the French were allowed to rally. They then attacked the archers in the flank, recapturing their culverins

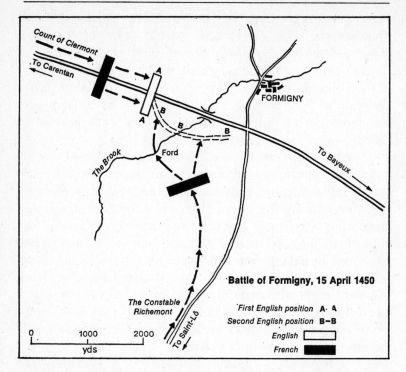

Battle of Formigny, 15 April 1450

First English position **A· A**
Second English position **B—B**

English
French

and engaging the English in a general mêlée. The English might still have won—but then the Constable appeared from the south without warning, with 1,200 fresh troops. Clermont disengaged his men to prepare a final charge in conjunction with Richemont. Kyriell must have seen that they were doomed, but he reformed his own troops into a semi-circular line—though this prevented the archers from concentrating their fire—to receive a concerted attack from both the west and the south. The English were already weakened and when the assault came, despite a brave defiance, they were driven back to the brook where they were broken. Matthew Gough and a few men managed to cut their way out and reach Bayeux, but Kyriell was captured and most of his men were slain. Next morning the heralds counted 3,774 English dead. Formigny was the first decisive battle lost by the English since Bannockburn in 1314.

In June 1450, Caen was besieged. After three weeks of bombardment, Somerset surrendered—one of Bureau's cannon-balls had smashed into a room occupied by the Duke's wife and children, which no doubt helped to make up his mind. He was allowed to retire to Calais. Vire, Bayeux and Avranches had already fallen. Falaise surrendered on 21 July—in return for Talbot being set at liberty—and Domfront did so ten days later.

The last stand was made at Cherbourg by Thomas Gower, who commanded a garrison of a thousand men. Bureau mounted his batteries on the sand on the seaward side, waterproofing them with greased hides when the tide came in and returning after it had gone out to continue the cannonade. 'The town received such a heavy battering from cannons and bombards that the like had never been seen before,' says the anonymous continuator of Monstrelet's chronicles. Gower fought with determination and many of the besiegers were killed, including the Admiral Prégent de Coëtivy. In England Sir John Fastolf was trying desperately to assemble a new army. But on 12 August 1450 Cherbourg surrendered. Save for the Channel Islands, the French had reconquered all Normandy.

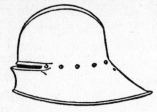

The End: 'A Dismal Fight' 1450–1453

> . . . a dismal fight
> Betwixt the stout Lord Talbot and the French.
>
> *King Henry VI*

> Is this the scourge of France?
> Is this the Talbot, so much fear'd abroad,
> That with his name the mothers still their babes?
> I see report is fabulous and false.
>
> *King Henry VI*

Talbot's expedition to Guyenne of 1452–1453 was a final effort by an exhausted England. The campaign demonstrated a revolution in military technology, French cannon proving more effective than English bows. Fittingly, of the two commanders the Frenchman was a self-made man and an artisan, the Englishman a great noble and *preux chevalier*.

The English could scarcely believe they had lost Normandy. But refugees were swarming across the Channel. Some of the officials found new posts in England, among them a few Normans—such as Raoul le Sage, Seigneur of Saint-Pierre, and the Abbot of Mont-Saint-Michel—while several became royal 'secretaries of the French tongue', employed for correspondence with France.

Others were not so lucky. Those who suffered most were the soldiers. Sir Andrew Ogard MP* did his best to help troops from his captaincy of Caen; in his will of 1454 he wrote how they 'came out of Normandy in great necessity as starving beggars'. The chronicler Robert Bate records how a large sum was raised to ship these men to Bordeaux 'to save and keep the King's right there', but the money was embezzled so they had to stay and 'became thieves and murderers in various places of this land'. It was not only the troops who suffered. In 1452 some 'churchmen, nobles, soldiers and others' from Maine petitioned Henry VI for relief; they had had to abandon 'their many benefices, lands, lordships, estates and pensions' in Maine and then during the conquest of Normandy had lost the movable goods upon which they and their families depended and 'at this moment the majority of them are utterly ruined and in a state of beggary'. A note written on the document says that the petition was not granted, adding sombrely that many petitioners had been reduced to destitution, that 'some for grief became ill and died; others were imprisoned for theft and condemned to death by law; while others still remain, as rebels, in the Kingdom of France'.

As soon as the French had invaded Normandy a rumour had spread throughout England that the duchy had been sold by Suffolk and his government. In January 1450 the Bishop of Chichester, Adam Moleyns—the former Privy Seal and a close friend of Suffolk—was murdered at

---

* Ogard was a Danish mercenary, his real name being Anders Pedersen. Born about 1400, he was the son of the Knight Peder Nielsen of Aargard, of the great Gyllenstierna family. By 1425 Ogard was serving in Anjou and in 1433 he was made Captain of Vire. He was naturalized in 1436. He served on the Councils of both Bedford and York and was twice an ambassador to the French. In 1450 he was appointed Captain of Caen, which he had the melancholy duty of surrendering. In 1443—in association with Fastolf—he had received a royal licence to 'empark' land near Ware in Hertfordshire and here with the money from his French spoils he built Rye House (to be the scene of a famous plot against Charles II). Sir Andrew's wife was a Norfolk heiress and in 1453 he was elected to Parliament for that county. He died the year after and was buried at Wymondham Abbey.

Portsmouth by Kyriell's troops when bringing them their pay, lynched as a traitor who had betrayed Normandy to the French. Before Moleyns died he seems to have said something implicating Suffolk. On 28 January the House of Commons accused the Duke of selling the realm to the French. In February they charged him with taking money for Orleans's release, plotting a French invasion, accepting bribes to stop reinforcements reaching Normandy and Guyenne, and selling secrets of English defences in France; in March he was impeached for treasonable relations with the French, corruption and mismanagement. King Henry tried to save him by banishing him, but when Suffolk attempted to flee to Calais in April he was intercepted by a ship called the *Nicholas* (possibly on the orders of the Duke of York); on 2 May he was taken into a dinghy and made to lay his neck on the gunwale, then his head was hacked off with six strokes of a rusty sword.

At the end of May, before Cherbourg had fallen, Jack Cade (or 'John Amend-all'), a reputed Irishman and undoubted murderer who had served very briefly in Normandy, raised the men of Kent in a peculiarly ugly rebellion. One of their grievances was the betrayal in France, Sir John Fastolf being unfairly accused of running down the garrisons. If there were other reasons, notably corrupt and extortionate government, the loss of Normandy was the spark. This rising, joined by a surprising number of local gentry and even by parish constables, was a far more dangerous affair than the Peasants' Revolt of 1381. The rebels reached Blackheath, then retreated before royal troops, but when the King withdrew to Kenilworth they came back, entering London on 3 July, freeing the prisoners in the Marshalsea and storming the Tower of London. There they found the Treasurer, Lord Saye and Sele, whom they dragged off to a tavern in the Cheap where they beheaded him. Many of Cade's followers were disillusioned by the looting, and after a fierce battle on London Bridge with government troops under 'the good old Lord Scales' and Sir Matthew Gough—fresh from Normandy—which lasted throughout the night of 5 July, the rebels fled from the capital. Cade was pursued to Sussex where he was caught and killed.

The Duke of Somerset was summoned from Calais to restore order. He was soon accused of being responsible for losing Normandy and spent a brief period in the Tower, but was saved by Queen Margaret who restored him to power. However, his government was too insecure and distracted to ward off new disasters in France. For Charles VII was now turning his attentions to Guyenne.

Here such peace had prevailed in recent years that between 1445–1449 Guyenne exported more wine to England than ever before. To begin with the French invasion met with little success; Guyenne had belonged to the Plantagenets for 300 years, not a mere thirty, and by and large the Guyennois remained loyal to the English Duke and his distant rule. Nevertheless, as soon as he had conquered Normandy, Charles held a council of war at Tours and although it was so late in the year decided on immediate invasion. The Count of Foix came down the valley of the river Adour to take fifteen towns round Bayonne, while the Count of Penthièvre, who had brought a strong artillery-train, took Bergerac in October, and Bazas. Penthièvre then advanced on Bordeaux, routing the city militia at Blanquefort in November before retiring to winter quarters. The English tried to assemble an army of relief under Lord Rivers, but it never set sail.

In April 1451 the Bastard of Orleans also invaded Guyenne, bringing with him Maître Bureau and an even more imposing artillery-train. He advanced on Bordeaux. He quickly took Blaye, Fronsac and Saint-Emilion, isolating the ducal capital, which he invested. Despite a brave defence by the Captal de Buch, Gaston de Foix KG, Bordeaux surrendered on 30 June. By the end of July only Bayonne held out for the Plantagenets, and that too fell on 20 August. Bribery contributed a good deal to the speed of the French conquest; Bergerac is said to have been betrayed by its Captain, Maurigon de Bideron—who also sold the castle of Biron—and the English Mayor of Bordeaux, Gadifer

Shorthose, received a pension for his disloyal services.

However, although some Gascon nobles at first welcomed the French, the Guyennois quickly began to hate their new masters. The northern French administrators and tax men proved harsh and efficient, contemptuous of the old ways, while Charles's troops behaved as unpleasantly as the English soldiers had in Normandy. In 1452 secret envoys reached London and promised the Duke of Somerset that Bordeaux would rise for him if he sent an army.

Somerset was overjoyed. The Commons had already accused him of causing the loss of Normandy, and when Guyenne had gone too there was uproar; the Duke of York had marched on London with an army and Somerset only retained power by the skin of his teeth. The recovery of Guyenne could well win him some desperately needed popularity.

The English still believed that one Englishman was worth two Frenchmen, and their hero Talbot shared this view. As has been seen, he was made a hostage in 1449 and was thus the one English commander in Normandy whose reputation had remained intact. Although an old man in his seventies by now—the French thought he was in his eighties—he was as vigorous as ever, retaining all his pugnacity and magnetism. The natural choice to lead the expedition, he was appointed the King's Lieutenant in Guyenne in September 1452. Yet the great Lord Talbot was now to meet his match.

If the French had no paladin of equal distinction, they did possess a technocrat—Maître Jean Bureau. Bishop Basin, who almost certainly met the great gunner, describes him as 'a man of humble origins and small stature, but of purpose and daring'. Bureau was a native of Champagne who came to Paris to become a lawyer and who is known to have been a legal official at the Châtelet in the days of the Duke of Bedford. In 1434 he left what was still the Anglo-French capital to enter the service of Charles VII, who appointed him Receiver of Paris two years later and promoted him to be Treasurer of France in 1443. It may seem odd that a lawyer and civil servant should also be a professional artillery expert, but during the fifteenth century master gunners were usually civilian specialists under contract who, like Bureau, founded their own cannon. According to Basin, Bureau had first served as a gunner with the English, and no doubt he and his brother Gaspard (who worked with him) were originally attracted to the profession largely by commercial considerations. However, they served Charles VII with outstanding success. Long before the Norman campaign, the Bureau brothers' guns had proved their worth—at Montereau in 1437, at Meaux in 1439, at Saint-Germain-en-Laye in 1440 and at Pontoise in 1441. In Jean Bureau one discerns a perfectionist with a methodical, mathematical mind, a brilliant administrator and an imaginative technician who knew how to get the best out of his primitive weapons.

During the fifteenth century the tools of the Bureau brothers' difficult and dangerous trade had slowly improved. The most important innovation was the powder mill, invented about 1429. Before then gunpowder had had to be mixed on the field, but now the new 'corned' powder-grains no longer disintegrated into their three separate components of sulphur, saltpetre and charcoal. The new powder increased velocity enormously. There had also been advances in casting cannon, in bronze, brass and, more rarely iron, even if the weapons were still apt to burst. (During the siege of Cherbourg it was a matter for congratulation that only four blew up.)

Moreover a cheap and reasonably effective manual firearm had been developed. These *batons-à-feu* or handguns were confusingly called culverins like the cannon of that name. They had barrels of brass or bronze, and straight wooden stocks and—mounted on a rest—were aimed from the chest instead of from the shoulder. They fired a lead bullet, using a special explosive powder twice as expensive as that for bigger guns. The firing mechanism was a 'serpentine', an S-shaped attachment of which one end acted as a trigger and the other held the match. (A serpentine was also a type of small cannon.) Although half the price of steel crossbows, such guns were not often used in the field as they were too cumbersome. However, mounted on a rampart they could be effective enough in siege warfare.

On 17 October 1452 Talbot landed in the Médoc with 3,000 troops. The French knew about the expedition but expected it to land in Normandy, so in consequence they had no proper army in Guyenne. As promised, the Bordelais rose against the Seneschal, Oliver de Coëtivy, turned out the French garrison and opened the gates. The English marched in on 21 October. All western Guyenne now rose and the few towns and castles garrisoned by the French were speedily overrun. Charles VII, taken completely by surprise, left Talbot in peace but spent the winter organizing a counter-attack for the following year. Before the end of the winter 3,000 more men reached Talbot, under his fourth and favourite son, Viscount Lisle.

By the spring of 1453 King Charles was ready. Three French armies invaded Guyenne, from the north-east, the east, and the south-east, all making for Bordeaux. Talbot's strategy was to wait and try to engage each one separately. In July the French army which was advancing from the east laid siege to the town of Castillon near Libourne on the Dordogne, about thirty miles up-river from Bordeaux. Talbot was inclined to leave the townsmen of Castillon to their fate, but they pleaded with him so eloquently that he reluctantly agreed to come and save them.

The enemy army in question consisted of about 9,000 troops. It had no designated commander and its senior officers were far from united. However in matters of gunnery they wisely deferred to Jean Bureau, who obviously had some sort of ascendancy over them. As was customary in siege warfare, he had built a fortified artillery park just out of range of Castillon's guns, his actual batteries being probably much nearer and connected to the park by communication trenches. This was not a revolutionary exercise in military engineering as has been suggested, but a routine precaution against sorties by the townsmen or relief forces. The actual park, which was constructed by 700 pioneers, consisted of a deep trench with a wall of earth behind it which was strengthened by tree-trunks; its most remarkable feature was the irregular, wavy line of the ditch and earthwork, which enabled the guns to enfilade any attackers. Bureau knew all about cross-fire. The park was about half a mile long and about 200 yards wide, lying parallel to the river Dordogne which was less than a mile away, while one side was completely protected by the Lidoire, a tributary of the Dordogne.

Bureau had brought 300 cannon with him, mainly culverins. It seems extremely likely that these were handguns. (Perhaps chroniclers were confused by 'culverins *with* serpentines' and heard 'culverins *and* serpentines' instead.) If so, the English military supremacy which had begun with bows was about to be ended by small arms. The guns were mounted on the earth wall.

On 16 July Talbot rode out from Bordeaux with his entire army, which included a Guyennois contingent and may have been as many as 10,000 men. He covered 20 miles, reaching Libourne by sunset though outdistancing his infantry and retaining only 500 men-at-arms and 800 mounted archers. At daybreak the following day he and his little force suddenly emerged from the woods near Castillon and annihilated a French detachment in a nearby priory. He then learnt of the artillery park and, after sending Sir Thomas Evringham to examine it and refreshing his men with a cask of wine, settled down to wait for the rest of his troops to catch up with him. But a messenger came from Castillon to say that the French were running; in fact the townsmen had seen a cloud of dust raised by the horses of enemy supernumeraries who had been sent away. Thinking the entire enemy army was in full retreat, Talbot at once led his men in an attack on the park. The only man to remain mounted, the veteran warrior, seventy-five years of age, must have been a striking figure in a gown of crimson satin, with a purple bonnet over his snowy hair. He had been forced to swear not to wear 'harness' (armour) against the French when they released him from his captivity in Normandy.

The English and Gascons charged the French camp,

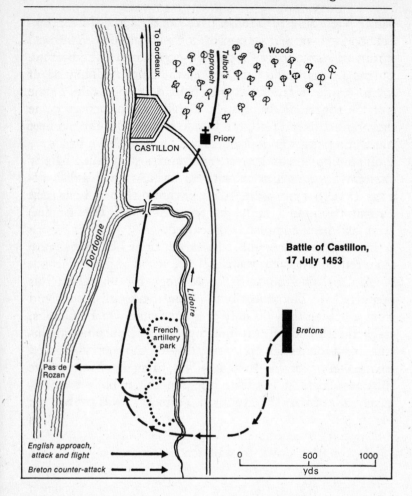

Battle of Castillon, 17 July 1453

shouting 'Talbot! St George!' Some managed to cross the ditch and a few scaled the earthworks, including the standard-bearer Sir Thomas Evringham who was at once shot dead. The enemy guns fired into the English at point-blank range—because of the enfilade one shot killed no less than six men. Despite impossible odds the assault lasted for nearly an hour, small detachments of Talbot's other troops coming up to join in the fight. Then a thousand Bretons appeared unexpectedly on the far side of the Lidoire, attacking the English from the south and crashing into their right flank. According to Monstrelet's continuator, the Bretons 'fell upon them and trampled all their banners underfoot'. But the issue was never in doubt—even without the Bretons, Bureau's guns would have broken the English. They began to run towards the Dordogne behind them, while Talbot and his son tried desperately to rally some men to cover their retreat over a ford, the Pas de Rozan. But the old hero was a good target and his horse was brought down by a gunshot, pinning him underneath; a French archer called Michel Perunin finished him off with an axe. A few English got away though most were killed, including Lord Lisle; the pursuit continuing as far as Saint-Emilion. The English army had been completely destroyed.

By the end of September Bordeaux alone held out against the French. The city was closely besieged and the Gironde blockaded. The Bordelais could hope for no relief from Somerset's feeble government; even the English survivors from Castillon thought only of going home. On 19 October 1453 the capital of Guyenne surrendered unconditionally, trusting—somewhat optimistically—to the mercy of King Charles. One of his first acts was to make Maître Jean Bureau Mayor of Bordeaux for life. But nobody seems to have realized that the Hundred Years War was over.

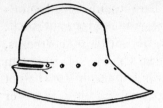

Epilogue

An if I live until I be a man,
I'll win our ancient right in France again,
Or die a soldier, as I liv'd a king.

King Richard III

to the intent that the honourable and
noble adventures of feats of arms, done
and achieved by the wars of France and
England, should notably be enregistered
and put in perpetual memory.

Lord Berners's translation of Froissart

In the end the Hundred Years War bankrupted the English
government and fatally discredited the Lancastrian dynasty,
though England herself may well have been richer from a
century of 'spoils won in France'. In August 1453 Henry VI
went mad and six months later the Duke of York became
Protector. When Henry recovered in 1455 and re-instated
the Beauforts, that long and murderous conflict known as
the Wars of the Roses broke out, veterans using the combat
skills they had learnt in France on each other. English noblemen had become accustomed to fighting as a way of life and
the men-at-arms and archers in their retinues desperately
needed employment. York and Somerset fell in battle,
Kyriell and Rivers died on the scaffold, Scales was lynched
by a Yorkist mob, and many of the men who were killed at

St Albans and Towton or even at Barnet and Tewkesbury had fought under Old Talbot. The rise of the House of York and the Wars of the Roses cannot be understood without some knowledge of the Hundred Years War.

At first the English regarded their expulsion from Normandy and Guyenne as purely temporary. At Bordeaux and Bayonne the French had to build citadels to cow the Guyennois, and in 1457 Charles VII wrote apprehensively to the King of Scots how he 'had to watch the coast daily'. In 1475 Edward IV (son of a Lieutenant General of France, and born at Rouen) at last marched out from Calais towards the Somme; however, at Picquigny he signed a seven-year truce with Louis XI, agreeing to withdraw for an indemnity of 75,000 crowns and an annual pension of 60,000. But no proper peace treaty was ever signed, and as late as 1487 Henry VII hoped to recover Guyenne; he intervened in Brittany the following year and invaded France in 1492. Henry VIII also took an army across the Channel, defeating the French at the Battle of the Spurs in 1513 and capturing Thérouanne and Tournai—the first French towns gained by English arms since the days of Bedford and Old Talbot. In 1523 he signed a secret treaty with the Duke of Bourbon and the Emperor Charles V, which would have given him the French crown together with Paris and the north-western provinces of France and would have restored the Lancastrian dual monarchy. This came to nothing, though in 1544 he took Boulogne. Even after the loss in 1558 of Calais, their last foothold, English monarchs continued to call themselves Kings or Queens of France until the Treaty of Amiens in 1802.

The only English memorials of the Hundred Years War are Lord Berners's majestic rendering of Froissart, and Shakespeare's historical plays. For the French it is a different story. France suffered horribly when England escaped unharmed—every local historian in northern and western France will show the tourist a château or a church which was sacked by the English. There is a strong case for maintaining that the origin of the uneasy relationship between

France in 1337

0 50 100 150
miles

— · — · — · Boundary of the Kingdom of France in 1337

English possessions

HOLLAND

Dordrecht

ENGLISH CHANNEL

Sluys
Bruges
Ghent
FLANDERS
Ypres
Schelde
BRABANT
ARTOIS
HAINAULT
Tournal
Cambrai
Crécy
PONTHIEU
Abbeville
Thiérache
Amiens
Somme
VERMANDOIS
PICARDY
Reims

Cologne
Coblenz
Rhine
Meuse
Moselle
THE EMPIRE

Cherbourg
La Hogue
Channel Is.
CAUX
Rouen
Marne
CHAMPAGNE

Caen
NORMANDY
EVREUX
Poissy
Meaux
Paris
Seine

Cotentin

Brest
DUCHY OF
BRITTANY
Quimperlé
Ploermel
Auray
Vannes
Nantes

Chartres
ÉTAMPES
Orléans
BLOIS
Loire
MAINE
ANJOU
Romorantin
Tours
TOURAINE
BERRY

DUCHY OF
BURGUNDY

COUNTY OF
BURGUNDY

Saône

POITOU
Poitiers

LA MARCHE
LIMOUSIN
BOURBON
AUVERGNE
Lyons

BAY OF
BISCAY

SAINTONGE
La Rochelle
Oléron
Saintes
Blaye
ANGOULÊME
Limoges

PÉRIGORD
Dordogne
Bergerac
La Réole
Cahors
AGENAIS
Agen
Garonne

Bordeaux
DUCHY OF
GUYENNE

Bayonne
BÉARN
KINGDOM OF
NAVARRE
ARMAGNAC
Toulouse
LANGUEDOC
Narbonne
Carcassonne

Rhône
Avignon

the two peoples can be found in the battles, sieges and the *chevauchées*, the ransoming and the looting, the *pâtis*, the burning and the killing by the English in France during the Hundred Years War.

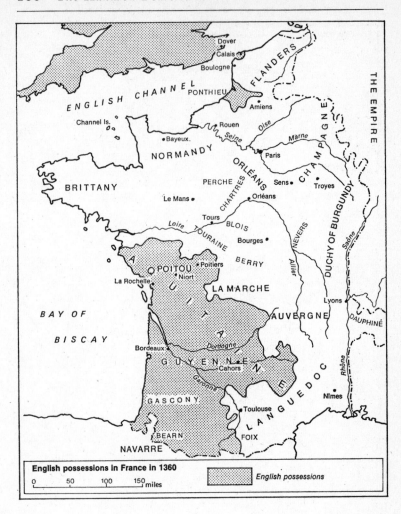

English possessions in France in 1360

0   50   100   150 miles

English possessions

English possessions in France in 1429

0 50 100 200 miles

░░░ *English possessions*

▒▒▒ *Burgundy (in France)*

▨▨▨ *France (loyal to Charles VII)*

Appendix
A Note on Currency

It is impossible to give even approximate estimates of the purchasing power of late-medieval money. We know from the income-tax returns of 1436 (imposed on incomes of more than £20) that the average income of a nobleman was £865, of a well-to-do knight £208, of a lesser knight £60, of an esquire £24, and of minor gentry, merchants, yeoman and important artisans from £15 to £19. At this date a good ploughman could make perhaps £4 a year, though before the Black Death he might have made as little as 10 shillings.

The English pound sterling of 20 shillings or 240 pence must not be confused with the French pound *tournois* of 20 *sous* or 240 *deniers*. (There was also the pound *parisis* and the pound *bordelaise*, but these are not used in this book.) The English mark of silver was worth 13s 4d sterling, the mark of gold £6 sterling. These pounds—sterling and *tournois*—and marks were all what was termed monies of account. The exchange rate between English and French monies of account was frequently adjusted by the two governments; in the fourteenth century a pound sterling was usually worth 6 pounds *tournois* but in the fifteenth century it rose to 9 pounds *tournois*.

The basic English gold coin was the noble of 6s 8d, originally weighing 7.77 gms but reduced to 6.99 gms in 1412. The French gold coins or crowns were, very roughly, equivalent in weight and value to an English half-noble; they consisted of the *mouton*, so called because it bore an *agnus dei*; the *franc*; and the *écu*. The beautiful Anglo-Gallic *salut* of the Lancastrians can also be equated with the half-noble, being worth 3s 4d sterling. Where mentioned, the florins of other European currencies should similarly be equated.

Most English troops would have been paid in silver, consisting of the groat (4d), the half-groat, and the penny and its sub-divisions. Sometimes they would have received French silver or base-metal coins instead, such as the *gros tournois* or the *blanc*.

1337 Edward III claims the throne of France
1340 French navy defeated at Sluys
1346 The English defeat the French at Crécy
1347 Calais falls to the English
1350 Death of Philip VI of France and succession of John II
1356 The Black Prince defeats and captures John II at Poitiers
1360 The Treaty of Brétigny—Aquitaine surrendered to the English
1364 Death of John II of France and succession of Charles V
1369 Charles V 'confiscates' Aquitaine—hostilities recommence
1372 Poitiers and La Rochelle admit French troops

1373 John of Gaunt leads his great *chevauchée* from Calais to Bordeaux

1376 Death of the Black Prince

1377 Death of Edward III and succession of Richard II

1380 Death of Charles V of France and succession of Charles VI

1381 Peasants' Revolt in England

1383 Expedition of the Bishop of Norwich to Flanders

1386 The French prepare to invade England but then abandon the plan

1389 Truce of Leulinghen between French and English

1399 Deposition of Richard II and succession of Henry IV

1407 Murder of the Duke of Orleans by agents of John, Duke of Burgundy

1412 The Duke of Clarence leads a *chevauchée* from Normandy to Bordeaux

1413 Death of Henry IV and succession of Henry V

1415 Henry V invades France, captures Harfleur and wins the battle of Agincourt

1417 Henry V begins the conquest of Normandy

1419 Rouen falls to the English. John, Duke of Burgundy is murdered by Armagnacs. Alliance between Burgundians and English

1420 Treaty of Troyes ; Charles VI recognizes Henry V as heir to the French throne and Regent of France. The English occupy Paris

1421 Duke of Clarence defeated and killed by the Armagnacs at Baugé

1422 Deaths of Henry V and Charles VI. Henry VI of England recognized as King of France north of the Loire while only France south of the Loire recognizes Charles VII

1423 The Earl of Salisbury defeats the Dauphinists at Cravant

1424 The Regent Bedford defeats the French at Verneuil

1428 The Earl of Salisbury begins the siege of Orleans

1429 Sir John Fastolf defeats the Dauphinists at the 'Battle of the Herrings'. Joan of Arc relieves Orleans and defeats

Fastolf and Lord Talbot at Patay. Charles VII crowned at Rheims, but Joan fails to recapture Paris

1430 Capture of Joan of Arc

1431 Burning of Joan of Arc. Coronation of Henry VI at Paris

1435 Death of the Regent Bedford. Treaty of Arras between Charles VII and the Burgundians who abandon the English alliance

1436 Charles VII recaptures Paris

1441 Fall of Pontoise to the French—the last English stronghold in the Ile de France

1444 Truce of Tours between French and English

1448 The English surrender Maine to the French

1449 Charles VII invades Normandy and takes Rouen

1450 English defeated at Formigny. All Normandy falls to the French

1451 Charles VII conquers Guyenne

1452 At the invitation of the Guyennois, Lord Talbot re-occupies Bordeaux

1453 English defeated at Castillon and finally lose Bordeaux

Select Bibliography

CHRONICLES AND OTHER CONTEMPORARY SOURCES

ADAM OF MURIMUTH, *Adae Murimuthensis, Continuatio Chronicarum* (ed E. M. Thompson), Rolls Series, 1889.

ADAM OF USK, *Chronicon Adae de Usk* (ed E. M. Thompson), London, 1876.

BASIN, THOMAS, *Histoire de Charles VII* (translated C. Samaran), Paris, 1964.

BAKER, GEOFFREY LE, *Chronicon Galfridi le Baker de Swynebroke* (ed E. M. Thompson), Oxford, 1889.

BEL, JEAN LE, *Chroniques* (ed J. Viard and E. Déprez), Paris, 1904–1905.

BLONDEL, ROBERT, 'De Reductione Normanniae' in *Letters and Papers* . . . (ed J. Stevenson), see below.

BONET, HONORÉ, *The Tree of Battles of Honoré Bonet* (translated G. W. Coopland), Liverpool, 1949.

BOUVIER, GILLES LE, 'Le Recouvrement de Normandie', in *Letters and Papers . . .* (ed J. Stevenson), see below.

CAPGRAVE, J., *The Chronicle of England* (translated F. C. Hingeston), Rolls Series, 1858.

CHANDOS HERALD, *The Black Prince: An Historical Poem, written in French by Chandos Herald*, Roxburghe Club, 1842.

CHASTELLAIN, GEORGES, *Oeuvres* (ed Kervyn de Lettenhove), Brussels, 1863–1866.

CHARTIER, JEAN, *Chronique de Charles VII* (ed V. de Viriville), Paris, 1858.

Chronicon de Lanercost (translated Lord Berners), in Tudor Translations, 1927–1928.

Chronique du Mont-Saint-Michel (1343–1468) (ed S. Luce), Paris, 1879–1883.

ELMHAM, THOMAS, *Henrici Quinti Angliae Regis Gesta*, English Historical Society, 1850.

ESCOUCHY, MATTHIEU D', *Chroniques de Matthieu d'Escouchy*, Paris, 1863–1864.

FROISSART, JEAN, *Oeuvres: Chroniques* (ed Kervyn de Lettenhove), Brussels, 1867–1877.

JUVENAL DES URSINS, JEAN, *Histoire de Charles VI 1380–1422*, Paris, 1841.

KNIGHTON, HENRY, *Chronicon Henrici Knighton*, Rolls Series, 1895.

LESCOT, RICHARD, *Chroniques de Richard Lescot* (ed J. Lemoine), Paris, 1896.

LEFEBVRE, J., SEIGNEUR DE SAINT-REMY, *Chronique de J. le Fèvre*, Paris, 1876–1881.

Letters and Papers illustrative of the Wars of the English in France during the Reign of Henry the Sixth, King of England (ed J. Stevenson), Rolls Series, 1861–1864.

LIVIUS, TITUS, *Vita Henrici Quinti* (translated as *The First English Life of King Henry V*, ed C. L. Kingsford), Oxford, 1911.

MONSTRELET, ENGUERRAND DE, *La Chronique*, Paris, 1857–1862.

PAGE, JOHN, 'The Siege of Rouen' in *The Historical Collections of a Citizen of London*, Camden Society, 1876.

Proceedings and Ordinances of the Privy Council of England (ed N. H. Nicolas), Record Commission, 1834–1837.

ROBERT OF AVESBURY, *De gestis mirabilibus regis Edwardi Tertii*, Rolls Series, 1889.

STRECCHE, JOHN, *The Chronicle of John Strecche for the reign of Henry V 1414–1422*, Manchester, 1932.

The Brut; or The Chronicles of England (ed F. Brie), Early English Text Society, 1906–1908.

The Libelle of Englyshe Polycye. A Poem on the use of Sea-Power, 1436 (ed. G. Warner), Oxford, 1926.

The Paston Letters (ed J. Gairdner), London, 1872–1875.

UPTON, NICHOLAS, *The Essential Portions of Nicholas Upton's De Studio Militari, before 1446* (ed F. P. Barnard), Oxford, 1931.

VENETTE, JEAN DE, *The Chronicle of Jean de Venette* (translated J. Birdsall), New York, 1953.

WALSINGHAM, THOMAS, *Historia Anglicana* (ed H. T. Riley), Rolls Series, 1863–1864.

——*Annales Ricardi Secundi et Henrici Quarti, regum Angliae*, Rolls Series, 1886.

WAVRIN, JEAN DE, *Recueil des croniques et anchiennes histoires de la Grant Bretaigne*, Rolls Series, 1864–1891.

GENERAL WORKS

BURNE, A. H., *The Crécy War. A Military History of the Hundred Years War from 1337 to the peace of Brétigny, 1360*, Eyre & Spottiswoode, 1955.

—— *The Agincourt War. A Military History of the latter part of the Hundred Years War from 1369 to 1453*, Eyre & Spottiswoode, 1956.

Cambridge Economic History, Vol I (ed J.H. Clapham), CUP, 1938.

Cambridge Economic History, Vol II (ed M. M. Postan and E. E. Rich), CUP, 1952.

CONTAMINE, P., *La guerre de cent ans,* Paris, 1968.

COVILLE, A., *Les Premiers Valois et la Guerre de Cent Ans 1328–1422,* in *Histoire de France* (ed Lavisse) Tom. IV (i), Paris, 1902.

DENIFLE, M., *La désolation des églises, monastères et hôpitaux en France pendant la Guerre de Cent Ans,* Paris, 1897–1899.

Europe in the Late Middle Ages (ed J. R. Hale, R. L. L. Highfield and B. Smalley), Faber & Faber, 1965.

FOWLER, K. E., *The Age of Plantagenet and Valois,* Elek, 1967.

JACOB, E. F., *Henry V and the Invasion of France,* Hodder & Stoughton, 1947.

—— *The Fifteenth Century,* Oxford, 1961.

KINGSFORD, C. L., *English Historical Literature in the Fifteenth Century,* Oxford, 1913.

LEWIS, P. S., *Later Mediaeval France: The Polity,* Macmillan, 1968.

LODGE, E. C., *Gascony under English Rule,* Methuen, 1926.

MCKISACK, M., *The Fourteenth Century,* OUP, 1959.

MYERS, A. R., *A History of England in the later Middle Ages,* Pelican, 1965.

NEWHALL, R. A., *The English Conquest of Normandy,* New Haven, 1924.

NICHOLSON, R., *Scotland: The Later Middle Ages,* Oliver & Boyd, 1973.

—— *Edward III and the Scots. The Formative Years of a Military Career, 1327–1335,* OUP, 1965.

OMAN, SIR C., *A History of the Art of War in the Middle Ages: II 1278–1485,* Methuen, 1924.

PALMER, J. J. N., *England, France and Christendom, 1377–99,* Routledge, 1972.

PERROY, E., *La Guerre de Cent Ans,* Paris, 1945. (Translated W. B. Wells, as *The Hundred Years War,* Eyre & Spottiswoode, 1951).

PETIT-DUTAILLIS, C., *Charles VII, Louis XI et les premières années de Charles VIII 1422–92,* in *Histoire de France* (ed E. Lavisse) Tom. IV (ii), Paris, 1902.

ROSS, C. D., *The Wars of the Roses*, Thames & Hudson, 1976.

RUSSELL, P. E. L. R., *The English Intervention in Spain and Portugal in the Time of Edward III and Richard II*, OUP, 1955.

Society at War: The Experience of England and France During the Hundred Years War (ed C. T. Allmand), Oliver & Boyd, 1973.

The Hundred Years War (ed. K. E. Fowler), Macmillan, 1971.

VALE, M. G. A., *English Gascony 1399–1453: A Study of War, Government and Politics during the Later Stages of the Hundred Years War*, OUP, 1970.

VICKERS, K. H., *England in the later Middle Ages*, Methuen, 1913.

War, Literature and Politics in the Late Middle Ages (ed C. T. Allmand), Liverpool University Press, 1976.

WYLIE, J. H., and WAUGH, W. T., *The Reign of Henry V*, CUP, 1914–1929.

SPECIALIST STUDIES

BLAIR, S. C., *European Armour circa 1066–circa 1700*, Batsford, 1958.

Catalogue of Rubbings of Brasses and Incised Slabs (ed M. Clayton), Victoria and Albert Museum, HMSO, 1968.

CREASEY, SIR E. S., *The Fifteen Decisive Battles of the World*, London, 1867.

FULLER, J. F. C., *The Decisive Battles of the Western World*, Eyre & Spottiswoode, 1954–1956.

HEWITT, H. J., *The Black Prince's Expedition of 1355–1357*, Manchester, 1958.

—— *The Organisation of War under Edward III*, Manchester, 1966.

JAMES, M. K. *Studies in the Mediaeval Wine Trade*, OUP, 1971.

LA RONCIÈRE, C. DE, *Histoire de la Marine française*, Paris, 1899–1934.

LELAND, J., *Itinerary in England and Wales*, Centaur, 1964.

MCFARLANE, K. B., *The Nobility of Mediaeval England*, OUP, 1973.

MACKLIN, H. W., *Monumental Brasses*, George Allen, 1953.

NICOLAS, N. H., *A History of the Royal Navy*, London, 1847.

—— *History of the Battle of Agincourt and of the Expedition of King Henry the Fifth in France in 1415*, London, 1832.

POWER, E., *The Wool Trade in English Mediaeval History*, OUP, 1941.

BIOGRAPHIES

BUCHAN, A., *Joan of Arc and the Recovery of France*, Hodder & Stoughton, 1948.

CALMETTE, J., *Les grands ducs de Bourgogne*, Paris, 1949.

CARLETON WILLIAMS, E., *My Lord of Bedford*, Longmans, 1963.

DELACHENAL, R., *Histoire de Charles V*, Paris, 1909–1931.

Dictionary of National Biography.

Dictionnaire de Biographie Française, Paris, 1933–1967.

FOWLER, K. E., *The King's Lieutenant. Henry of Grosmont, first Duke of Lancaster, 1310–1361*, Elek, 1969.

LUCIE-SMITH, E., *Joan of Arc*, Allen Lane, 1976.

MCLEOD, E., *Charles of Orleans: Prince and Poet*, Chatto & Windus, 1969.

MOWBRAY, SEGRAVE AND STOURTON, LORD, *The History of the Noble House of Stourton*, privately printed, 1899.

ROSS, C., *Edward IV*, Eyre Methuen, 1974.

STEEL, A. B., *Richard II*, CUP, 1941.

The Complete Peerage (ed G. E. Cockayne and V. Gibbs), St Catherine's Press, 1910–1959.

VALE, M. G. A., *Charles VII*, Eyre Methuen, 1974.

VAUGHAN, R., *Philip the Bold*, Longmans, 1962.

—— *John the Fearless*, Longmans, 1966.

—— *Philip the Good*, Longmans, 1970.

VICKERS, K. H., *Humphrey, Duke of Gloucester*, London, 1907.

WEDGWOOD, J. C., *History of Parliament, Biographies of Members of the Commons House, 1439–1509*, HMSO, 1936.

ARTICLES AND ESSAYS

Abbreviations
Econ. H.R.　*Economic History Review*
HYW　　　*The Hundred Years War* (ed Fowler)
HT　　　　*History Today*
TRHS　　　*Transactions of the Royal Historical Society*
ELMA　　　*Europe in the Late Middle Ages* (ed Hale etc)
EHR　　　　*English Historical Review*
WLP　　　　*War, Literature and Politics in the Late Middle Ages* (ed Allmand)
PP　　　　　*Past and Present*
BIHR　　　　*Bulletin of the Institute of Historical Research*
PBA　　　　*Proceedings of the British Academy*

ALLMAND, C. T., *The Lancastrian Land Settlement in Normandy*, Econ H.R. 2nd ser, 21 (1968)
——*The War and the Non-Combatant*, HYW
—— *War and Profit in the Late Middle Ages*, HT 15 (1965)
ARMSTRONG, C. A. J., *Sir John Fastolf and the Law of Arms*, WLP
CAMPBELL, J., *England, Scotland and the Hundred Years War in the Fourteenth Century*, ELMA
CONTAMINE, P., *The French Nobility and the War*, HYW
FOWLER, K. E., *War and Change in Late Mediaeval France and England*, HYW
—— *Truces*, HYW
HALE, J. R., *The Development of the Bastion, 1440–1534*, ELMA
HEWITT, H. J., *The Organisation of War*, HYW
KEEN, M. H., *Chivalry, Nobility and the Man at Arms*, WLP
LEWIS, P. S., *War Propaganda and Historiography in Fifteenth Century France and England*, TRHS 5th Ser, 15

MCFARLANE, K. B., *The Investment of Sir John Fastolf's Profits of War*, TRHS 5th ser, 7 (1957)
—— *A Business Partnership in War and Administration 1421–1445*, EHR 78 (1963)
—— *England and the Hundred Years War*, pp 22 (1963)
—— *The Wars of the Roses*, PBA 50 (1964)
—— *Bastard Feudalism*, BIHR 20 (1943–1945)
PALMER, J. J. N., 'English Foreign Policy 1388–99' in *The Reign of Richard II: Essays in Honour of May McKisack* (ed F. du Boulay and C. Barron) Athlone Press, 1971
—— *The War Aims of the Protagonists and the Negotiations for Peace*, HYW
PATOUREL, J. LE, *The King and the Princes in Fourteenth Century France*, ELMA
—— *The Origins of the War*, HYW
POSTAN, M. M., *Some Social Consequences of the Hundred Years War*, Econ. H.R. 1st ser, 12 (1942)
—— *The Costs of the Hundred Years War*, pp 27 (1964)
POWICKE, M., *The English Aristocracy and the War*, HYW
RICHMOND, C. F., *The War at Sea*, HYW
VALE, M. G. A., *New Techniques and Old Ideals: The Impact of Artillery on War and Chivalry at the end of the Hundred Years War*, WLP

Index